THE OTHER BARACK

THE OTHER BARACK

THE BOLD AND RECKLESS LIFE OF PRESIDENT OBAMA'S FATHER

SALLY H. JACOBS

PUBLICAFFAIRS

New York

Published in the United States by PublicAffairs,™
a Member of the Perseus Books Group

PublicAffairs books are available at special discounts for bulk purchases in the U.S. by corporations, institutions, and other organizations. For more information, please contact the Special Markets Department at the Perseus Books Group, 2300 Chestnut Street, Suite 200, Philadelphia, PA 19103, call (800) 810-4145, ext. 5000, or e-mail special.markets@perseusbooks.com.

Editorial production by the Book Factory

Library of Congress Cataloging-in-Publication Data

Jacobs, Sally H., 1957–
    The other Barack : the bold and reckless life of president Obama's father /
    Sally H. Jacobs.—1st ed.
      p. cm.
    ISBN 978-1-58648-793-5 (hardback)
    1. Obama, Barack Hussein, 1936–1982. 2. Obama, Barack—Family.
3. Economists—Kenya—Biography. 4. Luo (Kenyan and Tanzanian people)—
Biography. 5. Kenya—Biography. I. Title.
    E909.J34 2011
    973.932092—dc23
    [B]
                                                                    2011017340

First Edition

10 9 8 7 6 5 4 3 2

Grateful acknowledgment is made to the following for permission to reproduce photographs numbers 1, 12: Honolulu Star-Advertiser Library; 2, 5, 22, 24, 25, 27: courtesy Brendan Bannon; 3: Mooney Estate Collection; 4, 6–11: E. M. Kirk Family Estate; 13, 14: University of Hawaii Library; 15: Arthur Nachmanoff; 16: Anne Rand Library, International Longshore and Warehouse Union/Voice of the ILWU, Hawaii Local 142, Honolulu, May 1962 ; 17, 30, 32: Sally Jacobs; 18: Hulton/Deutsch Collection/CORBIS; 19: Anwar Hussein/Getty Images; 20: Buckingham Browne & Nichols School; 21: courtesy of Simmons College Archives; 23: Obama For America/Handout/Reuters/Corbis; 26: Hawa Auma; 28: AP Photo/Vincent Yu; 29: AP Photo/ Timur Emek; 31: Nation Media Group Limited.

For
Streett and Shi Shi
Whom I love

CONTENTS

PREFACE

Every man who has served as the president of the United States had parents who lived out their lives upon American soil.

Barack H. Obama did not. That fact has lent the president with the singular name both a hint of the exotic and—as his critics see it—a whiff of something decidedly un-American. The blood that makes Obama black flows from a place that is distinctly Other. His father, the other Barack H. Obama, did not come from somewhere known to most Americans, like England or Canada—places where the habits and manners are akin to that of America. Although several of the parents of early presidents were born in England or Ireland, they soon made their way across the channel and built their homes here. But Obama's paternal roots lie in far away Africa, specifically in the western region of Kenya that is populated by an ethnic group known as the Luo.

In Luoland, young men on reaching puberty routinely had their bottom six teeth removed as a coming of age ritual until well into the twentieth century. Polygamy is a long-standing practice, and men routinely take multiple wives to this day. The birth of twins is considered an ominous sign. At one time such a birth prompted a runner to streak to the home of the babies' grandmother, where he would secretly bury a hoe in an effort to stem the bad luck that the twins' arrival occasioned.

No other American president could say that about the land of their forefathers, nor would they likely brandish such information even if they could. Such a dramatic reflection of foreign roots—of "otherness"—is not exactly the kind of thing that wins the hearts and minds of voters in mainstream America.

It is partly for that reason that during Obama's determined march toward the White House in 2008 not a great deal was said about his father. Nor did the media produce a much more detailed portrait. At the time, his father's story was not easy to get, for the first Barack Obama had lived a disorganized life, one of fractured pieces that seemed to have little connective tissue. When he died in a car accident one night in 1982, even those close to him struggled to understand the chaotic forces that contributed to his end.

I played a role in that incomplete storytelling. In October of 2008 I wrote a profile of the elder Obama for *The Boston Globe*, where I had been a reporter for more than two decades. I was unable to go to Kenya to report the story but instead relied on dozens of telephone interviews and the contemporary journalist's tools of the trade—e-mail and text messages. The story accurately reflected the arc of the elder Obama's life, but there was much I could not understand without going to Kenya and walking the rocky plains that unfurl toward Lake Victoria and where his character was so deeply rooted. And yet the shadow of this mysterious presidential candidate's little-understood father riveted me. Even the candidate, who had written a memoir in large measure about the father he met only once in his life, seemed to yearn to know more about his enigmatic parent.

In the final weeks leading up to the election I resolved that if Obama made it to the White House, I would pursue the larger story. There was so much that was not known. How had Obama Sr., raised in the scrappy bush hundreds of miles from Nairobi, achieved the lofty heights that he did? With his superior intellectual abilities, why did he not get the Harvard University graduate degree for which he worked so hard and yearned so deeply? What were the deeper roots of his downfall? It was clear that his heavy consumption of alcohol played a part. Obama was given the nickname "Double-Double" due to his habit of ordering successive twin shots of whiskey at one sitting, sometimes accumulating up to sixteen shot glasses before him. But that there were far larger elements at play in the unfolding of his life's journey, not all of his own making, was also obvious. I knew from my initial reporting for the *Globe* that the older Obama's life was an extravagant journey, one inextricably linked to the

painful disappointments of Kenya's first presidency. The answers, somehow, must lie in the red dust of Luoland on the other side of the world.

I had never been to Africa before nor did I want to go in the slightest.
Eight years earlier a young relative of mine died in a brutal accident in a
game park in Botswana. Africa was the absolute last place in the world I
wanted to venture. And yet questions about the likely next president's
father continued to nag at me. Who he was and how the force of his personality had shaped his second son, even in his absence, seemed to be critical elements in the unfolding presidential drama. If Obama were to
become president, his largely unknown father lay at the core of a seismic
event that would bear upon developments around the globe for years and,
perhaps, even generations to come. I wanted to tell his story. Perhaps in
going to Africa I could also find some deeper understanding of what had
led to my family's personal tragedy as well.

In December of 2008, one month after Obama won the election, I was
on my way to the suburban town of Bracknell, west of London, to talk
with Obama's Sr.'s first wife, Grace Kezia. In her small apartment I heard
my first words of Dholuo, the language of the Luo tribe, as she recounted
for me how she met the new American president's father at a Christmas
dance more than a half-century ago. She showed me photographs of family gatherings at which the younger Obama had posed with half a dozen of
his relatives wearing vivid African dress—the kind of pictures that had not
figured remotely in the presidential campaign. That visit was the first step
in a long journey that took me to Hawaii, remote parts of the United
States, and Kenya time and again. By the end I had traveled seventy-five
thousand miles. I had spent days talking with dozens of Obamas in the village of Kanyadhiang, where the first Barack was born, and on one memo-
rable night I watched with them as a furious storm churned its way up
from Lake Victoria and lashed its wet fury upon their thatched-roof
homes. I had also broken two ribs, contracted salmonella poisoning from
a buffet in an elegant Nairobi hotel, and endured two bouts of pneumonia.
I had driven the torturous roads to countless remote homesteads bearing
rolls of barbed wire, machetes, and sacks of sugar, which were my gifts for
those generous enough to take their time from work to share their memories with me. On one of my last visits to Kanyadhiang, the goat I had

brought in the trunk of the car—the mode of transport for many an unlucky goat in Africa—was christened "Sally" in my honor. She was slaughtered shortly afterward—as is the fate of many an unlucky goat in Africa.

Not all Obamas were glad to see me. When the first Barack Obama died, he left behind a chaotic domestic tangle and a darkly checkered career. Some family members did not want his life's story told. But if it was going to be told, they wanted one of their own to do it. The last person they wanted writing about Obama's life was a *mzungu* (Swahili for a white person) from the United States. Several months after I started work on the book one Obama family member launched an e-mail campaign against the project, declaring that I was a Republican collaborator bent on bringing the president down and preventing him from running for another term. In the fall of 2009 Obama family members living near Kisumu, the principal city in western Kenya, received a flurry of such e-mails, and the e-mails' impact was chilling. There is no electricity in the village, which lies not far from Lake Victoria, but there are many cell phones, so the word traveled fast. By the following spring, when my car bounced down the rocky dirt road leading to the village, the reception was decidedly cool. Ironically, the barrage of e-mails was launched from Boston, Massachusetts, a little over one mile from my office at the *Boston Globe*.

Fortunately, the Obama extended family is as large as it is diverse. Although the international media has identified the home of the president's stepmother in Alego as the family's epicenter, there are many Obama relatives in both Kanyadhiang and Nairobi as well as in the United States. A good number of them understood that my interest in the family had nothing to do with politics and everything to do with expanding the historic record. They welcomed me into their homes, walked with me along tree-lined Harambee Avenue in Nairobi, where he worked for many years as a government economist, and introduced me to scores of people who had known him. They unfailingly responded to my succession of phone calls, texts, and e-mails over the course of two years. More important, they were unflinchingly honest in addressing both the triumphs and turbulence of Barack Obama's life. And when two Obama cousins accompanied me on my next journey to Kanyadhiang, the villagers moved beyond their wariness and once again agreed to talk.

The story of the president's father lies only partly in human memory. I was fortunate to find several repositories of documents that provided revealing windows on Obama's life both in Kenya and during the six years when he lived in the United States. On the back shelves of the Kenya National Archives in Nairobi there were hundreds of memos he wrote while working for the Ministry of Finance and Economic Planning and thick bundles of the minutes of meetings held during his years at the Kenya Tourist Development Corporation. In a storage facility in Lee's Summit, Missouri, where the paper records of what was once called the U.S. Immigration and Naturalization Service are stored, there is a folder bearing the name Barack H. Obama, alien registration number A11938537, which contained memos stretching from the time he arrived in Honolulu in 1959 until he was forced to leave Cambridge, Massachusetts, against his will in 1964. Assorted archives yielded still more. There were a dozen blue aerogrammes about Obama in the archives at Syracuse University and letters he had written to the popular Kenyan nationalist Tom Mboya stored at Stanford University. The paper trail was long.

What I found in the end was a story as unlikely as that of a certain Chicago lawyer who set his eyes on the White House and, despite the conventional wisdom that it couldn't be done, wound up being the first black man to live there. His father did something extraordinary as well.

The son of a cook for the British colonists in Nairobi, the first Barack Obama was a man of brilliance, one whose probing intellect enabled him to soar above his peers in the scrappy tropical bush in which he was raised. His destiny was to stand amongst a singular group of young Kenyans who were dispatched to America for an education and charged with shaping the course of the Kenya nation in the heady years after it achieved independence in 1963. Even among that handpicked group, Obama excelled. He was one of an elite cadre who was accepted for graduate study at the world's most prominent academic institution, Harvard University. As a young man, a path of limitless opportunity unfolded before him.

But Barack Obama was also a man prone to a certain reckless extreme. On his return to Nairobi, unable to hold down a handful of highly promising jobs, his astonishing early promise wilted. Confronted with the free-wheeling society of postcolonial Nairobi in the 1960s, Obama struggled to maintain his equilibrium. When he brazenly challenged the nation's steady drift to the political right and then courageously defied the country's autocratic first president when most others dared not, the momentum of his already faltering rise stalled. Just six years after he returned from the United States, the arc of his life had spun into a downward spiral from which he would never fully recover.

Some called him an impatient intellectual. Others saw him as an idealist, a man who could not square the political reality of the day with his heartfelt vision of a genuinely democratic Kenyan society. Whatever he is called, Barack Obama committed his life to the belief that the bounty and the burdens of the country he so loved should be shared by all. In the end what broke him was his disappointment in the failure of that dream.

1

THE OLD MAN

The sign is meant for tourists. But not many get this far.

It stands on the side of a red dirt road in western Kenya so pocked with holes that it is nearly impassable, its historic message shrouded in a thick coating of dust. "OBAMA OPIYO," it declares in blue capital letters, "Great grandfather of BARACK OBAMA Jr. (President, USA.)" A mere four generations does not begin to tell the story. This is Africa and so the forefathers must be acknowledged too. On the right side of the sign there is a list of the names of the past eight generations.

> NYANYODHI
> OCHWO
> OBONG'O
> OPIYO
> OBAMA −1
> HUSSEIN ONYANGO
> BARACK OBAMA SR.
> BARACK OBAMA Jr.
> (President, USA)

A red arrow points to the left, where the village of Kanyadhiang lies one teeth-jarring kilometer away. This is where the Obama side of an unlikely presidential epic begins. The American president's father, Barack Hussein Obama, was born here in a round mud hut with a thatched roof, a short distance from the once-bountiful waters of Lake Victoria. Nearly one hundred years before him a young farmer known as Obong'o decided to settle here in the mid 1800s, one finger of a vast diaspora of Luo pastoralists that came out of Sudan starting in the fifteenth century.[1] Although the earliest Obama ancestors, known as Jok' Owiny, had migrated to the lake's Winam Gulf region generations earlier, Obong'o was the one who established the family's home on the south side of the gulf, attracted by the rich fishing prospects and abundance of wild animals in the surrounding forests. The hut is long gone now, but several hundred Obamas still live in the shadow of the towering blue gum trees that the president's grandfather planted.

Since Obongo's arrival, little has changed in Kanyadhiang, which means "the place of the daughter of the cows" in the tribal language of Dholuo. There is no electricity, and people must still carry water by bucket up the hill from the muddy shores of the Awach River, although now they must treat it with purifying agents before it can be used. Cows and an occasional chicken wander the gently rolling terrain and pause to nibble the delicate yellow blossoms of the siala tree that hangs over Obama Opiyo's grave.

This is Luoland, the ancestral home of the Obama family's Luo tribe. It is a place where a young man's bottom six teeth were once routinely removed as a symbol of coming of age, and children are still often named for the conditions that prevailed at the time of their birth. In the Luo language "Onyango" means born in the early morning, whereas the common name "Okoth" means born while it is raining. In the weeks after the name Obama was engraved in history as the forty-fourth president of the United States, a great many babies were given the name. "Obama" is derived from the word *bam*, which means crooked or indirect.

The first Barack Obama is Kanyadhiang's greatest success story. Long before that name entered the global political lexicon, it carried great weight in these parts. Many among the older generation in the village remember Obama as a child swimming at Rapandu Beach, a point of the river reserved for men, and his prowess at the dance competitions in the lantern-lit dimness of the Kanyadhiang Social Hall. But Obama's mind was even faster than his feet, and he wielded his intelligence as a passport to transport him to the farthest reaches of the globe.

Ever since his son became a candidate for the U.S. presidency, a truncated version of the father's life story has become stock fodder. It goes like this: In the late 1950s, as Kenya was beginning to prepare to assume independence from the British colonial government that had occupied the country for over sixty years, Obama was one of a select cadre of young men and women chosen to travel to the United States to get a college education. He ventured to the University of Hawaii, where he met a young girl with luminous brown eyes named Ann, and in only three years he graduated Phi Beta Kappa. Then, incredibly, the boy who had walked barefoot five miles to school each day and whose job had been to lay a mix of cow dung and mud on the earthen floor to keep the dust down, won a scholarship to pursue his PhD in economics at Harvard University. On his return to Nairobi at age twenty-eight, Obama landed a job as an economist at Shell/BP and was poised to take his place among the *uhuru*, or "independence" generation charting the course for newly independent Kenya. With a wardrobe of tailored suits and a *mzungu*, the Swahili word for a white person, for a wife, Barack Obama was destined to be a Big Man, for sure. A photograph of him leaning against his blue Ford Fairlane and flanked by beaming villagers, which was taken on the day he returned from the United States, sits on a cousin's mantel in Kanyadhiang and is a cherished family possession.

As suddenly as it began, however, his ascent was over. Six years after he returned from the United States, Obama had been let go from one promising job and was fired from another, his career abruptly dead-ended. All three of his marriages had failed, and he was barely on speaking terms with any of his children. Penniless and increasingly dependent on his beloved Johnnie Walker Black, he collapsed at night on the floor at a series of friends' homes and lived for periods alone in a solitary hotel room. It was a monumental fall. Few, even among those closest to him, understood why it happened and the elements that contributed to it.

"Barack was a very upsetting case," said Wilson Ndolo Ayah, a schoolmate of Obama's who worked in a host of government ministries and served as a member of the Kenyan parliament. "He didn't commit a crime. He didn't do something wrong particularly. He just didn't finish the race. As schoolboys, we were always taught that you must finish the race no matter what. But he didn't. He just collapsed."

LATE ON A NOVEMBER evening in 1982, Obama was driving home when he rammed his white pickup truck headlong into the high stump of a eucalyptus tree at the side of the road and died instantly. He was forty-six. Obama's eight children, some of whom had not seen him for years, largely closed the door on the subject of their father. For better or worse, the Old Man was gone.

A quarter-century later another Barack Obama emerged, this one a cerebral U.S. Senator from Chicago who was angling, quixotically it seemed, for the Democratic nomination for the U.S. presidency. As that heavily laden name dominated the headlines and the nightly news, it triggered a flood of complex emotions among some of the elder Obama's children. They were struck at how oddly the younger Barack's name was pronounced. The Old Man had also been called *Barack*, but his was a working man's name, with the emphasis on the first syllable. The American pronunciation was heavy on the second syllable, giving the name a more formal, somewhat aristocratic cast. This particularly amused the elder Barack's three surviving wives—not that they were talking to each other.

Reporters scoured the younger Obama's background, and questions invariably arose about his namesake and the Kenyan family he had met on a handful of occasions. The phenomenon of Obama's candidacy and the worldwide prominence that his name achieved after he became America's first African American president prompted some of the children to begin rethinking their relationship with the Old Man and to grow curious about the elements of his chaotic life. Somehow they were all bound by that restless, bespectacled onslaught of a man who was their father and now to this gentler but no less intense version of him on the front pages of America's newspapers.

The questions led to more questions. Who was their father? And who, for that matter, were really his children? To get to the truth of the man, how could any of them penetrate the skein of lies and half-truths he had woven? Even the makeup of his immediate family was a confounding jumble. Three years after his death some of his children and wives became embroiled in a legal brawl aimed at establishing exactly who his legitimate heirs were and to which of his "wives" had he actually been married.

The colorful legal drama, which went on for years, pitted the first wife against the fourth, the eldest son against the youngest, and generally divided the family into two warring camps. At the heart of the matter was a claim by Obama's first wife, Grace Kezia Aoko Obama, that she had never divorced her husband and remained married to him at the time of his death.[2] If that were true, then none of his subsequent three marriages—including the one with the president's mother—would have been legitimate. A host of family members who took sides on the issue provided conflicting affidavits peppered with name-calling and insults. Even Obama's sixty-seven-year-old mother, frail and heartbroken over her first son's death, weighed in and declared that Grace had long ago divorced her son.[3] The Nairobi High Court judge considering the dizzying squabble apparently believed Obama's mother: In 1989 Judge J. F. Shields ruled that not only had Grace divorced her husband but also that two of the four children she claimed he had fathered with her were not his sons at all.[4] And that was just the first phase of the battle.

The name of Barack Hussein Obama II, the second son, crops up only incidentally in the bulging pink case files in Nairobi's High Court. No one in the case ever challenged the legitimacy of his paternity. But in July 1997 Barack Hussein Obama of Chicago, Illinois, deftly extracted himself from the matter with a brief letter to the court disavowing any claim he might have on the estate, which was worth about 410,500 Kenyan shillings, or $57,500, at the time his father died. He wrote the letter six months after he was sworn in to serve his first term in the Illinois Senate representing the 13th district.

Nearly a decade earlier, in the summer of 1988, Obama had launched his own effort to uncover the father about whom he had often wondered. At the time, his father had been dead for six years and he had just completed work as a community organizer in Chicago and was preparing to enter Harvard Law School. During a five-week visit to Kenya, Obama met many members of his sprawling clan for the first time and listened to their stories of his father's political frustrations and domestic travails. He also found that many of his relatives had no greater command of his father's essence than he had gleaned from his mother's recollections. The elder Obama seemed a baffling mystery to many with whom he had lived and worked, including his disparate tribe of children.

Although he was a master of the verbal parrying and one-upmanship that are the Luos' stock in trade and was famous for his legendary black velvet baritone, the elder Obama confided in virtually no one, not even those in his wide circle of drinking comrades. Talk of personal matters, and certainly of children, he considered to be a show of weakness. He mentioned the son he had fathered while in Hawaii to only a handful of his closest friends and family members, even though he kept a photograph of that little boy, riding a tricycle with a small cap perched jauntily on his head, on his bureau. Taken a couple of years after he had left his small family in Hawaii, the picture always followed him through his many moves and dislocations.[5]

His children may have understood him least of all. As Auma Obama, President Obama's half-sister, says in *Dreams from My Father*, "I can't say I really knew him, Barack. Maybe nobody did . . . not really. His life was so scattered. People only knew scraps and pieces, even his own children."[6]

Some of his children have pored over the letters and papers their father left behind, trying to pull all those inconclusive scraps and pieces together. Four of the five children indisputably fathered by Barack Obama have written books that are at least in part a rumination of the Old Man and his impact on their lives. Like *Dreams from My Father*, each of the works is a yearning of sorts, an effort to make some sense of their father's character and complex legacy.

Only his firstborn son, Abong'o Malik Obama, a volatile fifty-three-year-old who lives with his three wives near the family's compound in western Kenya, has not written a book about his father—at least not yet. Malik recently made headlines of his own when he took a nineteen-year-old schoolgirl as his third wife. He has also irritated some Obama family members when he built a small mosque on his property that the steady parade of tourists heading to the Obama compound pass daily. Some Obamas worry that such a glaring symbol of the family's Muslim faith will negatively impact the Obama presidency. Malik has accused others of trying to profit from his father's life and says that he intends eventually to write the definitive biography of his father himself.[7]

Auma Obama, Obama's only daughter and the second of his children born to his first wife, Grace Kezia, has painful recollections of a distant father who rarely spoke to her and often returned home from work drunk and irritable.[8] But as she read some of the newspaper accounts of his life, she found she wanted to understand more about the forces that shaped his experience and left him so embittered. She called Peter Oloo Aringo, a longtime friend of Obama's and then a member of Kenya's Parliament representing the Alego district where he spent his childhood, who recalled that Auma was "very troubled about [her father's] life. She had spent more time with him than most of the children, but she felt she had not known him at all. She wanted to know how we had gotten along, how we had been friends, that kind of thing. But mostly she wanted to understand what had led to his downfall."

Two months before the 2010 midterm elections in the United States, Auma published a memoir in the language of her adopted Germany, called *Das Leben kommt immer dazwischen*, or "Life Always Comes In Between." Her book is a deeply felt lamentation for a father so preoccupied with his own ambition, so riven by his own insecurity, that he barely sees the lonely little girl gazing up at him. When at last he reaches out for her toward the end of his life, she yearns for him but does not absolve him. "I simply could not forgive my father," Auma writes. "So much had gone wrong while we were together and in my eyes, then and now, it was his fault. . . . He never had time to listen but acted as if everything was alright. He had never asked us, and maybe himself, how we children were actually doing."[9]

Few were as profoundly affected by the Old Man as Mark Ndesandjo, the oldest of two boys born in Kenya to Obama Sr. and his third wife. By that time in his life, Obama Sr. was, according to Mark and his mother, a profoundly abusive husband who cheated on his mother repeatedly and often beat her. Deeply traumatized by his childhood years, Mark left Kenya to attend college in the United States in the 1980s and resolved to have nothing more to do with the hated Obama name.[10] When he met his half-brother Barack for the first time on a visit home to Kenya, Mark told him, "At a certain point I made a decision not to think about who my real father was. He was dead to me even when he was still alive. I knew that he was a drunk and showed no concern for his wife or children. That was enough."[11] Determined that he would be nothing like the cold and loveless man who haunted his childhood, Mark had blocked all memory of him.

By the time the presidential cavalcade came two decades later, Mark was a forty-three-year-old international marketing consultant living in Shenzhen, China, with a BA in physics from Brown University and master's degrees from Stanford and Emory Universities. At least once during the campaign he met with the half-brother he resembles markedly in both stature and expression. Obama describes his brother's appearance as though he were "looking into a foggy mirror." Like his siblings, Mark found himself propelled by his half-brother's inspiring success to reexamine the family's turbulent history and open doors he had long thought firmly closed behind him. He spent months reading the diaries that his mother kept during the seven years she was married to his father and began to ply her with questions he had never wanted to ask before.[12]

Years earlier Mark had begun work on a book that explored many of the same issues that Barack Obama wrestled with in *Dreams from My Father*. Mark was likewise struggling with questions about his own mixed-race identity, his relationship to his father, and his search for rootedness. Obama's election in November of 2008 is what moved him to complete his manuscript, and at the end of 2009 he wrote an autobiographical novel called *Nairobi to Shenzhen: A Novel of Love in the East* under the name Mark Okoth Obama Ndesandjo. The world's embrace of the Obama name had at last enabled him to take ownership of it as well.

In his book the father figure is a menacing and dangerous presence. His son—David in the book—remembers him as "the hulking man whose breath reeked of cheap Pilsner beer who had often beaten his mother. He had long searched for good memories of his father but had found none."[13] One night, the father turns violently on his wife while their six-year-old son cowers in the next bedroom listening in horror. "His mother's voice was screaming as if terrified," Mark wrote. "The child almost didn't recognize it. And then there were some thumps as of someone falling. His father's angry voice raised itself as if in a duet with the unrecognizable voice. . . . His mother was being attacked and he couldn't protect her."[14]

Nor did his conversations with his mother trigger particularly happy memories of his father. "I do not remember him ever smiling. Except when he drank," Mark said in an interview.

Yet, as with his older brother's memoir, even Mark found a resolution of sorts through his writing. In revisiting his experiences, he began to reflect on his own father's life and the hardships he too had endured. "I knew that my father had been through some traumatic experiences as a child and I began to realize that there must have been an emotional hardening in him that was not his fault," Mark explained. "When love is absent or you are physically abused as he was you develop a hard emotional skin. And that made me think differently about him."

Next in line is George Hussein Onyango, the youngest of the sibling tribe, now twenty-nine, who lives in the sprawling Nairobi slum of Huruma on the city's east side. In the final months of his life Obama Sr. moved in with a young woman less than half his age, named Jael Atieno Onyango. George, their only child, was born six months before Obama died and had little contact with other Obama family members until his political half-brother came on the stage. His mother's claim as an heir is what triggered the legal battle over the question of who was Barack Obama's wife at the time of his death.

George too has grappled with his enigmatic father. A year after Obama's election George wrote a memoir called *Homeland: An Extraordinary Story of Hope and Survival*. For George, the absence of his father initially propelled him downward, not up. But his tale is one of resurrection. It begins with a grim depiction of his youth: School expulsion is followed by the drinking of the alcoholic brew known as *chang'aa* and the smoking of weed which culminates in a prison stay on robbery charges that are ultimately dismissed. Confronted with Obama's inspirational Senate victory in 2004, however, George managed to bring an end to his ghetto lifestyle and recast himself as an advocate for Huruma's poor and dispossessed. Now, soccer is his passion.

Obama Sr. wafts through his book like the ghost that he was to his youngest son, materializing briefly in often heroic proportions. Family members describe him as famously generous, readily paying the school fees for a host of nieces and nephews and doling out fistfuls of cash on his visits back home. A man of abiding principle, Obama Sr. burned with a passionate faith in his country and a willingness to challenge its increasingly corrupt political leaders at a profound personal cost. He may not have always shown it—he was an African man, after all—but he felt deeply. As George flounders through his early teenage years in the book, family members are forever reminding him of the brilliant economist who was his father and urging him to follow in his father's footsteps. He quotes his mother as saying that Obama Sr. "would have been a role model for me if he were still alive. . . . She remarked what a tragic loss his death had been for her and the wider family, if not the country as a whole."[15]

Despite the sometimes brash tone of his book, in person George is a shy young man who seems a bit bewildered by the juggernaut of his American brother's success, not to mention the trail of international reporters who began to journey down the rutted dirt road to his shack in 2008, marveling in their stories at the disparity between his life and that of the president. The comparison was jarring on both ends, as each Obama son was cast at the radical end of an astonishingly unlikely spectrum.

Although George has mourned the lack of his father, the absence of much of his immediate family occupies him even more as he sits under a string of drying laundry in the makeshift tin shack in which he lives with several cousins. In fact, only when Obama visited Kenya in 2006 did George meet some of his relatives on his father's side for the first time and visit the home of his step-grandmother, known globally as Mama Sarah.[16] Jael has remarried and lives with her new family in an Atlanta, Georgia, suburb, though she has tried repeatedly without success to get him a visa to come to the United States.

In the churning alleys of Huruma, however, an Obama is still an Obama, and many in Kenya assume that must mean a link to the White House and all its power and riches. George is often accompanied by a heavy-set young man with blood-shot eyes whom he half-jokingly calls "my security man." But the truth is that George has little more access to the president than the tattered beggars who live next door to him in Huruma. George has met Barack Jr. on two occasions—once when Obama dropped in on his school when he was a five-year-old and again when he visited as a U.S. Senator.

George is hopeful that eventually he will get to talk to President Obama about their father. For when George himself wanted to learn about the Old Man, it was to *Dreams* that he turned. "I still have a lot of questions," George shrugs. "I'd like to know who my brothers are and I'd like to know who my father was. I'm proud of him. I think."

A YEAR AFTER HIS FATHER'S DEATH, Obama met him one night in his sleep, "in a cold cell, in a chamber of my dreams," he wrote in his memoir. He found his father locked in the cell alone, dressed only in a cloth wrapped around his waist, his face ashen and thin. The elder Obama appraised his son and told him how much he loved him. But when the son tried to depart with his father and insisted that they leave the cell together, Obama the father refused. Obama awoke weeping at the loss of his father but realized also that "even in his absence his strong image had given me some bulwark on which to grow up, an image to live up to, or disappoint."[17] Obama resolved then and there to search for his father, to somehow come to know him.

While still in his twenties, in the course of a search for his own identity that he chronicled in his memoir, Obama Jr. spent years inquiring about the father he met only once in his life. In talking with family members in Kenya, he made the painful discovery that his father had not been the towering success that he had been led to believe as a child. Although he gained a radically new perception of his father, Obama acknowledged in the end that "I still didn't know the man my father had been. What had happened to all his vigor, his promise? What had shaped his ambitions?"[18] Like many of his half-siblings on his father's side, ultimately Obama was unable to comprehend the forces that created and shaped the Old Man.

The person in the world best positioned to uncover the story of the first Barack Hussein Obama is, of course, the president of the United States. With infinite resources and manpower at his disposal, he could presumably assign a team of investigators to the task and have a comprehensive profile for his eyes only in short order. Family members who have presented sanitized narratives to the media or even refused to talk at all would likely be more inclined to share their blunter perceptions with one of their own. But, apparently, he has not done so. Despite the research he completed as he prepared to write *Dreams*, his old man remains a thinly understood character in his book, a brooding specter. Obama seems ambivalent about just how far he wants to go in probing his father's soul. There are many places he has not gone.

What he discovered on his Kenya sojourn was that Barack Senior was a man fundamentally flawed by his own inner demons and undone by his own fears, much like his own father, Hussein Onyango, before him. If he had been so inclined, the younger Obama might have gone one step further and discovered a curious reflection of himself, another "foggy mirror." After all, the two men have much in common. Both Baracks grew to be men of keen intellect and analytic ability. A boldness of ambition enabled each of them to imagine a life for themselves far beyond the proscribed circumstances of their birth. Each man exhibited hubris, some would call it arrogance, that enabled them to dream large—and they did so despite the fact that they had each been orphaned by a parent, left to explain that empty space as best they could. As it happened, the two of them came of age at a time when the currents of change revealed before them a life once thought impossible.

And each of them walked toward that opportunity without hesitation.

Barack Obama Sr. believed he had failed in his life, but the full scope of his existence was unknown to him. Had he been aware of the events to come a generation later, he might have appraised himself somewhat differently. For what greater success could a man aspire to than to have produced a child who would become the first black president of the United States, the person who stands at the helm of the world? One wonders what he might he have said if he had known of his own filial legacy. Neil Abercrombie, governor of Hawaii who was a student with Obama Sr. at the University of Hawaii, grasped his essence better than most. "If someone had come up to him and said, 'You know, your son might be the president one day,' he would have said, 'Well, of course. He's my son.'"[19]

2

WINYO PINY KIBORNE

"For a bird, the world is never too far."

The tribal prophet Kimnyole arap Turukat foretold its coming long before the white man knew of it himself. It would rear from the vast lake to the east, a lethal iron snake belching smoke and fire and uncoil across tribal lands before at last quenching its thirst in the waters to the west. The beast would bear with it a kind of foreigner never seen before, a "red stranger" who would one day rule the land. Kimnyole was right.

The white man called it the Uganda Railway, a 582-mile steel corridor that would link the coastal city of Mombasa to the shores of Lake Victoria and the dark heart of the African interior beyond. Launched by the imperial British government in 1896, it was the one of the largest engineering efforts in the empire's history. It was also a colossal financial disaster, costing more than double its original price tag of £2.2 million and requiring the importation of more than thirty thousand Indian laborers, many of whom were devoured by lions. As the beleaguered railroad inched across the arid African plain, the British press dubbed it the "Lunatic Line." But when it was complete, it dramatically altered the land that would become Kenya, propelling the nation into the twentieth century at a dizzying pace.

On December 21, 1901, the *Times* of London exultantly reported that the final rail plate had been laid at the terminal of Port Florence and the interior of East Africa was at last open to the world.[1] There was still a great deal to be done. Spurs and branch lines needed to be constructed. A fleet of steamers that could ferry passengers to the other side of the lake and return laden with the Ugandan riches of ivory, skins, and horns had yet to be assembled. And then there were the Africans. Since the iron snake's arrival, Kimnyole's people, fierce warriors called the Nandi, battled the beast as best they could, raiding the British outposts and stealing precious steel, wires, and supplies. But the imperial machine churned steadily forward, and many of the Nandi were slaughtered in a hail of British bullets.[2]

Word of the white man's coming traveled fast across the grassy plains of the Kavirondo region that sweeps down to the lake's edge, the home of what was then Kenya's third largest ethnic group, the Luo. Few had ever seen a white man but for the occasional missionary or Arab trader who came laden with sugar and cloth. They called the newcomer the "red stranger" for his curious skin tone, which seemed alternately pale or flushed, depending on how long he was in the sun. It was said that if you touched his skin, it would come off in your hand because it was so soft.[3] He had flat hair and his body was covered from neck to knee with clothing, whereas the Luo wore only a stretch of animal skin or loosely draped cloth. Many of the newcomers carried deadly metal sticks that erupted with fire.

In a small village fifty miles south of the railhead, the elders discussed these developments among themselves. It seemed best to stay away from the foreigners for the time being until their purpose could be understood. But at least one young man, a tall boy with curly dark hair, did not heed the elders' advice. His name was Onyango Obama, and he was the second of eight brothers born to Obama Opiyo in 1895, the same year that the British proclaimed the territory its East Africa Protectorate. He would be one of the first from his village to learn English and Swahili.

From the beginning Onyango was not like the other boys. He was solemn and rarely played with the other children in the village, preferring instead solitary pursuits of his own. He never sat still for more than a few minutes, and some laughed that he had "ants up his anus."[4] But he was intensely curious about many things and would often sit at the feet of the elders as they discussed the medicinal values of plants. In this way he learned the herbalist's secrets—useful knowledge in a land where magic and religion are entwined and spirits called night runners, or *jajuok*, streak through the darkness emitting chilling sounds.

Onyango was also curious about the white man and resolved to learn about him. One day, as a young teenager, he headed on foot to Port

Florence, which would be renamed Kisumu, and was not heard from for many months. On his return, he seemed a different person. He wore the pants and shirt of the white man, and his feet, unbelievably, were clad in shoes. When asked why he was wearing such strange skins, Onyango said nothing. His father concluded that Onyango's odd clothing was intended to conceal the fact that he had been circumcised, a grave violation of Luo custom, or was suffering from an outbreak of sores. Obama advised his other sons, "Don't go near this brother of yours. He is unclean."[5] Onyango returned to the provincial capital of Kisumu, where he would work alongside the white man for many years. His life would turn out to be a vivid chronicle of the repressive colonial years and Kenya's tumultuous drive for independence.

It was Onyango who would usher the family from the wilds of the African bush to the elegant parlors of Nairobi's finest homes, where he worked as a cook, a critical step in a long migration that had begun many generations earlier. The Obama family's ancestral journey was launched nearly a thousand miles northwest of Nairobi on the broad savannah grasslands of the Bahr-el-Ghazal Province in Sudan at the edge of the churning waters of the White Nile.[6] It was there that a nomadic people known as the River Lake Nilotes, believed to be the earliest ancestors of the Obama clan, lived for hundreds of years tending the cattle that were their lifeblood. At some point in the fifteenth century the Nilotes began to drift toward Uganda, apparently prompted by overcrowding from the east, in search of a less populated home. Their fitful migration continued for more than one hundred years, moving through northern Uganda and on into western Kenya, where they arrived sometime between 1500 and 1550.[7]

Historians believe there were four migrational surges into the Nyzanza Province that embraces Lake Victoria and was once known as Kavirondo, a stream of assorted clans and subclans that would eventually make up Kenya's Luo people.[8] The second surge was known as the Jok' Owiny, or the people of Owiny the Great, a fierce warrior who is President Obama's great-great-great-great-great-great-great-great-great-great-great grandfather and the first of his ancestors to live in Kenya.[9] On their arrival in Alego, where Onyango's widow, Sarah Ogwel, and other Obama relatives continue to live today, they encountered some hostile Bantu-speaking tribes. After lengthy combat, however, Owiny's descendants emerged victorious. Many of the Bantu remained and married into the Luo families, with whom the Bantu shared farming techniques and local knowledge of the land.

By the early 1800s Alego too had grown crowded, prompting fighting among the Luo, so some began to migrate again, this time drifting further south along Lake Victoria's eastern edge. Owiny's descendant, Obong'o, was one of them. As a young man he moved to the southeastern shores of the Winam Gulf, where he was able to make a living fishing the abundant tilapia and helping other men to clear their land.[10] Perhaps overwhelmed by the burden of his relocation and the huge amount of work it entailed, Obong'o died at a young age, but one of his sons later fathered a boy named Obama Opiyo. This grandson was the one who oversaw the building of the scores of homesteads that remain in Kanyadhiang today and fathered the president's own grandfather, Onyango Obama, with one of his five wives.[11]

The arrival of the British shortly after Onyango's birth marked a crucial juncture in Kenya's history, one that would usher in sweeping changes that radically altered the traditional African way of life. Sanctioned by the Congress of Berlin in 1884, which had brutally divided the African continent among the European powers with total disregard for indigenous peoples or topography, the British monarchy made its move into East Africa, propelled by a host of ambitions. At the top of the list was protecting the precious headwaters of the Nile in neighboring Uganda from Germany and other predators at all costs. Furthermore, the British railroad could serve to stem the continuing slave trade once and for all while also opening up trade routes that had previously operated over dirt tracks fraught with wild animals and hostile tribes. The British also believed firmly that Christianity and the white man's ways could help to illuminate the soul of Africa and bring civilization to the "heathen masses."

Inspired by their goal of both economic and human conquest, British administrators marched into rural Africa with their clipboards and their cherished Maxim machine guns in hand. The Uganda Railroad had already cost the British government far more than it had ever intended to spend, and the Tory leaders were adamant that the new protectorate was going to pay for itself just as the other colonies in its far-flung empire were required to do.[12] And so one of the first things the administrators did was to impose a system of taxation on its new subjects. Never mind that the Luo had long operated under a barter system and had no actual money—that would come soon enough.

Oginga Odinga, Luoland's political luminary and the country's preeminent opposition leader in the years after independence, was a young boy living in Central Nyanza in the formative years of British control. He recalls in his biography, *Not Yet Uhuru*, that Africans associated white people with five things: inoculations, forced labor, clothes, schools, and taxes. When government clerks came to the village, he wrote, the children, "watched them take a papyrus reed from the roof of each hut and cut it neatly in two. When the reeds were tied in neat bundles they represented the registration of that *boma*."[13] In this form of double accounting, one bundle of reeds was given to the chief and the clerk kept the other bundle. The tax collectors who accompanied the white man did not speak the Luo language of Dholuo and were not people of the tribe. They were called *okoche*.

Taxes were only the beginning. In the years leading up to World War I, Kenya was transformed from a loose association of clans and disparate ethnic groups into an administrative operation run by force and coercion. The machinery the British established to achieve that organizational structure brought an abrupt end to the Luo migration and disrupted many cultural patterns. Tribal chiefs, or *ruodhi*, were induced to be a part of the process and charged with keeping order and collecting taxes on behalf of the colonial government. Not only did this undermine the traditional authority of tribal elders, but the chiefs themselves were often prone to bribery and nepotism, which caused many Luos to lose faith in their leaders.[14]

But the more devastating and far-reaching changes had to do with land. In a parallel effort to finance the protectorate, the British launched a campaign to encourage European settlers to come to Kenya and grow crops that could be sold on the world market. They ran advertisements in newspapers extolling the region's fertile soil, ample sunshine, and abundant low-cost labor supply. One poster for the railway proclaimed that its observation cars "pass through the Greatest Natural GAME PRESERVE in the WORLD" and referred to the highlands as "a winter home for aristocrats."[15] Lured by the prospect of an untrammeled "White Man's Country," as author Elspeth Huxley dubbed the new colony, settlers came in a steady stream. The first to arrive were the white immigrants from South Africa, followed by the aristocratic stock from some of London's most notable families and later veterans of the world wars, all consumed by a vision of adventure and opportunity. Their hedonistic lifestyle and decadent ways cultivated in a region that came to be known as "Happy Valley," where drugs and multiple sex partners were de rigueur would become the subject of many a film and book.

For these agricultural settlers, the colonial government had targeted the protectorate's most luscious land, the fertile highlands in Central Province north of Nairobi that generations of the Masai and Kikuyu people had occupied. As the white settlers bought up the fertile tracts, the Africans were provided specially designated "native reserves," defined geographic areas that had been proscribed for each of Kenya's ethnic groups. For the Kikuyu, who ultimately lost over sixty thousand acres to the settlers in southern Kiambu, the displacement would have devastating consequences both materially and psychologically. As Caroline Elkins wrote in *Imperial Reckoning*, "To be a man or a woman—to move from childhood to adulthood—a Kikuyu had to have access to land.... A Kikuyu could not be a Kikuyu without land."[16] The reserves were soon crowded and lacked adequate space for the Kikuyu to grow enough food to be self-sufficient, thus forcing some to work for the settlers on the very land on which they had once lived. Called "squatters," they were initially free to grow crops and graze their animals, but they soon found themselves subject to draconian restrictions.

Once the settlers had committed to the White Man's Country, the colonial government had to make good on its promise of cheap labor. A hut tax was imposed on each dwelling, forcing the occupants to work off the debt through physical labor or to earn wages that could retire the debt. The deeply despised tax marked the beginning of a cash economy that had wide-ranging impact. When voluntary labor was insufficient for the settlers' needs, chiefs and headmen served as labor recruiters and scoured their areas for able-bodied men who were then forced into low-paying work contracts. With the halt to migratory patterns that traditionally enabled the Luo to move as they needed so as to secure additional fertile land, many in Nyanza were forced to work outside the reserves in order to earn cash. As Odinga wrote in his biography, "The toll that White rule exacted from Nyanza was labour, not land. Our province became the country's largest labor reserve."[17]

To ensure that workers traveling to their jobs remained manageable and pliant, the British devised a compulsory registration system that by 1920 required all African males over age sixteen to carry an identification pass called a *kipande* when not on their reserve. The pass contained not only identifying information such as a person's name and fingerprint but also an employer's evaluation of the individual's work performance. By 1928 the number of Kenyans carrying the kipande had reached 675,000.[18] The small dog-eared cards were easily the most reviled tentacle in the colonial government's elaborate web of far-reaching controls.

As a house servant in Nairobi, Onyango Obama was also required to register with the government. Onyango was given a small rust-colored book the size of a passport that, like the kipande, contained a range of detailed personal information. Each book contained a stern warning reminding those who failed to carry their books at all times that they would be, "liable to a fine not exceeding one hundred shillings or to imprisonment not exceeding six months or to both." Onyango's personal details follow, penned in an elegant script.[19]

Native Registration Ordinance No.: Rwl A NBI 0976717.
Race or Tribe: Ja'Luo
Usual Place of Residence When not Employed: Kisumu.
Sex: M
Age: 35
Height and Build: 6'0" Medium.
Complexion: Dark.
Nose: Flat.
Mouth: Large.
Hair: Curly.
Teeth: Six missing.
Scars, Tribal Markings or Other Peculiarities: None.

At the back of the book, several of Onyango's employers wrote assessments of their servant, which were largely positive. Onyango held a series of jobs for which he was paid about 60 East African Shillings a month, equal to about $145 today.[20] Capt. C. Harford of Nairobi's Government House wrote that Onyango "performed his duties as personal boy with admirable diligence." Mr. A. G. Dickson gushed that "he can read and write English and follows any recipes . . . apart from other things his pastries are excellent." But he lamented that he would no longer need Onyango because "I am no longer on Safari." But Mr. Arthur W. H. Cole of the East Africa Survey Group was distinctly unhappy with his houseboy after one week on the job and declared that Onyango "was found to be unsuitable and certainly not worth 60 shillings per month."[21]

Although he lived much of the time in Nairobi, Onyango regularly returned to Kendu Bay, the larger township near Kanyadhiang, walking the entire 220-mile journey on foot. Onyango had carefully saved his money and built himself a home not far from those of his brothers. However, he lived in a manner that was so different from his siblings, so unlike that of any other villager, that he became the object of great curiosity and conversation. In leaving the confines of the village and adopting some of the white man's ways, Onyango had begun to hold himself apart from some of his own people, thus becoming alien to their ways. At times he was no longer at ease with his neighbors, and his stratification between the two cultures was a foreshadowing of the kind of dislocation that his son would experience in an even more extreme way.

Onyango had learned a great deal more from his *mzungu* employers than how to bake scones or on which side of a plate setting to put the knife or fork. Onyango was now a clean man, one nearly obsessed with hygiene and orderliness. He washed himself constantly and demanded that people rinse their feet before they enter his hut. His home, too, was immaculate, and he demanded that things be returned to their proper place. Whereas the villagers regularly ate *ugali*, a staple porridge of maize and water, or *sukuma wiki*, a plate of cooked greens, Onyango prepared for himself aromatic breads and scrambled eggs in butter. He did not allow cows anywhere near his hut because he felt the flies that accompanied them were unsanitary.

A man of few words, Onyango had an elaborate set of rules governing how things should be done. Charles Oluoch, a village elder whose grandfather was one of Onyango's seven brothers, recalls that at mealtimes Onyango insisted that others wait to wash their hands until after he had washed his own. He would then eat his meal alone, "and no one could sit down at the table until he was done," explained Oluoch, fifty-six and still living in Kanyadhiang.* When Onyango visited the homes of his brothers, he instructed their wives on how to cook their food and demanded that only a single measure of water ever be put in a pot, with no additional liquid allowed.[22] He did not like people visiting his home. And if a person wished to see him, he required that they make an appointment. And when they arrived at the arranged time, if he consented to see them at all, they had better have something specific to address, or beware.

"You would fear facing him," recalled Arthur Reuben Owino, seventy-nine, who attended school with Barack, Onyango's son. "You would think *very* carefully what you wanted to say to him. He was a very frank person and if he didn't like what you were saying he would tell you point blank. He liked to argue. He'd say, 'No, no no. It's not like that,' or, 'It's not done that way.' Even if it was your way of doing it. You had to do it *his* way. That was the *right* way."

With his impressive city job and fluency in English and Swahili, Onyango was a man of significant stature in the village. But his manner instilled more fear than respect. The two words that people invariably use to describe him are *kwiny*, meaning harsh, or *ger*, which means about the same but in a different dialect. Onyango could not bear the sound of a crying child, and if a mother failed to keep her baby quiet, he would promptly strike her with his cane. Likewise, a woman who did not answer his summons on the first call would feel the weight of his cane or, worse, the four-lashed whip made of stiff hippopotamus hide that he kept at the ready beside his door. Hawa Auma, one of his nine children, remembers that when women in the household heard his voice as he approached the house, they would hide behind large pots, or *dak*, so he could not see them. "My dad was very harsh," Hawa Auma declared in Swahili. "If he was caning one of his children and someone happened to ask him why he was doing so, he would turn around and cane them senselessly, too."

Obama Madoho remembers the sting of the dreaded whip all too well. Seventy-three and curved with age, Madoho was eleven years old when he

---

*All ages in the book reflect the individual's age at the time this book was published.

made the mistake of allowing his cows—and their attendant flies—to stray too near to Onyango's hut. He recalls his age because he had just begun to wear clothes for the first time. "The whip had four straps to it, so when he hit you, it was like he was hitting you four times at once," explained Madoho, who lives next door to the Obama compound in Alego. "I can tell you I was never so foolish as to take the cows near to him again."

Nor was Onyango like most other Kenyan men in another significant aspect: his religion. During his childhood in the early 1900s Christian missionaries were just beginning to set up the schools that would provide an education for many Kenyan schoolchildren, including Onyango himself. At the time many were eager to learn the ways of the white man and therefore readily converted to Christianity, which is now the dominant religion in Luoland.

But the mission teachers also taught a submissiveness bred of Christian doctrine, one that colonial administrators wholly endorsed. A good and forgiving Christian was to "turn the other cheek" and "forgive your enemies." The missionary teachers also declared un-Christian many African practices of which they disapproved, such as polygamy and witchcraft, and insisted these practices be abandoned immediately. The Africans, who had traditionally regarded multiple wives as a status symbol reflecting a man's wealth, were made to feel ashamed of their behavior and uncertain about their own beliefs. Christian doctrine reinforced that sense of inferiority by proscribing that Africans accept their lot in life as ordained by the Almighty and bend to the fate that befell them. Passivity was the mantra, and the colonial administrators were glad of it. As the esteemed Kenyan historian Bethwell A. Ogot put it, "Thus both the Government and the Missionaries aimed at producing obedient and meek Africans who believed that the white man was always right because he was morally superior."[23]

But Onyango was not buying it. Although he respected the white man's discipline and organizational strength, he considered many of the *mzungu*'s practices unjust and their cultural affectations foolish. To him, such Christian homilies had never rung true. Who was a Jesus who could wash away a man's sins? Only a fool would show mercy toward an enemy.

Like some 165,000 other Africans,[24] Onyango was enlisted to aid the British when they battled the neighboring Germans in East Africa during

World War I. For nearly four years Onyango worked with road crews in Tanganyika, the German protectorate, which included Rwanda, Burundi, and almost all of Tanzania, before winding up on the island of Zanzibar, which was also under British control. There he discovered the Islamic faith, a set of beliefs that appealed to him far more than Christianity or Nyasaye, the god and ubiquitous spiritual force that many Luos tradition-ally revered.

Onyango was so drawn to Islam's goal of religious and moral perfection as well as its highly disciplined practices that he converted and took the name Hussein. In doing so, he became part of a religious minority that many Luos regarded with suspicion. Although Muslim traders began arriv-ing on the coast of East Africa in the eighth century, not until after the rail-road reached the Lake Victoria region in the early 1900s did Islam gain a foothold inland. When Onyango returned from the war, there were still only about twenty Muslim families in the district, representing a tiny fraction of the local population.[25] Although Islam would become more common in the area in coming decades due to widespread Muslim proselytizing in the later part of the 1920s, it had to overcome some significant cultural hurdles. One of the main impediments among Luos was the requirement that Muslim males be circumcised, a practice Luos traditionally do not believe in. And so it was that on his return home, Hussein Onyango, as he now called himself, was seen as stranger more than ever before.

By then Onyango was in his mid-twenties and it was beyond time for him to marry. Given his demanding ways and eccentric habits, finding a wife was not going to be easy. That Onyango had taken to wearing a long red *kanzu*, a traditional robe worn by Arab men, did not help the matter. Onyango paid the traditional dowry of a dozen cows or more for several young women, but when he beat them for falling short of his rigid house-keeping standards, they fled back to their parents' homes. One girl, who the senior members of the Obama clan only dimly recalled, did become his wife, but soon she too fled. Finally, late in the 1920s Onyango found a docile young woman named Helima who was able to endure his harsh ways and moved in with him. But when she was unable to have children after a few years, he was on the prowl again.[26]

One day while walking in the woods, he spotted a beautiful young woman with broad cheeks and deep-set brown eyes carrying a basket of fish. Although another man had already claimed her, Onyango managed to talk her father into rejecting the other man's offer and accepting a dowry offer of fifteen cattle. The following day he captured the girl on her way to the market and dragged her back to his hut. Her name was Akumu Njoga. Onyango soon persuaded her to convert to Islam and she took the name of Habiba, a variation of the Arabic name for "loved one." But Akumu never forgave Onyango for abducting her, and their marriage was tempestuous from the start.

Their first child was a girl, Sarah Nyaoke. Then, blessedly, three years later the first boy arrived in June of 1936.[27] In the Luo patrilineal culture, ancestry is defined through the father's family line, and the birth of a son is a much-celebrated event. Males are generally more highly valued than females, and in many family trees the names of a man's wives are not even recorded. Male babies, for example, would be kept indoors for four days before being taken outdoors, whereas female babies could go outside after only three days.[28] Firstborn sons in particular were prized and anointed with weighty responsibilities. Referred to as *kadier ng'eya*, meaning "my back" in Dholuo, a first son was to literally watch his father's back both in terms of protecting him and also learning from him. He would be the custodian of the family's cultural knowledge and their interrelationships with other clans. The family's general well-being would be his responsibility for as long as he lived.

Onyango's baby son was gifted with his mother's attractive features. His face was broad like hers, and his brown eyes were so deep that his mother was fond of saying they were "entered in" his face. His parents named him Baraka, meaning "blessing" in Arabic.

As the firstborn son, Baraka was bound to partake in certain rituals with his father, designated just for the two of them. When a new home was built, for example, the eldest son was designated to go to the site with his father and prepare it for their home. The father would carry a cock, symbolizing male power or polygamy, and the son carried a new axe on a new handle, signifying his growing autonomy. The first wife brought fire.[29] When the first son eventually had a family of his own and built his own house, he was given a location of some honor set to the right of the father's homestead. The second son's home would be positioned farther out from the father's house but to the left. The third son went to the right and so on in a physical manifestation of the family tree.[30] On this sacred familial land, which the members of an extended clan held collectively subject to shifting seasonal claims, both the placentas of newborns and the bodies of the dead would ultimately be buried.

Even the curmudgeonly Onyango was taken with the wide-eyed little Baraka. On his return from work in Nairobi, he brought him special fabric for clothes and mosquito netting for his crib. When Onyango and his son traveled outside the village, he dressed the boy in a white kanzu like his own with a matching white cap. Keenly aware of the benefits an education could bring, he taught his son to read at an early age and told him stories of his far-flung travels. As the family grew with the addition of a third child, Hawa Auma, Onyango took to addressing only his son Baraka and would often refuse to talk to his daughters. The girls, after all, would soon move on with husbands of their own. "He would talk only to Barack because he was the boy," recalled Joseph Akello, a childhood friend of Barack's. "He would say to the girls, 'Ladies, you are all going to go away from this home. You are going to get married and not stay in this place.' And so then he would not talk to them."

Hawa Auma, the third child born to Onyango and Akumu and the only one still alive, lives in the village of Oyugis about an hour's rough drive from Kendu Bay. As she remembers it, Barack was treated like *dhahabu ya nyota*, or "the gold of the stars" in Swahili. But she, too, adored her older brother. A widow, she spends most of her days sitting at the edge of the dirt road next to a pile of charcoal stubs that she sells for about 30 Ksh for a tin of two kilograms, or about forty cents, if she's lucky. Flashing her broad toothless smile, she delights in showing a visitor the interior of her tiny dark house where a photograph of President Obama, her nephew, and his family hang next to a row of dirt-encrusted axes. One of her prized possessions is a set of six water glasses that bear the seal of the U.S. Senate, which she says then-senator Obama presented to her along with 10,000 Kenyan shillings, or about $140, when he visited Alego in 2006. She wonders aloud if he will pay to get her teeth fixed one of these days.

Like all of Onyango's children and many of his grandchildren, Hawa Auma was raised as a Muslim. The front of her small house bears the painted black crescent and star featured on many Islamic flags along with the name of her dead husband. She speaks reverently of a recent trip she made to Mecca with several other family members, although she is more interested in discussing the airplane they took than the Holy City of Islam. "That plane was all white and so beautiful," she declared. "There was a toilet, a bed, just like a hotel. And all the time, tea with milk."

Her brother Baraka, as she recalls, converted to Christianity when he was about six years old and changed his name to the more Christian-sounding Barack because the Christian missionaries at the early schools he attended insisted that he do so. They were not discriminating against his faith in particular; rather, the missionaries required all non-Christians to leave their rival faith at the door and embrace Christianity if they hoped to go to school. Many young Kenyans who were baptized during the early twentieth century were given both African and Christian names, and the latter were often heavily Biblical ones such as Obadiah or Ezra. Later in life many of them abandoned those Christian names, considering them relics of an oppressive past.

Furious at the church's requirement but determined that his son be educated, Onyango did not openly challenge the missionaries. For his daughters, the situation was much simpler. Because they, like many girls, did not attend school, they did not have to trouble themselves with changing their names or renouncing the family faith. Barack, as Hawa Auma tells it, did not particularly care what religion he was ascribed; instead, he cared about not being different from the other children, and he cared enough about that to stand up to their bullish father. "Our father would say, 'You are a Muslim. Why do you say you are something else?'" says Hawa Auma. "But Barack was very bold and he stood up to him. He would say, 'I do not see anyone like that in the school where I am learning. I see only Christians.'"

Excluding matters of faith, Barack and his two sisters were raised largely according to longstanding Luo custom and tradition much as their parents had been. Although Barack would live as an urban man of the twentieth century when he became an adult, the tribal habits that defined rural Africa of the century past shaped his earliest years.

The Obama family lived in a typical Luo homestead composed of a collection of round, thatched dwellings arranged in a circular formation. Each of the structures had a designated function. Onyango occupied the central house, called a *duol*, although he was more often with one of his wives than in his own hut. Although second in number, Helima acted as a first wife, who is called a *mikayi*, and lived in a larger hut in the middle of the compound. It was she who oversaw the running of affairs, no matter how many other wives might be added to the family. The man of a family would routinely have two or more wives, and their huts were positioned in descending hierarchal order in front of the first wife's house, just as the sons' homes were laid out before the father's hut.[31] When Onyango married Habiba, she became his third wife, or *reru*, and lived in a separate hut of her own. She and Helima together cared for Sarah and Barack when they were born.

Girls generally slept in their own mother's homes until they reached puberty and then moved into a home with their grandmother called a *siwindhe* where they remained until they married. Boys moved into a bachelor house called a *samba* when they reached their teenage years. Between the ages of eleven and thirteen, boys would undergo the ritual removal of their six lower teeth, signifying their entry into adulthood. Although, fortunately for Barack, the practice began to die out around the time he was born, as did many customs of which the missionaries disapproved, many older men in Luoland still bear the telltale dental gap. Today, death remains one of the Luos' primary cultural expressions, marked by several days of elaborate ritual and the burial of the corpse. The body goes to the left of the door to the main dwelling in the case of a female and to the right in the case of the male. When a married man dies, the wooden pole extending from the roof of the main dwelling called an *osuri* is broken in a signal of his passing. One of his brothers will then "inherit" his widow, or if there are no brothers, another male in the family will do so.

Elaborate protocols continue to govern relations among Luo men and women, particularly those between a man and his mother-in-law. A wife's mother, for example, is to keep her distance from her daughter's spouse. She is not to hug him closely or even to cook food for him in her daughter's home. And she is never, ever to spend the night in her son-in-law's home. If she does, the young couple will be afflicted by a *chira* disease, an illness triggered by the breaking of cultural norms and marked by progressive wasting. When Michelle Obama's mother, Marian Robinson, moved into the White House to help take care of her granddaughters not long after the 2009 inauguration, many Luos around Lake Victoria grumbled in disapproval and predicted that disaster would surely follow.

Barack was teethed on the varied musical forms that echo in Luoland at an early age. By the early 1940s Kendu Bay had become known as a musical center featuring the popular fast-paced *mach* melodies and percussion-based rhumbas. Despite Onyango's severe ways, most family events were accompanied by performances on a lyre-like instrument called the *nyatiti*, then common among Luo families. Often the music would evolve into a popular form of verbal entertainment involving "praise names," a string of laudatory words a person uses to describe themselves or someone else. A *pakruok* is another form of self-glorification that employs metaphors or similes and often uses symbols from the environment, such as plants or animals. On overhearing a Luo enjoying his Tusker beer while uttering a string of complimentary adjectives describing himself, a non-Luo might concur with the Kenyan truism that Luos are as supremely arrogant as they are intellectual. But among Luos, such talk is more game than brag, although of course there might be the *slightest* bit of truth to those elaborate appraisals. Barack would often approach friends in later years declaring himself "*an wuod Akumu nya Njoga, wuod nyar ber*," or "I am the son of Akumu, the daughter of Njoga, a beautiful woman." Or he might say, "*an wuon nyithindo mabeyo*," meaning "I am the father of beautiful children." It was a childhood habit that entertained him, and like many other practices learned from his childhood—not all of them as benign—he never abandoned it.

The addition of some home brew invariably enlivened such addresses. Although the Muslim faith prohibits the drinking of alcohol, Onyango was nonetheless a large consumer of *chang'aa*, a traditional alcoholic drink distilled from grains such as maize or sorghum.[32] Another popular drink made at the family compound was *busaa*, brewed from millet or sorghum.

But Hussein Onyango typically put strict limits on entertainment, for he was determined that his son get the kind of formal education that he himself had tasted in the earliest mission schools. By the time Barack came of school age in the 1940s, those mission schools dominated education in East Africa, where the agenda was predominantly focused on reading, writing, and teachings from the Bible. Barack attended the

Gendia Primary School, started by the Seventh Day Adventist church in 1906 and located about three miles from his home. Each morning, he would fall in with the straggling groups of children who strode the wide dirt paths to school. In the absence of motor vehicles, Kenyan schoolchildren routinely walked many miles to their school in small groups, often singing praise songs along the way. Sometimes, on their way home, Barack and other boys would play a popular form of hockey called *adhula*, in which sticks made from date trees were used to shoot a ball into a rival clan's territory.[33]

Barack was fortunate that, due to his father's job, he often had shoes to wear on those long walks to school, unlike many children whose families were unable to afford such a luxury. So precious were those shoes, however, that children often carried them to school rather than wear them out on the rock-strewn journey. But in most other respects Onyango was a difficult and exacting father who did not hesitate to cane his children if they disobeyed him or to intimidate them with the threat of his infamous whip. His greatest expectations were reserved for Barack. Because Onyango had achieved much for himself and was one of the most accomplished men in the village, he was determined that Barack surpass him. "Sometimes Onyango would pull him aside and say, 'I want you to go beyond where I am,'" said Arthur Reuben Owino. "'People have respected me, so you also will be respected much more than me. You must study hard and pay attention. And always take care of your appearance.'"

Onyango kept a watchful eye on Barack's studies, particularly in the subject of math, for he had learned from the *mzungu* the importance of calculations and record keeping. On Barack's return from school each day, his father required him to perform his math sums out loud while standing beside a table laden with dinner. If he was unable to complete his work perfectly, he was forbidden to sit down and eat. Or he was locked in his room for the night. "Even as a young boy, Barack was very smart and prone to mischief and sometimes he would skip class because he did not feel he needed to go," explained Wilfred Obama Kobilo, a first cousin to Barack and a businessman now living in Nairobi. "But Barack always made sure that he knew his math homework before he went home because he knew his father was waiting for him there. He knew that his father had very high expectations of him."

Regardless of whether there was homework to be done or not, other children were forbidden to visit the Obama compound. Onyango considered them unkempt and ill-mannered, and he could not endure the noise they made. Nor were his own children permitted to visit other households to play with their friends. Once, when Barack ignored the rule and stopped at a friend's house, Joseph Akello recalls that Onyango was furious and shouted at him when he got home, "Why would you go to someone else's home when you have all the mangos and guavas you need *here*?" he demanded. "We have everything you need right here and so you must stay here."

But every rule has its exception, even Onyango's. When one of his employers was leaving town to head to another posting, he gave Onyango some photographs they no longer wanted. The photos, simple poses of white ladies sitting in a drawing room, were of immense curiosity back in Luoland, where many women and children had never seen a white person and cameras were the stuff of lore. A few dared to inch close to Onyango's compound in hopes of getting a glimpse of the pale-faced ladies hanging on the walls inside, only to have him shoo them away. These white women, posed for photographs, were among the first Barack had ever seen. He gazed upon them in his childhood home, mysterious and alluring creatures that belonged to a world about which he could only imagine.

Onyango had also been given an abandoned RCA gramophone, one of the earliest record players, which trumpeted sound through a conical metal horn. Crank the handle on the side and the horn suddenly emitted a thundering torrent of Zulu drumbeats or the cascading strains of a Beethoven sonata. Turn the dial on the side of the box and suddenly the music got louder. Villagers were rapt. Immensely proud of the machine, Onyango permitted a select group to come and listen, but they had to abide by his strict rules. The gramophone was set on a stool in the middle of the compound, and children were instructed to sit quietly in front of it. Adults could come as close as the compound gate to listen, but no closer. As the strains of music swelled over the dusty yard and the panicked chickens frantically ran from the noise, Barack often leapt impulsively to his feet and began to twirl to the rhythm, but Onyango swatted him back down to the ground. No dancing was allowed. No singing, either. And after two or three songs, he abruptly shut off the machine and ordered everyone back to work.

"Barack always wanted to dance. He had the rhythm in him," said Akello. "But Onyango only let him have so much. A couple of songs. One record. Then it was over."

HABIBA AKUMU DREAMED of running away.

An independent spirit, she had never been happy with her domineering husband. She chafed at his incessant rules and deeply resented his tyrannical ways. Even in the highly chauvinist Luo culture of the time, in which wife beating was not uncommon, Onyango was severe. When he summoned Habiba, he insisted that she must come at his first call or face a harsh beating. He constantly complained that she did not keep their home sufficiently tidy. And when they began to have children, the tension between them grew worse.

Onyango demanded that the babies always be clad in the fine clothing that he had brought back from Nairobi. If they cried, Habiba must stop them immediately. And when he was dissatisfied with her mothering, as he frequently was, he would cane her. Twice Habiba fled back to her parents' home in nearby Kolonde, after the births of Sarah and then Barack, and two times Onyango followed her and brought her back to Kanyadhiang. Because Habiba now belonged to Onyango, her family sided with her husband and would not let her stay with them. At least not at first.[34]

Nor did Onyango approve of his wife's gregarious manner. Habiba was an outgoing and social person who liked to go visit her friends around the village, but Onyango forbade her to engage in such frivolous behavior. Habiba did not cross him directly, for she had learned to take advantage of his long absences while working in Nairobi. When he finally left, she would head out and visit as often and as long as she pleased. During the rainy season in particular, she liked to pick mushrooms and take them to her friends' houses, where they would chat while preparing the food. But when Onyango returned, someone would whisper to him of his wife's doings. Once again the harsh crack of his whip breaking against her skin and her beseeching cries could be heard throughout the compound.

As Habiba turned increasingly inward in the face of her husband's brutal treatment, Onyango began to take comfort in the arms of other women. One of them, a young Muslim girl from Kendu Bay named Sarah Ogwel, stayed with him in Nairobi and eventually became his fourth wife. Today, she is known worldwide as "Mama Sarah," the American president's step-grandmother. Photographs of her clad in traditional African dress, poised beneath the mango tree that Onyango planted outside their home, first appeared in news stories in 2008. Now a routine stop on the tourist circuit near Lake Victoria, she often poses with a life-size paper cutout of President Obama in return for a handful of shillings.

In 1939, as the drumbeat of war again sounded around the globe, Habiba got the reprieve she'd been waiting for. When Germany began its lethal march through Europe that triggered World War II, the British empire again turned to its African troops for reinforcement. This time, the empire's African colonies would provide over 320,000 *askaris*, or soldiers, to the African regiment known as the King's African Rifles to fight in the Ethiopian and Burmese theaters of war.[35] Hussein Onyango did not hesitate to sign up for global adventure once again. Assigned to cook for a British captain, Onyango traveled for three years visiting the fronts in Burma, Ceylon, and Europe.[36] During his absence his wives and three children lived in relative peace, despite the mounting financial difficulties many Africans experienced during the war years. The hippo whip, at last, lay blessedly coiled.

By the time World War II wound to an end, the world was a vastly different place than that into which Barack had been born. The bloody conflicts of war may have seemed far removed from the bucolic shores of Lake Victoria, but the war marked the collapse of an old world order that opened the door to a new era not only in Kenya but also across much of the African continent. Barack would come of age in the throes of a revolution that would lift his country out from under the yoke of colonial oppression. And from that, he would find himself presented with the kind of opportunities that neither he nor his father could have ever imagined.

It would take nearly fifteen years to get there. By the time the war ended in 1945, much of Europe lay in a state of physical devastation. Despite being on the winning side, the British Empire was left in economic ruin and was forced into a period of retreat that triggered the gradual dissolution of Britain's colonial holdings. Decolonization would be a long and drawn-out process lasting nearly three decades, beginning with the surrender of the empire's jewel of India in 1947. As the African troops began returning home, they carried with them the seeds of a fierce political nationalism that would erupt violently in a matter of months.

The returning Kenyan soldiers were changed men. Not only had they witnessed the once-vaunted white man in a state of vulnerability and retreat, but they had also gained an appreciation of political self-determination that whetted their own simmering discontent. Further exacerbating their frustrations, they came home to find conditions even worse than what they had left. Although the British recruiters who had conscripted many of them had promised better paying jobs and additional land for settlement on their return, none of that came to pass. On the contrary, taxes had increased at all levels along with the cost of living, and land was scarcer than ever.[37] Meanwhile, a flood of *mzungu* war veterans, induced by more government settler schemes, began arriving to make their claim in the highlands, further squeezing the Kikuyu on the intolerably crowded reserves. Far from being rewarded for their military service, the returning Kenyan soldiers were made to feel ever more like second-class citizens in a White Man's Country, where neither their opinions nor their most fundamental needs were taken into consideration.

Popular discontent with the colonial government and its repressive practices had taken tentative root in Kenyan soil many years earlier. In the years following World War I a group of young mission-educated men had boldly taken steps to challenge colonial authorities with mixed results. In Nyanza the Young Kavirondo Association was created in 1921 in protest of forced labor camps and ever-increasing taxation. At the same time the Kikuyu Central Association (KCA) took on the issues of progressive land confiscation and the deteriorating conditions in the Kikuyu reserves. Its general secretary was a young man named Johnstone Kenyatta, a passionate Kikuyu who would become the country's first president and the most dominant figure in Kenyan politics for over a half-century to come. By the late 1930s the KCA was the most prominent of a host of ethnic organizations fueled by the early churning of nationalist sentiment. There were others such as the Luo Union, the Abaluyia Association and the Nandi-Kipsigis Union, all of which gave voice to mounting unrest and a surging nationalist fervor.[38]

But the Kikuyu's persistent agitation through the bureaucratic channels of petitions and appeals was what infuriated the colonial powers that be. And at the onset of World War II the government outlawed the KCA and declared the organization a threat to the empire's security. Throughout the war virtually all rumblings of opposition were muted as the course of war riveted the world's focus—including that of Kenya.

As the European generals began assessing the full scope of damage they had sustained at the war's end, the Kikuyu politicians resurfaced with a far more ambitious agenda. No longer were they seeking change within the existing administrative system, but as Ogot wrote, "They were now questioning the legitimacy of colonialism itself."[39] In 1944, the Kenya African Union (KAU) was formed, and three years later Kenyatta, now calling himself Jomo, or "flaming spear," was named its president. Kenyatta, who had been living in London studying for fifteen years, triggered a huge surge of interest in the party, and the talk quickly turned to independence. The KAU seized on the political ferment gripping the country and would become inextricably linked to the bloody and protracted uprising known as the Mau Mau rebellion.

In its early years of existence the KAU focused largely on the Kikuyu's demand that their "stolen lands" be returned and was highly centralized in Nairobi. As a result the party did not develop a strong following in Nyanza Province.[40] Many Luos turned for support from the Luo Union, a welfare association started in the 1920s to organize disparate Luo groups and workers who had been forced into a far-flung diaspora by the colonists' demands for taxes and labor.[41] The Luo Union, however, was a largely nonpolitical organization, and any challenges to the colonial administrators and their hand-picked chiefs in the immediate postwar years in Luoland were more likely to be manifest on a personal basis rather than an overtly political one. Not long after his return from the front, Hussein Onyango engaged in just such a struggle with the presiding chief of the Karachuonyo division in south Nyanza, the outcome of which would cause a dramatic upheaval in his already troubled family life.

On his return from the war, Onyango too seemed a changed man. Now nearing fifty, he still had a formidable temper, but age and experience had relaxed him somewhat. Travel had taught him much about the ways of other peoples, and he had developed a green thumb like no other. Tucked in his satchel he had brought home seedlings of pineapple plants, Blue Gum trees, and other exotic vines that he planted around the compound. He had also learned novel farming techniques and more advanced forms of the herbal medicine that he had come to know as a youth. As he was generous with his newfound knowledge, many came to him for treatments and advice. But as with many returning veterans, Onyango was also deeply disappointed in the grim economic conditions that plagued Luoland and the failure of administrators to make good on their promises. And he did not hesitate to challenge the local chief who was the face of the British in the Karachuonyo district.

His name was Paul Mboya, and like Onyango, he was as feared as he was admired. Once a pastor in the Seventh Day Adventist Church, Mboya had been educated in the missionary schools and modeled himself on the white man, as evidenced from his tailored suit and tie to his cherished cup of morning tea. Although he deeply admired the British and would attend the coronation of the Queen Elizabeth II of England in 1953, he also cherished indigenous traditions and worried that the influx of foreigners would erode the Luo way of life. In 1938 he wrote a seminal book on Luo culture and history called *Luo Kitgi Gi Timbegi*, or "Luo Customs and Traditions," which remains a highly respected work to this day. In his own way he did much to encourage resistance to foreign domination and encouraged Africans to take pride in their culture.[42] And yet, chosen by colonial administrators in the mid-1930s to serve as chief of the district, he simultaneously assumed the duties of collecting taxes and conscripting ablebodied men for work projects and military service on the British behalf.

Mboya was a strict disciplinarian and one of the most decorated African administrators who took the British orders one step further. During his watch, villagers were required to not only pay their taxes but also brush their teeth, dig pit latrines outside their huts, and send their children to school. If they failed to do so, they would be publicly humiliated and possibly whipped by one of Mboya's squadron of security guards. When his long, blue Chevrolet rumbled down the dirt road, many villagers fled in hopes that "Ja British," as they had nicknamed him, would not be able to find them.

Many in the district also believed that Mboya, like many others among the colonial government's network of chiefs, lined his own pockets through the performance of his administrative chores. When he or his assistants collected taxes, they often demanded sums much higher than the official levy or insisted on "gifts" of grains or eggs. Men and women who were forced to participate in public works projects often received only a portion of the contracted wage or were given no payment at all. Hussein Onyango was one of very few who dared to challenge Mboya in the public meetings, or *barazas*, and was swiftly branded a troublemaker. Some whispered that another reason for Mboya's intense dislike of Onyango stemmed from the fact that his clever son Barack regularly out-did Mboya's boy at the Gendia school. But money was the issue over which they most frequently crossed horns.[43]

"The police would take cows for taxes, but when they went to Hussein Onyango, he refused to pay. He said Mboya was not giving them to the government but was keeping the cows himself," said Elly Yonga Adhi-ambo, an Obama cousin. "Then the police would come and order the young men to work on the roads for free, and Onyango would say, 'You cannot do that. You go tell the chief that these young men must be paid to work.' Paul Mboya was very angry with him."

Not long after Onyango returned from the battlefront, the tension between the two men finally came to an explosive head. There are many versions of the story told in Nyanza, each of which varies slightly, but the storyline is fundamentally the same. As it is related by Joash Muga Okumu, a classmate of the elder Barack who lived in Kital Village in Kara-chuonyo, their final collision erupted over a trophy that Hussein Onyango had been awarded for athletic prowess during competitions held among the soldiers during the war.

Each year Paul Mboya sponsored a soccer contest among rival villages in Nyanza Province. When the competition rolled around in 1943, Mboya requested Onyango to donate the trophy so that it might be given to the victorious team under the name of "The Karachuyonyo Trophy." An annoyed Onyango crisply informed the local council of elders, who still retained some clout in village affairs, that he would agree to the trophy's use but only if it was called "The Hussein Onyango Trophy." Infuriated by Onyango's effrontery, Mboya declared in a public meeting with the elders that a *jadak* such as Onyango who would refuse local authorities could not be trusted. A jadak is a foreigner or a transient dweller, someone who does not belong in a place. Among the Luo, a people intimately attached to their land, such a term can be profoundly offensive. Indeed, Mboya's words enraged Onyango. "Onyango was furious that Mboya would question his integrity," said Okumu. "He said, 'Doesn't Mboya know of my lineage, that I have lived in Nyanza for many generations?' And he resolved that he would move back 'home' to Alego Kogelo at once."

That is exactly what he did. Within days, Onyango and his family had packed a few items and made their way to the northeast side of the lake where his ancestors of the Kogelo clan had lived nearly one hundred and fifty years earlier. The move was impetuous, a decision fueled by wounded Luo pride. None of Onyango's wives were happy about it. Because Helima was getting on in years and could not be expected to help in establishing a new home, Onyango permitted her to remain with her family in Kendu Bay. Alego was a much fiercer area, where leopards roamed freely and would sometimes boldly scratch at the door. The land was also thick with heavy brush, and a great deal of work was needed to be done before it could be planted. Habiba in particular was fearful of animals lurking in the dense foliage, and when Onyango returned to Nairobi to work for the *mzungu* again, she often cried into the night.

As it turned out, Habiba had just as much reason to be afraid when her husband was at home as when he was away. Despite Onyango's mellower ways, he continued to complain about Habiba's housekeeping, and their quarrels raged on. Nor did the addition of Sarah to the family mix help matters in the slightest, for the two women had their own differences. Feeling displaced by a younger wife, Habiba was dejected and often lonely with only her three children for company in Alego. Onyango, however, continued to cane his wives at the slightest annoyance until one day he completely lost control during a disagreement with Habiba.

Furious at her stubbornness, Onyango grabbed a shovel and stalked to the compound's edge, where a deep trench ran the length of the property. He dug steadily until at last he had cleared out a space the size of a grave. He stormed back to the house, seized Habiba, and dragged her to the side of the grave, where he pulled out the Somali sword he had nicknamed "Kogelo" in reference to his clan. Just as he was lifting his sword to slice Habiba's throat and throw her into the grave that he had dug, a neighbor caught sight of the two of them and ran screaming at Onyango to stop.

"My father had my mother on the ground and was about to cut her neck when the neighbor came by," said Hawa Auma. "He said, 'Onyango, don't you know you are about to commit a terrible taboo?'" Habiba hastily threw her small daughter in a nearby sisal bush, presumably fearful that her husband would next attack their child. Auma added, "I was just a little baby and my father's cat alerted people to my being there. Later they rescued me."

For Habiba, the marriage was finally over. She did not act right away but again bided her time until the moment was right. Onyango went about building a new compound on the family's land that other relatives had occupied. With the shillings he had carefully saved, he constructed a house so different from any other that villagers still recall it in fine detail. Unlike their round dwellings, Onyango's house was square and had separate rooms for sleeping and cooking. It had a tin roof that made a "pinging" sound in the rain but kept everything dry. Even the chicken hut had a small metal roof protecting the birds from the elements. As Onyango and Sarah fussed over the compound and planted lush mango and banana trees, Habiba plotted her escape.

One night Habiba pulled twelve-year-old Sarah and nine-year-old Barack aside and told them devastating news. They had lived in Alego for two years, but she told them that if she was going to survive their father's rage, she had to run away to her family in Kolonde. Although the journey was too arduous for them to accompany her, she urged them to follow her when they got older. Then, leaving all three of her children alone in her hut, she slipped into the night.

Barack and Sarah were heartbroken. Not only did they miss their mother deeply, but their father's wife Sarah was far too busy with an infant of her own and their own younger sister to pay them much attention. Within weeks of their mother's departure, Barack and Sarah decided to set out on their own to see if they could find Habiba and bring her back, leaving little Hawa Auma behind.

They walked through the darkness of night. Although the eyes of hungry hyenas and leopards surely fixed on their small moving forms as they passed through the dense bush, the children decided that if they traveled during the day, adults would likely see them and promptly send them back home. With the elder Sarah in the lead, they took two weeks to cover the roughly one hundred miles from Alego to Kanyadhiang. They slept in open fields during the day and lived off the fruit they could scavenge and the small amount of ugali they carried with them. By the time they reached the village their feet were bleeding and their clothes were in tatters. A relative promptly sent word to their father that the children had been found, and when he came and saw them, the tears streamed down his face. It was the only time anyone ever saw him cry. "He did not beat them. But he told them that they could not stay. They had to come home with him," said Rajab Ouko Obama, who lives in Nairobi and is the son of Sarah Nyaoke. "They tried to get Habiba to go back with them, but she would not."

Barack and Sarah's failed pursuit of their mother would mark each of them indelibly, leaving a void that shaped the course of their childhood. Although they would see her occasionally during their youth and far more when they were adults, they were left to the ministrations of their kwiny father and his remaining wife. The young Sarah would grow to be a fiercely independent woman and the single mother of several children. She would often tell her children of her journey to find her mother, as though she found some solace in its retelling. Barack rarely spoke of it to anyone.

As they set out on their long walk back to Alego the following day, Onyango, observing his headstrong son, impulsively coined the pakruok: *winyo piny kiborne*, meaning "for the bird the world is never too far." He understood that even as a boy, Barack was prepared to travel great distances toward goals to which others might never aspire. Onyango would prove to be right, for his son would indeed journey an unimaginable distance from his humble beginnings, and the nickname stuck.

But as the years unfolded, Barack was forever in want of something precious that he lost on the night that his mother left him. For the rest of his life he would be haunted by a sense of unworthiness that made it difficult for him to commit himself to anyone, including his wives and children.

3

A MASENO BOY, ALMOST

B arack Obama had his first run-in with a woman in a lush, open field
beneath the sprawling arms of an ancient fig tree. He was eleven
years old.

She was not a romantic interest. She was his teacher at the Nyang'oma
Kogelo Primary School, and every day she sat in the shade and taught
reading and writing to a solemn group of children. The school had no
building, so the great tree served as a classroom for the fledgling school
that the Anglican Church had started a decade earlier.

During the years of the colonial administration, only those African
children who showed extraordinary promise and whose parents could
afford to pay school fees were able to attend school. But after just one week
there, Obama refused to go anymore. He was a man, he declared, and he
was not going to be taught by a mere woman who could not possibly have
anything to teach him that he did not already know. A man must be taught
by a man. He was, after all, the son of Hussein Onyango. If some of the
other boys secretly felt much the same way, they said nothing of it. Instead,
they watched in astonishment as Obama abruptly stood up and headed
back home. "We all felt that women teachers were not as good as men
teachers because that is what we had been taught," said Joseph Akello,
Obama's childhood friend. "Barack said he was not getting the information he wanted from that lady and so he wanted to go to another school
farther up the road."

Nyang'oma Kogelo would not be the last school nor its instructors the
last women with whom Obama would find fault. Although his teachers in
the years to follow were invariably impressed with his facile mind and

intellectual curiosity, his reckless behavior and critical commentary often disappointed them. At a time when education was virtually the only avenue to a life beyond the village gate, Obama frequently played a high-stakes game with school administrators, pushing their tolerance to its far-thest edge. As an adult, he would do much the same thing with anyone who claimed authority over him.

When Obama refused to be taught by a woman, Onyango did not dis-agree. Within days Obama was transferred to another Anglican school on the road toward Kisumu called the Ng'iya School. There Obama discov-ered a male teacher whom he liked, and he soon became one of the school's most enthusiastic pupils—at least temporarily. Each day he eagerly pulled on his uniform of tan pants and a white shirt bearing the school's shield of a blue cross on its pocket. He packed in his pocket a small meal for midday and headed out to run the five-mile journey to school. Neighbors, impressed with his speed as much as his enthusiasm as he sprinted barefoot along the dirt road, often referred to him as a *guok jarikni*, or "swift dog," and shouted out, *piyo, piyo*, or "faster, faster."[1]

Typical of the mission schools, the program at Ng'iya was a blend of academics, religious study, and vocational training designed to mold good Christian followers. At the beginning and end of each day, students read from the Bible and prayed together under the elegant limbs of the lilac jacaranda trees outside the main administration building. The daily pas-toral program also included a variety of Christian teachings and songs, most of them new to Obama.

In addition to their math and English studies, students learned useful skills. Boys studied rope tying, a skill useful in caring for animals, whereas girls learned to make bowls. Students were responsible for a host of chores. They swept the corridors each morning, and in the after-noon some students helped the teachers maintain a large garden that supplied the school staff with vegetables. And every other Friday a handful of boys were charged with the task of smearing a layer of cow dung mixed with dirt on the school's earthen floors in order to keep the dust down. For a time, Obama was assigned the job of bell ringer, signal-ing a change of lessons.[2]

Onyango's early math tutoring of his son paid off handsomely, as Obama was soon identified as one of the smartest students in the school.

John Rabuku, one of Obama's teachers and later the school's principal, remembers Obama's voracious appetite for learning and still calls him "the brightest boy in the school." When reading, he could distill large amounts of text in a short period and succinctly explain its major points. But math was his forte. With only the slightest direction, Obama was able to perform sophisticated functions far in advance of what his peers were doing.

But the missionary teachers valued academic ability only up to a point. They had little interest in any inquiries that might call into question their personal authority or that of their teachings. A good student in the mission school was one who listened closely and followed the rules. Students who raised too many questions or attempted to take their inquiry beyond what was taught in the classroom were considered mischievous or impudent. School administrators were careful not to mete out excessive canings or beatings, as they had learned that students so disciplined often stopped coming to school.[3] But too many questions could easily earn a student a trip to the school headmaster's office for a little discussion about the importance of compliance.

This was a lesson that Obama had great difficulty absorbing. Even as a young boy, Obama flaunted his intelligence and challenged those around him on any matter or subject. Arthur Reuben Owino, a childhood friend who attended the Ng'iya school as well, remembers Obama as always asking, "Why not?" When they were young boys and Owino was taking his cows out to pasture, Obama would ask him why he was going to a certain field. "And I'd say I was taking the cows there because the long grass is there. And Barack would say, 'No, no, you must go elsewhere for the long grass. You know, they're not going to chew it well where you are going. You must go this way.' And if you argued with him, he'd say, 'You don't know *what* you are talking about. I'm telling you what I *know*.' And then you would be arguing with him endlessly, endlessly."

Owino grew accustomed to Obama's verbal drilling, and in later years he often found his friend's hard-edged interrogations more endearing than offensive. But the missionary teachers considered his battery of questions disobedient. What they found particularly annoying was Obama's habit of seeming to listen closely to their lessons, only to leap to his feet and declare it all untrue. "He'd say, 'Why not this way,' or 'Why not that way.' Or just, 'Why?'" recalled Owino. "But the missionaries would get upset and they'd say, 'No, no, no. You are not ready to ask those things or make those suggestions. You are to read what we are telling you to read and believe what we are telling you to believe. You are not to go beyond that.'"

But Obama persisted with his queries and cross-examinations. Sometimes he dared to question a teacher in front of the entire class. Even when the teacher admonished him, Obama refused to back down. But as time passed, the novelty of the game wore off. At age eight Obama began skipping classes and refusing to go to school for weeks at a time. Only Onyango's harsh words sent him scurrying down the road again. All that missed class time didn't seem to impact his performance in the slightest. When exams rolled around, Obama would pore over a classmate's notes and absorb in only a few hours what other students took many days to learn. When the grades came in, Obama would run home and boast that, even without attending classes, he was still number one.[4]

Nor was his challenging nature the only thing that got him into trouble at the Ng'iya school. When the time came for the students to head back home at the end of the day, Obama often mysteriously disappeared. When Onyango appeared at the school's doors looking for his son, as he often did, Rabuku would dispatch a team of boys to search for Obama in the dense brush outside the school's perimeter. Sometimes they found him playing not far away and turned him over to Onyango, who led him home to a sure beating. But other times the boys could not find their classmate no matter how hard they looked. Rabuku began to realize that Obama was reluctant to go home, perhaps anxious about what awaited him there. And then one day, when the school's gate swung open at the end of the day, he noted that Obama walked in the opposite direction from his home. On those days Obama would spend the night eating guavas and sleeping in the high trees so that the hyenas would not get him. "When we brought him down the next morning, I could never bring myself to cane him," sighed Rabuku. "He was so amusing and I quite liked him. I think sometimes he was afraid to go home."

As he approached adolescence, it was becoming apparent that Obama had absorbed the lesson of his father's example all too well. Although extraordinarily gifted, his often unyielding posture and refusal to concede his own fallibility did not bode well; indeed, Obama's exceptional intelligence seemed to give him license to ignore the rules that bound other mere mortals. Although Obama had a deeply generous heart, he was already showing a lack of emotional grounding needed to navigate the sweeping changes that would alter Kenyan society in the years to come.

When Obama turned thirteen in 1949, he faced a crucial turning point in his academic career. At the time, each school selected its brightest students to sit for the rigorous Common Entrance Exam to determine if they were qualified for a spot at one of Kenya's handful of secondary schools reserved for exceptionally bright students and the sons of chiefs. For the vast majority of students at a school such as Ng'iya, graduation marked the end of their formal education. Even if some of those students could have passed the test, very few of their families could have afforded the fees at the premiere schools. Obama was not only selected to take the test, but he also passed with flying colors and was accepted to the prestigious Maseno School for boys, a twenty-five-mile walk from his home. No one was more pleased than Hussein Onyango, who slaughtered his plumpest chicken for a feast and even invited Rabuku to his house to celebrate. "Onyango never liked people to come to his house, but this time he made an exception," recalled Rabuku. "Barack and Onyango were so very excited. We had roasted chicken and tea."

Acceptance at Maseno instantly put Obama on elite footing. One of Kenya's oldest educational institutions, the Anglican Church Missionary Society founded Maseno in 1906 for the sons of four Luo chiefs and boasted a roster of attendees that included some of the most sterling names in Kenyan history. Among them were Oginga Odinga, the country's first vice president and its preeminent opposition leader in the 1960s; Bethwell A. Ogot, the nation's premiere historian; and Achieng Oneko, a freedom fighter and one of the celebrated "Kapenguria Six" who were arrested for allegedly supporting the Mau Mau rebel movement in the 1950s.[5]

Along with a handful of other prestigious secondary schools such as the Alliance High School and St. Mary's, Maseno produced a good number of the first wave of Kenya's nationalists on its bucolic campus, where students were exposed to critical thinking and met for the first time Luos from other parts of Nyanza Province. Educated in the array of mission schools that dotted the country, the first generation of political leaders, including first president Jomo Kenyatta, who attended the Church of Scotland mission school in Thogoto, were often dubbed the "mission boys." Obama's class produced its own educated elite, and a good number of the boys whom he met during his four years at Maseno would go on to claim some of the highest-ranking jobs in Kenyan government and business.

The school's graduates had a proud history. Maseno students were among those who in 1921 founded one of the nation's earliest political protest organizations called the Young Kavirondo Association, dedicated to protesting the oppressive colonial rule. Bitterly opposed to the *kipande*—or the identification pass—rising taxes, and the government's forced labor practices, these young men were part of a new generation that would soon displace the tribal chiefs. Their angry voices of discontent were echoed by another group of mission boys in Nairobi founded in the same year, called the Young Kikuyu Association. When the Kikuyu group's leader, Harry Thuku, was arrested on charges of sedition in 1922, twenty-five of the thousands of protestors outside the jail were gunned down in what became Kenya's first political protest. Three decades later those early rumblings of nationalist sentiment would erupt in widespread rebellion.

Life on the Maseno campus, a trim expanse of playing fields and brick dormitories located a few hundred yards from the equator, was modeled closely on the ways of the British public school system. Students wore uniforms of khaki shorts and white shirts, and teachers were clad in bush jackets and shorts with long stockings hugging their calves.[6] Discipline was the watchword, and those who strayed off the pathway and onto the closely cropped grass or who failed to nod in deference to a passing teacher would find themselves cleaning the latrines or being publicly whipped. Prayers were held promptly before breakfast and again after dinner, and readings from the Bible were part of the daily routine. The curriculum, taught largely by European teachers, provided a liberal serving of British literature, including the works of Anthony Trollope, Charles Dickens, and Thomas Hardy.[7] When Obama entered in 1949,[8] the principal was Mr. A. W. Mayor, whom Ogot describes in his biography, *My Footprints on the Sands of Time*, as "a lean, mean-looking and pipe-smoking person who taught us English language and literature."[9]

Their experience at Maseno marked students so deeply that decades later some graduates claim to still be able to identify "a Maseno boy" with

ease. Part of it is the crisp British accent that many carried into adulthood, and part of it is an imperceptible bearing that they alone could dis-
tinguish. "You know we were highly Anglicanized. We tried to behave
like upper-class Englishmen, which was silly, but we admired them," said
Wilson Ndolo Ayah, a former member of Parliament and Minister of Foreign Affairs in the early 1990s, who was two years ahead of Obama at
Maseno. "There are just certain behaviors you do not get involved in
because you are from the school. You can tell from a person's language,
their demeanor, and that kind of thing that they went to Maseno. The
behavior is very restrained, very disciplined. I would say the discipline
was effortless."

However, not all graduates saw the net effect of a Maseno education in
quite the same way. In his biography, *Not Yet Uhuru*, Odinga declares that
both the colonial government and settlers were upset that the missions
produced "jumped-up Englishmen" rather than the "quiescent tribal subjects" that they would have preferred. But the outspoken Odinga also
noted that the independent thinkers who walked out the mission schools'
doors soon lost their bite. They became, he wrote, "tame middle men,
shadows and subjects of White mission men, and any stirrings in them to
become independent leaders of their people were suppressed by their allegiance to the mission hierarchy and the fact that, once educated, they were
absorbed into the government machine."[10]

Into this highly regimented academic training ground came the teenage
Obama. Muslim by birth, contrarian by nature, and survivor of a tumultuous youth, he was a problematic fit. The twenty-five-mile distance to
school, which he walked a couple of times a year, was the easy part. Like
any other student, Obama trekked there with a band of others heading to
their different institutions, his clothes carried over his head in a wooden
suitcase. Students would often pause for the night at the home of family
members or others willing to lend a hand toward the educational cause.
As usual, Obama excelled at his studies. On the small, brown card that is
his school record—Index No. 3422—it is noted that he was promoted
from Class B to Class A, which was reserved for the brightest students.
Principal B. L. Bowers, who by then had replaced Mayor, wrote in neat
script that Obama was "very keen, steady, trustworthy and friendly. Con-
centrates, reliable and out-going."[11]

Nowhere did Obama excel with more flourish than on the school's debate team, which regularly squared off with some of the other top-notch schools. The topics ranged widely, but some of the students' favorite subjects related to the European colonial rule. Debater A would take the African side: The Europeans had robbed the Africans of the finest agricultural land in the White Highlands and pocketed profits that rightly belonged to the African. Debater B would take the British side: The settlers had brought improved farming techniques and were providing a better grade of beans and maize for the Kenyans. Or the subject of polygamy: On the one hand it was an un-Christian practice that should be abandoned immediately, and on the other hand it was a valued cultural tradition that would swell the ranks of Kenyans who hoped to contain the European presence. Obama had no proscribed point of view, as his classmates recall it. For him, the push back was the point, the intellectual gamesmanship the aim. "He wouldn't miss a single debate," recalled Owino, his hair parted neatly to the side in a classic style one sported by politicians and called the "lorry" as it requires a barber to cut a path through the hair big enough for a truck, or British lorry, to pass through.[12] "I think what he stood for was alternative reasoning. If you say *this,* he would insist *that.* He was a very persuasive man, and he will in the end get you on his side. But he could be foolishly frank, you know, because if you want to hit your head against a stone, you know in the end what you will have: a broken head."

After one year at Maseno, Obama boldly began to direct his alternative reasoning at his teachers and the student prefects charged with keeping order. He soon gained a reputation for chronic misbehavior. When a prefect once ordered him to clean a classroom as penalty for being late to class, Obama arrogantly pointed out that his own grades were superior to the prefect's and flatly refused. As his schoolmate Oyiro Ayoro, a school captain in charge of discipline, recalls it, "Barack said, 'I will not do it. After all, what number were you last term? Your job is cleanliness, not mine. I repeat, what number were you?'"

Obama's offenses, his schoolmates recall, were many. He refused to wipe his dinner dishes dry as was required, insisting instead on laying them in the sun. He was chronically late to class and complained about the school's diet of cabbage and *ugali,* a staple porridge of cornmeal and water.

Although notoriously lax in his own reading, he admonished other boys for not reading more diligently. He sneaked off campus with a friend and got drunk with some village rowdies. And he perpetually committed the cardinal sin: He walked on the school's immaculate green lawn. Once, when a prefect came upon Obama indolently lying upon the manicured carpet of grass, his shirt stained green, he demanded to know what Obama was doing. "'This school has given us nothing comfortable to sit on, that is why I am lying here,' Ayoro recalls Obama saying. "'We should have more comfortable chairs to sit on while studying.'"

School administrators were taking note. At the conclusion of each school day, the entire student body gathered outside the chapel for evening prayers. As the students stood in half circles with their dormitory mates, the principal routinely reviewed the events of the day and made announcements about the day to come. In his concluding remarks he commented on any students who had exhibited problematic behavior during the day. "Barack was very disobedient and his name came up often," recalled Yekohada Francis Masakhalia, a close friend of Obama's and an economist who served as Permanent Secretary of the Ministry of Finance and Economic Planning in the 1980s. "[Principal] Mayor would announce very clearly that Barack Obama was a very bright student but he had problems with his character. The rest of us tried to avoid being named in such a way."

Obama was already being singled out for his oppositional nature, but there were other things that set him apart as well. Ndolo Ayah, who was a neighbor of Obama's in later years, often wondered if Obama's Muslim background made him feel different from the other boys at school, presumably none of whom had been raised in the Muslim faith. Most of the students, who had been taught the ways of the Christian church early on, accepted the strict discipline at Maseno with ease. But not Obama. "I always had the feeling that maybe his Muslim background had some kind of effect on his Maseno days because there is no reason why he would have behaved the way he did. Maybe because he grew up not having to go to church or read the Bible, it struck him differently when he did have to do those things."

Toward the end of Obama's fourth year at Maseno, a letter arrived in Principal Bowers's office. The handwritten letter, which was unsigned, was a lengthy rant against the school, its faculty, and traditions, according to Leo Odera Omolo, a friend of Obama's and a veteran Kenyan journalist. The mail service was inadequate, the food served inedible. The faculty was second rate, and the uniforms antiquated and unnecessary. The list was long.

Bowers, a heavyset former biology teacher who was easily exasperated, detected a familiar tone in the cascade of complaints that sounded suspiciously like one of his more notorious students. He decided to turn the matter over to a special investigative branch of the police to examine the handwriting on the letter. But before the police could look into the situation, Bowers decided to take action of his own.

At the end of every academic year, Maseno's principal reviewed each student's report card and made a recommendation whether they continue to the next level of study or not. The procedure was largely routine, as virtually all the boys were referred to a higher level. But when Obama's name came up in the spring of 1953, Bowers penned a definitive rejection on his file, apparently irate at Obama's behavior and suspecting he was the author of the critical letter. Obama, he wrote, was not to complete his studies at Maseno. What's more, he was "not recommended to join any other high school in Kenya," according to Ayoro, one of several students who recall the incident.

Bowers terse words were damning. Without the school's endorsement, Obama, then sixteen, could not take the next step in his education or obtain the Cambridge School Certificate that he urgently needed to apply for college. That fact would sabotage his fervent efforts to seek higher education in the years ahead. On hearing that his son had left Maseno in disgrace, Hussein Onyango was beside himself. And when Obama appeared at his compound a week later, Onyango beat him so hard with a stick that the boy's back bled. A furious Onyango ordered him to go to Mombasa, where he would live with a cousin and earn his own living. "You will learn the value of education now," Onyango called after him. "I will see how you enjoy yourself, earning your own meals."[13]

DURING THE YEARS OBAMA had spent on Maseno's serene campus, a single name had come to dominate the Kenyan colony. It struck fear in the hearts of British administrators as well as their compatriots back in

London, who read about it in the tabloids. Few shuddered more at its mention than the tribal chiefs who worked at their behest. But to many of the Kikuyu, the ethnic group that had historically farmed the southern part of the fertile highlands at the colony's heart for generations before the European settlers arrived, the name was a declaration of defiance, a sounding of hope in the long and grueling ordeal of British occupation.

The name was Mau Mau.

Although historians dispute the origins of the term, the Mau Mau movement of the late 1940s came to be associated with a violent uprising of Kikuyu rebels dedicated to expelling the Europeans from the country and reclaiming what they regarded as their stolen lands. The movement began with the administration of the traditional Kikuyu oath, a ritual that was invoked in the face of war or grave difficulty. But as the colonists' land seizures pushed the Kikuyu to the brink of desperation, mass oathing evolved into a secretive and violent campaign of murder and destruction that engendered an equally brutal response from the British.

By 1952, when Obama was completing his third year at Maseno, the conflict had mushroomed into an internal war that would ultimately recast the balance of power within the colony. The British tried hard to dismiss Mau Mau as an aberrant movement led by a troublesome few, but in the end the conflict would clear the way for the next stage of the battle for independence. Although the British soldiers crushed the movement militarily within a few years, they were forced to concede that the status quo in Kenya was no longer tenable. The Africans, they realized, had to be given greater representation in the country's political and economic structures, if only to establish a moderate alternative to the rebel route.

That path of protest had been first laid open many years earlier. The seeds of Kenyan nationalism were rooted in the experience of the African soldiers who served in World War I, for their far-flung travels had given them a greater understanding of their subservient role in the colonial hierarchy. It also exposed their British rulers as imperfect humans and not the omnipotent icons they had considered them to be. But it was not until the closing days of World War II that their mounting grievances against the colonial government's labor policies and restrictive agricultural practices reached a boiling point.

Part of the complaint stemmed from the successive humiliations of everyday life under colonial rule. Throughout the country Africans were routinely excluded from a host of locations and services available to Europeans. Many of Nairobi's finest hotels and restaurants exhibited signs declaring, "No Africans or Dogs Allowed." Nor could most Africans even consider living in the city's better neighborhoods such as Muthaiga or Lavington, which were reserved largely for whites and far removed from most Africans' modest ability to pay. Instead, the natives were ushered to the crowded slums to the east, which were plagued by unsanitary conditions and intermittent police raids. And should an African happen to vex his *mzungu* employer in some way, he could only hope that the employer would not rip up his kipande, making it impossible to get other work.

No issue was more passionately contested than that of land. In the years after the war ended, the Kikuyu found that the reserves onto which they were squeezed were approaching a state of ecological exhaustion after decades of heavy farming. A postwar surge in the settlers' agricultural production that further limited the Kikuyu's ability to grow and market their own crops further worsened their situation. The arrival of mechanization struck another blow at the Kikuyu heart, as the more efficient farming techniques forced many who had toiled as "squatters" on the verdant highlands off their farms. Some returned to the already overcrowded reserves, while thousands fled to Nairobi, where unemployment and inflation had generated flammable discontent. When the Mau Mau militants offered them a way to fight for *ithaka na wiyathi*, or land and freedom, many did not hesitate.

The violence began in the countryside, where settlers' cattle were sporadically found maimed and unexplained fires erupted on their property. Local chiefs, called "loyalists" who sided with the British and had long been reviled for their brutal and corrupt ways, were discovered mysteriously dead. Widespread discontent gave rise to a form of mass oathing, in which the participants committed to the rebels' cause. One common oath was, "If I know of any enemy of our organization and fail to kill him, may this oath kill me." Another pledge was, "If I reveal this oath to any European, may this oath kill me."[14] Although the British government banned Mau Mau in 1950, the movement continued to gain widespread support in both the crowded urban centers and the Kikuyu reserves. In the mean-time, the militants' path of destruction expanded.

By 1952 the tide of violence reached crisis proportions. As the frantic settler community insisted that the government take aggressive action, the papers were chock-full of reports of crop burnings, murder attempts, and robberies. And then it got worse. In October Senior Chief Waruhiu wa Kungu, one of the highest-ranking officials under the colonial admin-istration and a fierce critic of the Mau Mau movement, was shot dead in the backseat of his dark brown Hudson sedan. Supporters of Mau Mau, who had arranged the assassination, celebrated Waruhiu's death with songs and festivities. The killing sent waves of terror through the settler community and caused British administrators to abruptly escalate their response.

The Mau Mau war was waged largely by the Kikuyu and supporting factions of the Embu and Meru tribes against the British colonists in the highlands and the greater Nairobi area. But some of the deep-seated resentments that had given rise to it were also felt among the other ethnic groups, including the Luo. In the aftermath of World War II, many sol-diers returned home to mounting frustrations just as their predecessors had in the previous war. The ex-servicemen opposed the African chiefs, as the historian William R. Ochieng wrote, "whom they considered as noth-ing but the *mzungu*'s stooges. These returned soldiers began a campaign to 'liberate' the masses of their fear of the white man."[15]

Organizations such as the Kenya African Union and the Nyanza Ex-Soldiers Association were formed to express the Africans' discontent with the soaring cost of living and mounting taxation. And as the conflagration of the late 1940s spread across the country, it came to have a direct impact on the Obama family. Hussein Onyango agreed with many of the posi-tions that the early African political groups took and was a staunch oppo-nent of the profiteering loyalists. But he had grave doubts that the African could overcome the white man's armies. As he explained to his eldest son: "The white man alone is like an ant. He can be easily crushed. But like an ant, the white man works together. . . . He will follow his leaders and not question orders. Black men are not like this. Even the most foolish black man thinks he knows better than the wise man. That is why the black man will always lose."[16]

Nonetheless, Mama Sarah, Onyango's fourth wife, says that her husband's name was put on a list of political activists and that in 1949 he was confined to a detention camp for six months. In *Dreams from My Father*, Mama Sarah reports that his name had been turned over to British authorities by a man who worked for the district commissioner whom Onyango had admonished for demanding excessive taxes from local people and keeping the money for himself.[17] During the 2008 U.S. presidential campaign, as a steady stream of reporters journeyed to the Obama family compound, Mama Sarah told a reporter for the *Times* of London that British guards had brutally tortured her husband in order to gain information about the insurgency.

"The African warders were instructed by the white soldiers to whip him every morning and evening till he confessed," the *Times* reported Sarah Hussein Obama as saying. The white soldiers, she continued, visited the prison regularly to carry out "disciplinary action" on the Africans confined there. "[Onyango] said they would sometimes squeeze his testicles with parallel metallic rods. They also pierced his nails and buttocks with a sharp pin, with his hands and legs tied together with his head facing down." It was then, she added, "we realized that the British were actually not friends but, instead, enemies."[18]

Although Sarah's recollection echoes several accounts of the torture inflicted on the Kikuyu detainees in the later years of the rebellion, it is problematic. The detention centers that the British used to hold Mau Mau supporters were not established until 1952. While it is possible that Onyango might have been charged with being a subversive and imprisoned, no family member has identified the location where he was held. Several close relatives say they do not believe that he was confined at all. Although Mama Sarah told her grandson Barack Hussein Obama in the 1990s that Onyango had been detained in a camp for six months, she said in the *Times* interview that he was held for two years. But whatever the exact circumstances of his confinement, that he was confined somewhere is possible. He supposedly returned home from the camp thin, dirty, and greatly changed. As Obama quotes Mama Sarah in *Dreams*, "He had difficulty walking, and his head was full of lice. He was so ashamed, he refused to enter his house or tell us what had happened."[19] Barack Obama Sr. was at the Maseno School at the time and did not learn of the detention until later.

While Barack was defying school authorities, government officials in Nairobi were preparing an aggressive crackdown on the insurgents. Less than one week after Waruhiu's murder, Kenya's new governor of a matter of days, Sir Evelyn Baring, received approval from London to declare a state of emergency. Under the emergency legislation and subsequent regulations, the government was free to detain suspects, deploy the military in order to maintain civil administration, and impose other laws without checking in with London.

In the early morning of October 21, 1952, the same day the emergency went into effect, Baring unleashed a surprise police roundup that was code-named Operation Jock Scott, arresting one hundred eighty suspected Mau Mau militants and activists with the Kenya African Union. Nairobi police, assisted by British reinforcements, loaded the offenders into their trucks and carted them ceremoniously to the Nairobi police station. Baring's hope was that a dramatic show of force would bring the movement to its knees and convince the settlers—if not the world—that the British authorities were in control.

One of the biggest catches of the roundup was Jomo Kenyatta, the Kikuyu president of the KAU, whom Baring and other government administrators erroneously believed was the mastermind behind the Mau Mau uprising. In fact, Kenyatta, one of the elders of the Kikuyu political oligarchy, had long tried to repress the rebels at the forefront of Mau Mau.[20] Kenyatta had emerged as a moderate nationalist among the "mission boys" of the 1920s, and he regarded the fierce, young militants who had spearheaded the Mau Mau movement as impetuous and their radical tactics unwise. Although he had spoken against their violent methods, British authorities turned a deaf ear to his words, just as they did to the grievances of the Kikuyu people; instead, the highly visible and popular Kenyatta had been targeted as a prime instigator. The British authorities reasoned that his public prosecution would send a loud message to both the settlers and the other militants. The authorities' miscalculation would have far-reaching consequences and, ironically, served to enshrine the aging statesman as the presiding symbol of the nationalist cause.

Charged with "managing an unlawful society," Kenyatta and five others were taken to the remote northern town of Kapenguria near the Ugandan border—a location that enabled the government to maintain strict control on the comings and goings at their sensational trial. The government selected conservative British Judge Ransley Thacker to hear the case. There was no jury. Thacker was given £20,000 for his service and the inconvenience of the location, a payment that was widely regarded as a bribe intended to ensure a guilty verdict. Despite little real evidence with which to prosecute the defendant group, known as the "Kapenguria Six," Kenyatta and the others were found guilty in April of 1953 and sentenced to seven years imprisonment with hard labor followed by a lifetime of restriction. On his release in 1959, Kenyatta, then in his late sixties,[21] had become the country's most prominent champion for the cause of freedom as well as its undisputed leader.

Far from bringing an end to the insurgency, however, Kenyatta's arrest only exacerbated the ongoing conflict. Within months of the declaration of emergency, bands of armed freedom fighters based in the Aberdare Mountain range and the forests of Mount Kenya stepped up their campaign in earnest. There followed a series of highly visible murders, the most notorious of which was the slaying of the Ruck family. In January 1953 Kikuyu fighters hacked to death Esme and Roger Ruck, a hardworking and well-liked young British couple, on their remote farm. Their six-year-old son, Michael, was slaughtered as he lay in his bed. The sordid killings, photographs of which appeared the world over, marked a critical turning point in the war.

In the months following the Rucks' deaths, the government implemented a draconian series of measures that further inflamed the situation. The Emergency Regulations authorized collective punishments, detention without trial, the seizure of convicts' property, and the suspension of due process. In addition, the range of offenses for which capital punishment could be imposed was vastly expanded. The purpose of these extreme measures was to reestablish colonial domination and to satisfy the settlers' near-hysterical calls for dramatic actions against the rebels.

Over the next two years the British brought their military might to bear upon the rebels and by 1955 eventually gained the upper hand. But they did not lift the state of emergency for another five years. The net result was a staggering degree of human dislocation and suffering, as legions of Mau Mau suspects were detained without any trial and often brutally tortured in detention camps. Although the government put the number of those Kikuyu detained at 80,000, historians have subsequently reported that the actual tally more likely ranges from 150,000 to 320,000.[22] The estimated number of Kikuyu rebels who died in the war also varies widely. Although the official tally rests at 12,000, Oxford historian David Anderson estimates that in fact more than 20,000 Kikuyu fighters died. But Caroline Elkins, a Harvard historian, contends in her Pulitzer Prize–winning book, *Imperial Reckoning: The Untold Story of Britain's Gulag in Kenya*, contends that the figure was far higher than Anderson's. She concludes that the colonial government launched "a murderous campaign to eliminate Kikuyu people, a campaign that left tens of thousands, perhaps hundreds of thousands dead."[23] Whatever the final numbers, the Mau Mau war was, by any assessment, as Anderson writes in his book, *Histories of the Hanged: The Dirty War in Kenya and the End of Empire*, "a story of atrocity and excess on both sides, a dirty war from which no one emerged with much pride, and certainly, no glory."[24]

Working in Mombasa nearly three hundred miles away on the Kenyan coast, Obama was far removed from the crisis gripping the highlands, though he was surely keenly attuned to the ongoing conflict. He also had some pressing problems of his own. The first job he had landed, working as a clerk for an Arab merchant, came to an end when Obama quarreled with his boss and angrily quit without being paid. He managed to find another job, although at significantly lower pay. Onyango learned of his son's difficulties from a Mombasa relative, and when Obama came home for a visit, Onyango railed at him for his impetuous behavior. The headstrong Obama insisted that he was now employed in a job that paid much more money, but when Onyango demanded to see his wage book, Obama could only stand silently before him. His father ordered him away, saying he had brought shame upon him.[25]

Uncertain where to turn in 1954, Obama headed to Nairobi, where he had friends from his school days and hoped that he would find another job—and perhaps some adventure. In a few weeks Obama again secured work as a clerk, this time with an Indian law firm, but he soon found the churning life of the city far more consuming. During the emergency years many city residents vented their frustration with chronic unemployment and low wages through the evolving trade union movement. Although the Kenya Labor Department closely monitored the formation of employee organizations to ensure they were not being used for political ends, it discreetly encouraged the growth of collective bargaining in part to counter the extremism of the radicals' appeal.[26] Generally, the government hoped to encourage the development of a middle class that would have a tempering influence on African politics and might eventually serve as a bulwark against radical elements such as Mau Mau.

When Obama arrived in the city, one young man's name was inextricably linked to the emerging trade union movement: Tom Mboya. He was, like Obama, a Luo, and a very ambitious one at that. The two men would develop a friendship, drawn to one another by their deep ethnic roots and rapidly developing political passions. Six years older than Obama, Mboya would act as Obama's mentor during a critical juncture in his life, a kind of benevolent father figure of the sort that Obama had never had.

The son of a sisal plantation overseer from Rusinga Island in Lake Victoria, the engaging and polished Mboya had already established himself as an officer with the Kenya African Union and was a prominent union activist by the time Obama arrived in the city. Only twenty-four, the moon-faced organizer had begun his career three years earlier as a sanitation inspector for the Nairobi City Council when an incident occurred that would become a favorite anecdote reflecting the racist attitudes of the time. Mboya was alone in the city health department testing milk samples when a European woman entered. As he turned to greet her, the woman stared directly through him and loudly asked, "Is there *anybody* here?" Highly offended, Mboya could not contain himself. "Madame," he said, "Is there something wrong with your eyes?"[27]

Mboya had long been an admirer of Kenyatta but had decided he would find greater opportunity as a young man in labor organizing rather than the more conventional political routes.[28] Although he would evolve into a liberal internationalist with decidedly capitalist leanings, as a young man he was a devout champion of the working man. Obama would wind up farther to the left than his mentor, ardently defending aspects of a socialist model in the early years of Kenya's independence. But in the 1950s they found common cause in their conviction that

Africans had a right to self-determination and that the era of imperial rule must come to an end.

Mboya's rise was as meteoric as would be his end. When Kenyatta was sent to prison in 1953 and dozens of other KAU leaders were arrested, Mboya was unexpectedly snapped up to fill the party's empty acting treasurer's seat. Several months later he was made the general secretary of the prominent Kenya Federation of Registered Trade Unions (KFRTU), and his rapid advance was much talked about in the African sections of the city. In the years leading up to independence, Mboya's passionate and sophisticated articulation of Kenya's political ambitions would usher him to the highest ranks of the Kenyan government and make him an international celebrity on the emerging Pan-African scene.

But Mboya was also an eligible young bachelor who liked to pull on his immaculate white tuxedo and escort some of the city's beautiful young ladies to dance competitions around town. A resident of the Kaloleni estate, a neighborhood populated by middle-class and educated Africans, most of whom were Luos, Mboya invariably drew a crowd when he appeared at parties and dances there. It was at one of those that he apparently met Obama, then living in the nearby African estate of Shauri Moyo. They were both excellent dancers who could invariably be found twirling across the dance floor to the guitar bands that were popular. Each of them sported a highly polished Western appearance, although Obama took some years to master the tailored poise that Mboya so artfully cultivated. They also shared a certain haughtiness, off-putting to others but a characteristic that apparently echoed positively between the two of them. Mboya's biographer, David Goldsworthy, wrote that Mboya was so aware of his own abilities that at times "lesser men were treated with contempt."[29] Goldsworthy could be describing the young Obama at his most withering.

Although Obama was not particularly interested in holding political office himself, he was absorbed in the political conversation of the day. And for that, Kaloleni was the place to be. He attended many of the evening debates there that featured the emerging nationalist heavyweights such as C. M. G. Argwings-Kodhek, then the only African lawyer and a prominent champion of human rights; Apolo Milton Obote, a vocal construction worker from Uganda who went on to become prime minister and president of his country; and Mboya, who was becoming an increasingly powerful orator. Obama, as ever, took his contrarian viewpoints with him. "Obama was not somebody to be brought easily into anything," explained Were Dibo Ogutu, the longtime national secretary of the General Chemical Allied Workers Union in Nairobi. "As a young man he would ask many questions even of those large men before he would accept their policies or ideas. But the one thing he really believed in was that the majority mattered. He very much believed that the people needed to be listened to."

Mboya left Kenya in 1955 to attend Ruskin College in Oxford, England, and on his return he and Obama got to know one another well. They had both attended tempestuous labor organizing meetings after national political parties were banned in 1953. Mboya had developed a more worldly manner during his time overseas, and his vision for Kenya's future was more defined. Although he assumed a more paternal role toward Obama, the two men maintained their friendship. As Obama struggled with the question of where he fit into the churning political scene, Mboya became a cherished elder—albeit only by six years—to whom Obama regularly turned in the years to come. Obama was one of many who dropped into Mboya's house for a drink to talk of the turbulent politics of the time, and they shared many of the same friends who would go on to hold key posts in both government and private enterprise.

They also had in common a deep rootedness in the red soil of Luoland. Obama regularly returned to Kendu Bay, the lakeside town nearby to the village of his birth and famous for its musicians and exuberant dances. Kendu Bay was a prominent port that drew steamers from as far away as Uganda and Tanzania. The eclectic mix of traders and travelers who stepped onto the town's piers contributed their favored rhythms to the musical mix there. A far more subdued locale today, Kendu Bay was once considered the entertainment capital of the region and was home to the popular "Kendu Show," a well-attended local event that showcased bands and musicians from across the country.

In nearby Kanyadhiang, the Social Hall on the road leading into town hosted a succession of evening dances and competitions. Obama, who often returned to his childhood home on the weekends, was a regular at the lantern-lit events and often claimed the evening title for best dancer.

On one legendary occasion when he was still a teenager, Obama and another young man were chosen as the two finalists in an evening competition. As a packed audience watched intently in the dim light, the two of them performed alternately one after the other before an informal panel of judges. First a rhumba, then a chorus dance or tango, then a dance of their choice. The dueling dancers kept at it for over an hour, their brows streaming with sweat. In the end, Obama was declared the winner.[30]

Many elderly residents there remember his lithe form bumping out a rhumba or twirling his partner in the fast paced *mach* dance, his ever-present Sportsman cigarette angled rakishly from his full lips. Two of his favorite songs were "*Simbi Nyaima*," named for the crater lake a few miles from Lake Victoria, and "*Kiduogi Dala*," or "Can't You Come Home." Obama's movement was astonishingly fluid, his limbs always in syncopation with the music. As his neighbor Obama Madoho described it, "he seemed to be boneless."

"Barack was the best dancer in the whole region for a while," recalled Alfred Obama Oguta, an elderly cousin from Kanyadhiang. "He was very, very proud of that. After all, what lady did not want to dance with a man who could move like *that*. If he asked someone to dance, she would never turn him down."

Another common style of dance event was held in a makeshift hall in the village square, where papyrus mats served as fencing secured by a temporary gate. The dance floor was bare earth that became so dusty during the hot season that revelers would be prompted to declare at a song's end, "*amiel ma buru ema dum!*" or "I have danced until I kicked up dust." Posters were placed around town announcing the impending event and couples would start practicing weeks in advance. The most popular dances were held during school holidays in August and December, and many young men would journey back home from their jobs in nearby villages or Nairobi to attend. The entrance fee was one Kenyan shilling. At one of these dances in Kendu Bay on Christmas Day in 1956, Obama, then twenty, met his first wife in the midst of a pulsing rhumba.[31]

Grace Kezia Nyandega was sixteen years old, a shy young woman with a beatific smile from the village of Gendia. As she stood nervously at the edge of the crowded dance floor wearing her holiday outfit of a peppermint pink skirt and a crisp white blouse her eyes fell upon Obama. "I was looking for someone who could dance, and then I saw him," exclaimed Kezia, a seventy-one-year-old grandmother living in the suburban town of Bracknell outside London. "He was such a lovely boy. So smart. And he could dance like no one else. We danced all night."

Kezia's escort to the dance was a cousin of Obama's named William. The following morning Obama dispatched William to her house to ask if he could formally introduce Obama to her. It is a Luo custom that in certain delicate matters a go-between is used to negotiate between two adults, as a direct encounter is regarded as far too aggressive. In the first stage of a relationship between a man and a woman, both sides generally have a family member serve as a go-between, called a *jagam*, to communicate between the two parties in order to get information about the other person, such as their habits and tastes. They could also serve as important witnesses later if the dowry, which was usually presented in the form of cows and other gifts, had to be returned for some reason. After the go-betweens finished their investigations and both sides accepted an introduction, the man was permitted to visit the girl.[32]

But on hearing William's proposal, Kezia refused. "I was very shy with men, so I said, no, no, no," recalled Kezia. "But William came back the next day and the day after that. Finally, I decided to go with Barack. I did not tell my parents because I knew they would say no, as I was so young."

When the couple arrived in Nairobi, Obama took Kezia to meet his father, who was working as a cook for an American family living in Muthaiga, one of the toniest suburbs reserved exclusively for whites. The head of the family was Gordon Hagberg, the public affairs officer with the Nairobi office of the U.S. Information Service (USIS) office, a division of the State Department dedicated to public diplomacy. By coincidence, Hagberg was well acquainted with many of the city's rising young nationalists, for he had been in lengthy discussions with Tom Mboya about a possible scholarship program for Kenyan students. Onyango walked the young couple outside Hagberg's house so that he could examine his son's choice of a bride, and he was not pleased. Although Obama was only four years older than Kezia, Onyango declared that the girl was far too young to marry. "He told Barack, 'Why do you bring someone so young? She is like a babysitter. Go find someone older whom you can marry,'" said Kezia. "He told everyone Barack had chosen a babysitter."

Undeterred by Onyango, Obama returned to Kendu Bay to seek permission from Kezia's parents, which they granted, and eventually Onyango agreed to the union. A lengthy process of dowry payments were then made to Kezia's family. In all, fourteen cows were walked from Kanyadhiang to Gendia and presented as "bridewealth." Family elders delivered the first pair of cows. One of Onyango's brothers delivered another set. And a final pair were delivered by a seven-year-old cousin, Wilfred Obama Kobilo, who was thrilled at the responsibility. "I had always looked up to Barack and it was a great adventure to take the cows across the river," recalled Kobilo, who was sixty-one and a businessman in Nairobi. "We delivered them and then we went right back home."

Obama and his bride married in 1957 under Luo customary law, an elaborate process involving go-betweens, dowry installments, and sometimes the literal capture, or *mako*, of the bride.[33] As such, no court of law or house of worship sanctioned their union, only communal consent. If they were ever to separate or desired their union to end, they were required to present their case to a council of elders that would consider if there were sufficient grounds. Terminations were allowed if the wife turned out to be a food thief, a witch, or extremely lazy. The marriage could also be ended if the husband was found to be "a wizard, impotent, a thief or if he interfered in the kitchen or served himself from the pot," as it is spelled out in the revered encyclopedia of Luo ways Paul Mboya wrote in 1938, *Luo Kitigi Gi Timbegi*, or "Luo Customs and Traditions."[34] Under certain conditions, the dowry would be returned to the husband's family, a process called *waro dhok*.

Some Luo customs relaxed with the passage of years, and marriages were at times terminated without the approval of an elders' council. As men increasingly took up residence in Nairobi or other urban centers far from their tribal homes in the years after independence, they occasionally claimed to have dissolved their marriages merely by declaring them ended. Several years after Obama married Kezia and was contemplating marriage to the president's mother, that is precisely what he did. Kezia, however, claims that the two remained married at the time of his death and continue to be joined to this day. "Even now, I know I am his wife," declared Kezia, tapping the floor with her foot to indicate Obama buried underground. "He is dead down there, but I know he is thinking about me. He always came back to me. And then he realized that I am the wife, the real wife, always."

In the joyful months after their marriage, however, such matters were years away. Obama and his bride moved into a home near to the Kaloleni estate on the east side of the city with several other Obama cousins and began their life together. It was a fitting place to begin, for Kaloleni's multitude of single-story brownstone homes was a cherished refuge for Luos. Many of their most prominent politicians lived there, and after weekend football games at the neighboring city stadium, scores of Luos would flood the bars and restaurants. Obama felt deeply at home there, and he would remain a habitué there until the final hours of his life.

At the time the Obamas were settling into their new routine together, the mood of the city had begun to change markedly. Even before the military defeat of the Mau Mau was accomplished by 1955, the colonial government had come to realize that the status quo was no longer a viable arrangement. Toward the end of 1954 a halting reform process had begun, with a series of initiatives intended to promote the development of an African leadership that would supplant Mau Mau and its followers. By allowing a controlled degree of political expression, British administrators hoped to stifle the burning embers of nationalism. One of the most significant of these initiatives was the Lyttelton Constitution of 1954, which introduced a new government structure that included African and Asian ministers and, more critically, embraced the principle of representational parity for different racial groups.[35] Under the constitution a defined stratum of voters would eventually be able to select eight Africans to sit on Kenya's Legislative Council, known as LEGCO.

The following year another door opened. Convinced that self-government for Kenya was still many years away, in 1955 the government cautiously moved to relax the ban on African political activity. Political organizations could be formed but only on a district level, and not in Central Province, which was the domain of the Kikuyu. But colonial administrators failed to take into account, as they had throughout the Mau Mau conflict, that the grievances that gave rise to the war were felt not just by a handful of weapon-toting rebels but instead ran deeply through the Kenyan heartland. And so it was that local leaders began to surge onto the political scene, eager to participate in the first African election, which was to be held in 1957. Most of the candidates had a very definite agenda on their minds, and compromise with the colonial government was not on their list. Mau Mau may have been defeated in the forests and in the cities, but the balance of power was slowly shifting from the Europeans to the Africans—and both sides knew it.

Tom Mboya, aligned with the Nairobi Peoples Convention Party (NPCP), of which he would eventually become president, was one of four candidates running for a seat representing Nairobi. With a highly disciplined organization behind him, Mboya campaigned on many of the positions outlined in a political manifesto he had penned while at Ruskin College called, "The Kenya Question: An African Answer." He wanted an end to the emergency regulations. There must be a one-person, one-vote franchise for Africans and a lifting of the limitation on national political organizations for Africans. Kenya was for Kenyans. His slogan: "To hell with European Domination."[36]

The handsome young Kenyan's bold posture caught the attention of the American media in general and American labor leaders in particular. In the fall of 1956 the American Committee on Africa (ACOA), a group of liberal Americans and prominent black leaders interested in developing relations between the United States and Africa, invited Mboya to make a speaking tour of American college campuses. Mboya eagerly accepted. During his highly successful visit he forged a host of relationships that would blossom into a program of unique academic opportunity for hundreds of young Kenyans in the coming years.

During that trip it is also rumored that the Central Intelligence Agency recruited Mboya through his numerous labor contacts in the United States. In 1959 Mboya, the general secretary of the Kenya Federation of Labor, became a member of the board of the International Confederation of Free Trade Unions (ICFTU), a group of international unions financed by American labor and the U.S. government with the aim of opposing communism. Mboya worked closely with the ICFTU and received their ongoing financial support for years.

A 1969 article in the liberal magazine *Ramparts*, published only weeks before Mboya was assassinated, appraised the situation like this: "The

CIA's program in Kenya could be summed up as one of selective libera-tion. The chief beneficiary was Tom Mboya. . . . Mboya was ideal for the CIA's purposes—the main nationalist hero and eventual chief of state, Jomo Kenyatta, not being considered sufficiently safe."[37]

Mboya's biographer points out that Mboya consistently declared that he never "knowingly" had any dealings with the CIA. But he also acknowl-edges that the young nationalist was determined to achieve his aims. Mboya's attitude, Goldsworthy added, was, "just as expedient as the Amer-icans'. Quite simply, he wanted the money for domestic political purposes and had no qualms about its sources."[38]

Such relationships were strictly behind the scenes and were of little matter to the many who rallied around Mboya in his bid for office. Even Obama, a nonjoiner by nature, was swept up by the enthusiasm that engulfed the legislative race. When he was not at his desk at the law firm, Obama headed to Mboya's office to help strategize and galvanize support among the Luo community. The NPCP was fast becoming one of the strongest political organizations in the country, despite the ban on colony-wide organizations, and during his days working on Mboya's campaign Obama met many activists who would take key roles in the coming days of independence. Obama wanted to be one of them. Here, at last, was a direc-tion in which he could funnel his ambition and intelligence and also have a hand in shaping his country's development as an independent nation. Increasingly, Obama began to adopt the Western dress and urban style that the nationalist crowd sported.

"Tom always surrounded himself with very smart people who helped him to develop strategies, and Barack was one of them," recalled Phoebe M. Asiyo, a former member of the Kenyan parliament representing the Karachuonyo constituency in Nyanza Province for nearly two decades and a childhood friend of Obama's. "Barack was always there with him. He was very dedicated to Tom."

And yet Obama was characteristically dissatisfied. He did not like his job and was adamant that he should be engaged in more challenging work. Although the pay was reasonable, he chafed at working for an Indian boss and had to rein in his sharp tongue every time he was given an assign-ment. More galling, many of his friends from the Maseno school were heading to Makerere University in Kampala or even overseas to seek higher degrees. When they weren't talking about the impending election, his friends were debating the relative merits of schools in the United States versus those in the Soviet Union. Education was the key to everything. But because of his expulsion from Maseno, Obama could not even consider such options even though he easily qualified intellectually. Then there was the Old Man. Obama was keenly aware of his father's disappointment in him, and he was tired of listening to his father's litany of complaints. Lately, Obama had stopped dropping by the Hagberg's home to visit him.

Nor did it seem likely that anything was going to improve. Not long after the election, Kezia discovered that she was pregnant with their first child and was already talking about the clothes the baby would need. Obama was intrigued at the thought that he might soon have a son, but he knew that a child was going to add considerably to his financial burden. Some days Obama was despondent, fearing he would be stuck in a tedious clerk's job for the rest of his life. How could this have ever happened to *him*, Barack Obama, the son of Hussein Onyango and the smartest boy in the class?

What he couldn't know was that change was right around the corner. And it was coming in flats and a floral skirt.

4

MISS MOONEY

The crowd at Makadara Hall had been waiting for nearly half an hour. It was a humid Sunday in 1957, and over a thousand men and women were eager to see their political hero, Tom Mboya, take the stage. Craning for a glimpse of the presumed next president of the Nairobi Peoples Convention Party, the crowd churned against the sheet-metal walls that framed Nairobi's largest social hall, chanting bits of song, ever watchful of the European police officers stationed at the doorways.

Mboya was often late, but he always showed up at this weekly event, easily one of the city's most popular political meetings. Just as the crowd was growing impatient, a figure stepped on the stage. But it was not Mboya in his trademark red windbreaker. It was a woman. More astonishing, it was a *mzungu*. She was barely over five feet tall, her floral skirt falling just above her pale ankles, a tentative smile playing across her angular face. The crowd grew abruptly quiet, uncertain as Mboya appeared on the stage behind her. What did this mean? Surely, this could not bode well.

But when the white woman began to speak, with Mboya acting as her interpreter, they listened. Her name was Elizabeth Mooney. And she had come to change their lives.

The forty-three-year-old Texas native was a literacy teacher who the Kenyan government had employed under a U.S.-sponsored program to teach Kenyans how to read and write. In the four months since she had arrived, Mooney had had difficulty spreading word of her program. And so when the immensely popular Mboya, an ardent advocate of education, had offered to let her appear on stage, Mooney jumped at the chance.

Mooney made good use of her few minutes, explaining to the impatient crowd how easy it could be to learn how to read and write and exactly how her classes were taught. Although her appearance prompted much fluttering in the U.S. Consulate office and a reprimand in one of the local papers—both parties were distraught at the impropriety of her appearing on stage with such a high-profile politician—her mission had been accomplished. Her words that day turned the tide in her favor, and the numbers in her classroom tripled the following week. During her two-year stay in Kenya, Mooney would change the course of hundreds of Africans' lives, but none so completely as that of a young man named Barack Obama. In a matter of months Mooney not only helped give focus to his wandering ambition, but at a time when many doors seemed closed to him, she provided the critical assistance that ultimately put him on a plane to America, thus planting the seed of a political upheaval to come a generation later.

They had crossed paths several times in the city, for Obama often attended Mboya's afternoon addresses. But one afternoon, not long after her appearance at Makadara Hall, Mooney happened to visit the cramped office of the Indian law firm where Obama worked as a clerk typist taking dictation. This time they began to talk. Eager to staff her Spartan office on Ribeiro Street in the heart of Nairobi, Mooney observed that Obama was both fast and accurate at the keyboard as he worked. She promptly offered him a position as her secretary, and Obama started work for her a few days later.

Mooney was a colleague of world-renowned literacy expert, Dr. Frank C. Laubach of New York, who had recommended her for the Kenyan post and helped to fund the project. After paying Obama for several months out of her office expense fund, she turned to Laubach for the money to pay him on a more regular basis. Mooney was impressed with his performance. In a letter, she asked for $100 a month "for salary for Barack O'Bama for six months if possible," she wrote, adding an Irish twist to the spelling of his name.[1]

Laubach agreed. And early in 1959 Mooney wrote to thank him. "Thank you so much for the secretarial help," she wrote to Laubach. "Barack is a whiz and types so fast that I have a hard time keeping ahead of him. I think I better bring him along and let him be your Secretary in the USA."[2]

Obama could not have had less in common with his new boss. Sara Elizabeth Mooney, known as Betty, was the granddaughter of the cofounder of the Texas Christian University in Fort Worth, Texas. Single, she had spent virtually all of her life teaching. At age thirty, she met Laubach, a congregational minister and the father of a global literacy program known as "Each One, Teach One," a method by which each new reader teaches another person what they have learned, thus passing on the new skill one person at a time. Inspired by his personal faith in God and messianic zeal, Mooney committed herself to literacy. For eight years she worked in India, first running a mission boarding school and then teaching in an adult literacy center. Before accepting the post in Kenya, she spent two years as the supervisor of a literacy training program at the Koinonia Foundation in Baltimore, Maryland, at the time a Christian-based training center for literacy workers. Laubach served as president of the board of Koinonia.

A straightforward woman with a tight cap of brown curls, Mooney was prone to prim cotton dresses and flat shoes. A "spinster" in the jargon of the day, family members believed she had long ago given up on the idea of marriage. She was a deeply committed Christian who believed that God had brought her to Kenya on a "literacy safari,"[3] as she described it, to empower people to read. She said devotions daily.

Then there was Obama. He was twenty-one years old, a racehorse at the gate, already sporting the "academic" look that was in vogue in some Nairobi circles. His jacket was finely cut, his glasses a donnish horn rimmed, and the occasional pipe provided the crowning touch. Never mind that once he put the pipe down he invariably resumed his chronic chain smoking. On the brink of becoming a father for the first time, he was consumed with a single burning passion, which was to be a player in the development of a newly independent Kenya. But with a record already marred by rejection from Maseno and a series of small, short-lived jobs on his résumé, his prospects were moderate at best.

Mboya had urged Kenyans to think practically as they prepared for independence. He wanted them to get training in the fields that would be of service to the country, particularly in areas such as economics and administration. With his impressive mathematical skills, Obama was convinced his calling was to serve as an economist who could help develop the country's fiscal foundations and project its needs in the future. All he needed to do was find some way to get a university degree, possibly even at a college overseas as some of his friends were planning to do. Mooney was the first person—other than the Old Man—who tried to channel his strengths in such a direction rather than punish him for his audaciousness. That she was a white woman only added intrigue to the relationship.

Mooney had been hired to help the Kenya Department of Education set up a pilot literacy program, funded by the U.S. International Cooperation Administration (ICA), then an arm of the U.S. Department of State that administered aid for a host of development purposes. Her job, for which she was paid $6,355 a year, was to develop a country-wide literacy campaign that would instruct adults how to read and write first in their native language and then in English. The first step was to assemble a skilled administrative staff and launch a series of classes both in Nairobi and in the field.

The need was huge. Eight out of ten African adults in Kenya could neither read nor write,[4] a fact that loomed as a huge impediment to a nation fast approaching independence. Another one of Mooney's tasks was to produce reading materials and primers written in the tribal languages, such as Dholuo and Masai, that could be used in the classroom. The Laubach method used a series of familiar pictures coupled with related sound associations to teach words. Once the student grasped the relationship between the sound and the thing, they could then master syllables and, ultimately, the words. For the millions of Kenyans who could neither read nor write in the 1950s, the political implications of such a campaign were huge, as Laubach well knew. "You think it is a pity they cannot read, but the real tragedy is that they have no voice in public affairs, they never vote, they are never represented in any conference, they are the silent victims, the forgotten men," Laubach wrote in his 1943 book, *The Silent Billion Speak.*[5]

Mooney launched the Literacy Center in a pair of rooms—No. 19 and 20—in Ribeiro House in the heart of Nairobi. She was soon assisted by another white woman, Helen Roberts, who had left her home in Palo Alto, California, in the summer of 1958 to volunteer as a literacy teacher. Roberts, a grandmother of eleven and the author of children's books, had heard Laubach speak and soon learned his method herself. Although

Mooney was a skilled manager, Roberts, her senior by more than a decade, was the "people person," and the two worked well as a team.

They were a curious pair—two middle-aged women navigating the crowded city streets in Roberts's blue Volkswagen Bug. Undaunted, they soon managed to introduce themselves to an emerging group of Kenyans who had begun to address the country's dire need for educational opportunities. Mooney and Roberts also traveled widely "up country" to hold teacher training courses and distribute readers.

Although the Laubach method caught on quickly and Mooney's classrooms were soon packed with adult students, getting started had been challenging. In the beginning most Kenyans regarded Mooney with a deep-seated suspicion, wary of anything that hinted of the colonial government's largesse, one of the legacies of the bloody Mau Mau years. Although many Kenyans were hungry for education, they were fearful of the government publicity vans and radio announcements that broadcast the program under the banner "*Kusoma Ni Faida*," Swahili for "reading is profitable."[6] Most were convinced it was all part of a scheme to raise taxes or move them elsewhere, just as they had been forcibly relocated to the brutal detention camps during the Emergency.

Indeed, Mooney's appearance in the politically charged atmosphere of the day prompted a flutter of suspicion far beyond the audience at Makadara Hall as well. Days later a columnist for the *Sunday Post*, a Nairobi weekly newspaper, sniffed at the impropriety of her appeal, writing, "I know that Miss Mooney merely talked about Adult Literacy but a political platform is not the place for such talk by a representative of a Government Department—particularly a representative of a nation who are on record as being against the idea of the Colonies."[7] And a week after her address a member of Nairobi's Criminal Investigation Department dropped by her office to "discuss" her breach of protocol. But Mooney, an earnest law abider, had acquired approval from educational authorities before she made her appearance.

Deeply moved by the plight of those who could not read or write, Mooney was sure that her mission was divinely led. In a letter she wrote several weeks after she arrived, Mooney described watching a group of illiterate women leaving a community hall and heading "over the fresh green hillside to their homes, some of them ten miles away. And at last I felt that my own trail had stopped going in circles and had led me to the reason for being here. . . . I no longer doubt God's time table. There is some reason for my being here at this particular time."[8]

Mooney's efforts attracted the interest of two of Kenya's most prominent college graduates, who were among a tiny handful of Kenyans who could boast of college degrees. One was Dr. Julius Gikonyo Kiano, who had earned a PhD from the University of California at Berkley in 1956 and was the first Kenyan to receive a doctoral degree, and the other was Kariuki Karanja Njiiri, who earned a Master's of Arts degree from Lincoln University in Pennsylvania.[9] Kiano, a savvy Kikuyu economist, helped Mooney overcome the Kenyan people's widespread mistrust of government and guided her in the recruitment of teachers. Njiiri, the son of a senior Kikuyu chief who had his pick of jobs on his return in 1959, became her chief assistant. Both men would be instrumental in assisting Tom Mboya to raise money and select candidates for the student airlifts. One of the names that would come across their desks for consideration would be Barack Obama.

In the crowded Ribeiro Street office, Obama started out as a low-level clerk assigned to basic office tasks. He took dictation, helped organize the office, and assisted with translations in Luo and Swahili. But he was soon promoted to the writing committee, composed of half a dozen young men assigned to write elementary adult readers in their native language. Dressed in jacket and tie, Obama and the other writers sat at long wooden tables, carefully penning the pamphlets used as follow-up to the literary primers. If the high-arching Obama grumbled that the work was somewhat menial, he also realized that the job was a critical first step toward fulfilling his dream. First, the work was exceptionally well paying. But more important, teaching literacy was a critical component in the advance toward independence.

In all, Obama wrote three books in Luo that employed "Otieno" the wise man as a model instructor. The first book was *Otieno Jarieko, Kitabu Mokuongo: Yore Mabeyo Mag Rito Ngima*, or "Otieno Jarieko, the Wise Man, the First Book: Wise Ways of Health." Otieno describes a variety of healthy foods, demonstrates how to use a knife and fork, and gives instruction in the proper way to build a latrine. The second and third books center on Otieno's teachings of the wise ways of farming and citizenship, respectively. Obama worked on the three books almost the entire year and a half that he assisted Mooney, and he proudly included them on his résumé.

Working closely with the American women and a handful of their Kenyan assistants, Obama kept his bravado under close wraps and toed the line. The style in the office was highly cooperative and the staff represented a host of different tribes, due in part to the need for materials written in varied tribal languages. Obama worked closely with one of Mooney's early hires, a young Kikuyu named George Wanyee, who recently returned from India with a BA. Wanyee helped prepare Kikuyu charts and was the first editor of the *Key*, a newsletter for new readers.

A photograph of Obama, in the fifth issue of the *Key*, shows him at the chalkboard in the Center during Laubach's visit in the fall of 1958. Obama is at the ready with his chalk, helping to write the story of Jesus's birth in Luo, a project he worked on for several weeks. Part of the point of the project was the religious story itself, but Laubach also noted that "the 1,000 most common English words are used in such stories."[10] Obama impressed Laubach, who chose him to appear in his farewell photograph with a group including Laubach, Njiiri, and Mooney.

A highly organized person, Mooney ran a tight ship on Ribeiro Street and was well aware that the eyes of both the Kenyan and British governments were on her after her appearance at Makadara Hall. But she was also deeply interested in the lives of the Kenyans she was working with and went out of her way to help many of them achieve their personal goals. In addition to Obama, she assisted nearly a dozen other young Kenyans accomplish their educational goals. She kept a running "wish list" of projects and people for whom she hoped to find funding or contacts, often turning to Laubach for help. Even after she returned to the United States, she was instrumental in assisting another young Kenyan to enroll in a high school just outside Bohemia, New York, where he lived with her brother for two years.

Over the course of long hours spent poring over the evolving texts with Obama, the serious-minded Mooney gradually warmed to Obama's ironic sense of humor. In Obama she found a keenly intelligent student bristling with potential, one who also happened to have a powerful magnetism with women. That he was desperately eager to perfect his English and advance the rudimentary social skills the Old Man had taught him may have drawn her to him even more. At the time they met, Obama was just coming into his manhood. Obama was now a young father, for early in 1958 Kezia had given birth to his first son. They named him Roy Abongo Obama, although he later assumed the name Malik. Kezia took care of the baby almost entirely herself, but Obama was aware of his responsibilities as the father of an infant son. Mooney had no children of her own, but she delighted in young people and took a great interest in Obama's small family.

Although not a tall man, his broad face and often earnest expression gave Obama a commanding appearance. Along with his elegant demeanor, he possessed an intense physical allure. The same fluidity that drew admiring stares on the Kendu Bay dance floor of his youth was now present in an everyday grace of movement. The power of his appeal, however, had as much to do with his aura of self-confidence and ebullience as it did with his physical attributes, at least as a young man. And then there was the trumpeting voice, now matured, that could snap a sleepy room to attention from a corridor away. Obama, clearly, was not to be passed over.

What Obama found in Mooney was more complex. Part of her appeal for him was certainly the job. Working at the Literacy Center provided both social standing and the opportunity to rise. But Mooney and Obama also spent time together outside the office, enjoying rural drives and attending some of the popular evening dances. And that association brought a different kind of benefit for Obama. Among a certain kind of African man, just keeping company with a white woman provided considerable social status. Doing so was a bold act, the behavior of a man who no longer intended to blindly knuckle to European social mores. Although certain elements among both the colonists and the Africans disapproved of interracial unions, others felt it was high time that things began to change. C. M. G. Argwings-Kodhek, the lawyer who squared off with Mboya in colorful political debates, had openly thrown down a gauntlet when he married a white woman while he was studying outside the country in the early 1950s, a time when, in Kenya, it was against the law to do so. Kenyatta had also married a white woman in England, although he did not bring her home until after independence. And if others speculated about the precise nature of the relationship between Mooney and Obama, well, all the better from Obama's point of view.

Several of Obama's friends recall Mooney and Obama touring through town in her 1956 Plymouth or pulled off on the side of the road with Obama repairing one of the car's seemingly perpetual flat tires. And when Obama stopped in at meetings of the Kogelo Union Association, a group that looked after affairs of interest to the Kogelo clan and provided support to the needy, she would wait patiently behind the wheel while he went inside.

Mooney waited outside partly because the discussion concerned union business and was held strictly in Luo. There would surely also have been an element of social propriety being observed on her part as well. Just six years earlier, relations between African men and white women were strictly circumscribed by law. Under the Penal Code of the Protectorate of Kenya, a man or a woman engaging in sexual relations with a person of another race could be subject to up to five years in prison. The interactions between white women and African men in particular had long been closely scrutinized. With the influx of a growing number of *wazungu* in the 1950s, including educators and government advisers, black and white relations had become somewhat less extraordinary. But though the law forbidding such unions had been repealed in 1951 and the situation was more relaxed, mixed couples still raised eyebrows on the streets of Nairobi. On the back roads leading through the countryside, Obama and Mooney drew astonished stares.

Obama minded not at all. Although many a Kenyan man would have shredded his identity card before asking a white woman to dance, Obama did not hesitate. When he came across Mooney at one of the dances at the Railway Hall not long after he started working for her, he tucked his cigarette jauntily between his lips, and extended his hand. "At that time, to go and beg a dance from a white lady, you must be very brave," said Arthur Reuben Owino. "You must be well behaved and well dressed—you know, civilized. But Obama was all of that. And when he asked that white lady to dance, she said 'yes.'"

And she said yes more than once. Despite the raised eyebrows, Obama and Mooney clearly took great pleasure in dancing together. He was the one who escorted her to an invitation-only evening at the prestigious African Club, an elegant event featuring classical music and an impressive list of guests clad in their most elegant silks and smoking jackets. In a letter to friends back home, Roberts wrote, "Well, the dance was a wonderful affair. The band was excellent and the quality of guests was very high. . . . Betty danced many dances, without harm to her back, tho she got very tired."[11]

Obama confided in a few of his friends that he was not sure how far to take the friendship, so they observed the evolving situation with keen interest. Obama, of course, paid little mind to rules or social niceties, but a middle-aged *mzungu*? One working for the government? This was a whole new level of daring. Or something.

Richard Muga, a childhood friend of Obama's who lived with Obama during the first year he worked at the Literacy Center, recalls that Obama often visited Mooney in her two-bedroom flat. A tireless letter writer and amateur photographer, Mooney took many photographs of Obama that she kept throughout her life. They are a curious collection of largely posed shots, possibly taken to be used with school or job applications overseas. In a couple of them he stands in her flat next to her boxy, brown radio, staring intently into the camera, his expression pensive. In another he frowns in a lineup with other members of the literacy staff, standing on a Nairobi street. One shows him smiling whimsically—and completely uncharacteristically—at a white flower that he appears to have just plucked. "They were so close, no air passed between them," said Muga. "They cooked together. They spent time together. And a lot of people noticed that Barack's English got much better during that time. The Mooney lady helped him very much with that."

Kezia, preoccupied with her new baby back at their home, seemed wholly unaware of such observations about her husband. On occasion she and Roy were included on outings with Mooney and several others from the office. As was the custom in Nairobi of the time, men routinely socialized in the evenings without their wives. Far from resenting this *mzungu*'s close association with her husband, Kezia was glad that he had a job and was hopeful that the connection might bring even greater opportunity. Although Kezia acknowledges that her husband had a roving eye even from the start, she does not believe that Mooney was one of his romantic interests.

Despite the speculation of some of Obama's friends, that Mooney would have had a physical relationship with Obama seems unlikely for a multitude of reasons. For starters, her religious convictions would have put any married man off-limits. What's more, Mooney was friendly with Obama's young family. She and other members of the office staff would sometimes picnic on the outskirts of Nairobi along with Kezia, baby Roy, and Mooney's assistant, Wanyee. Mooney herself had experienced first-hand the pain of a broken home after her father left her mother when she was a teenager, and she was deeply opposed to extramarital affairs. Mooney often declared that she was waiting to find someone as reliable as one of her two older brothers, who had long-standing marriages, for her to marry.

Soon enough, another consuming interest united Obama and Mooney, one that was sweeping the country. By the beginning of 1959, just as Obama was completing the second Otieno book, the drive for advanced education for Kenyans had begun in earnest. Education was not only an ideal; it was a practical necessity if the country was to govern itself. As independence loomed and the handover of the reins of government from the British administrators to Kenyans inched ever closer, the need for Africans trained in a host of professions became urgent, as Mboya often emphasized. In the tumultuous months of 1959 literacy became a subject central not only to Kenya's future but also to the expanding reach of the Cold War.

The numbers told part of the story. Although European missionaries had helped to spread reading and writing throughout the country since their arrival in the mid-1800s, educational opportunities for Kenyans remained extremely limited well into the twentieth century. Just as the missionary schools were devoted largely to evangelical aims, the British government schools had their own self-serving design. Most schools the colonists inaugurated were intended to produce a low-level workforce that would supply semiskilled laborers to assist the white-run farms or civil servants to aid in government administration. The last thing the colonists wanted—or so most Kenyans believed—were independent or critical thinkers.[12]

Most Kenyans were lucky to get several years of schooling before encountering a bottleneck in the educational system. In 1958, of those completing eight years of school, only 13 percent were able to continue on to secondary school because there were neither the schools nor the teachers to accept them, as Mboya wrote in his biography, *Freedom and After*.[13] For the few who did manage to make it through secondary school, the opportunities for undergraduate, let alone graduate-level education, were virtually nonexistent.

At the end of the 1950s there were two institutions of higher learning available to Kenyans: Makerere University in Kampala and the Royal Technical College of East Africa in Nairobi, which only began admitting students in 1956. But both Makerere and the Technical College, later to be called the University of Nairobi, were two-year institutions and offered the equivalent of a high school diploma only. Nor were their enrollments substantial. In 1955 Makerere, then the only college in East Africa, admitted a total of 205 students from the entire region. In 1957 there were a total of 251 students at Makerere, and another 57 students were admitted to the Royal Technical College in Nairobi.[14] Those who wanted higher education had to go overseas, but few had the finances or ability to do so.

By 1958 fewer than two hundred Kenyans were studying for university degrees outside the country, seventy-four in Great Britain, seventy-five in India and Pakistan, and a few dozen in the United States.[15] Kenyan students began to trickle into the United States during the mid 1950s, and by 1957 there were at least thirty-four enrolled in colleges or universities, and in 1958 another thirty-nine arrived. However, all but a handful of those were privately sponsored students. In 1957 only seven U.S. scholarships were given to Kenyan students, with another nine were awarded in 1958.[16] All told, only several hundred Kenyans had university degrees out of a population of just over eight million toward the decade's end.[17] This tiny group was hardly enough to supply the doctors and lawyers and bankers and teachers and the thousands of other professionals that would be needed to run the country when independence arrived. Critics among the rising tide of nationalists argued that this was no accident. They charged that the colonists had deliberately crafted an educational system that served their labor needs while keeping the bulk of Kenyans chained by their own illiteracy to brute labor or low-level administrative tasks.

Part of the problem was the shortage of Kenyan secondary schools, the equivalent of American junior high schools. Another impediment to those few who had managed to get a secondary school certificate was the British government's reluctance to have Kenyan students study in U.S. schools, which it considered inferior to its own.[18] That prejudice had taken cultural hold within Kenya, and a British education was generally regarded as superior to any other well into the 1950s. But as the first graduates of American institutions began to trickle back home to Kenya and then swiftly rise to the highest posts an African was afforded, the thinking began to change. Here were Africans with university degrees who looked the white man right in the eye. Their arrival fanned mounting frustration with the colonial regime, and this was swiftly translated into political expression. America, it now seemed, might be an option after all.

Although few in number, their impact was profound. The return of these students, fresh with stories of America's relative freedom and modern ways, coincided with an accelerating urgency in the tenor of Kenyan politics. In 1957 the first LEGCO elections open to Africans had introduced a new generation of Kenyan politicians to the scene. They included Mboya; Oginga Odinga of Central Nyanza, a former teacher and president of the Luo Union; Ronald G. Ngala of the Coast, also a former teacher and a member of the Mombasa Municipal Board; and Daniel T. arap Moi, a member of the Kalenjin tribe who was already a LEGCO member representing the Rift Valley. Upon their election, the group of eight immediately formed the African Elected Members Organization (AEMO) and went on the offensive.

Just days before the Kenyan elections, a critical African milestone had been reached after the Gold Coast achieved independence from Great Britain on March 6, 1957. The country was given the African name Ghana, which was chosen to reflect the ancient empire of Ghana that had once covered much of West Africa. Kwame Nkrumah was appointed Prime Minister as he trumpeted that Ghana "our beloved country is free forever." It was the first sub-Saharan African country to gain independence from colonial rule, and it galvanized countless others across the continent to persevere against their imperial rulers. Coupled with the stirring stories of the students returning from the United States, the Ghanian triumph inspired the Kenyan nationalists like nothing else. As Mboya wrote to friends in London, "The battle is on."[19]

AEMO had a short but determined list of demands. Members of the group would not accept any ministerial posts unless the Africans were granted a legislative majority over the European and Asian members. They also wanted a clear articulation of the British government's plans for Kenya's future. Although the African representation was subsequently increased to fourteen seats under the Lennox-Boyd Constitution in October 1957, AEMO rejected that as well, opting instead to hold out for a more complete response to their demands.

By 1959 the tide begun to shift in favor of the African nationalists. Determined to move the government's hand, the entire group of African and Asian members of the LEGCO walked out and formed a united front behind the Constituency Elected Members Organization (CEMO). As the tempo of the political debate grew ever more aggressive, the group sent a delegation to London headed by Odinga to demand an immediate end to the Emergency and a release of all veteran political leaders. Although the British government remained noncommittal on some of their demands and refused to discuss Kenyatta's release, it consented to the need for a constitutional conference. The colonial government, it seemed, was in retreat.

Mboya would normally have been a part of the delegation, but he had earlier accepted an invitation from the American Committee on Africa, which had sponsored his first visit to the United States, to return for an April speaking tour. By not going on the trip to London, Mboya risked the possibility that Odinga, who was clearly emerging as a rival in the bid for national leadership, would benefit politically at home if the discussions were fruitful—and even if they were not. It was a risk he was willing to take. Being a politician blessed with an astute sense of timing, Mboya seized the moment for a return to the United States.

In April 1959 Mboya made his second visit to the United States, landing in New York to a hero's welcome. He was by now a figure of immense global popularity, and his first few days in the United States were crammed with speeches, press conferences, and meetings with Vice President Richard Nixon, Adlai Stevenson, and Senator John Kennedy. Handsome, a centrist compared to some of his rivals back home, and intellectually astute, Mboya was clearly an African that Americans could love.

With the flames of Pan-Africanism sweeping the globe and the embryonic seeds of the civil rights movement beginning to take root at home, U.S. leaders were keeping a close eye on the creep of independence across Africa. As tensions between the United States and Soviet Union rose steadily, the British colonies emerging from domination were seen as being up for grabs politically. Determined that those new nations not fall under Communist rule, the government was poised to intervene in any way that might bolster its posture in the simmering Cold War. In his increasingly fiery oratory before labor leaders and rapt college students, Mboya repeatedly drove home the link between education and political self-determination for the African nations. "A main theme in Mboya's speeches was the lambasting of the European powers' attempts at continuing their domination in Africa through denying Africans access to higher education, which, he contended, prevented the training of the sort of educated leaders who could take new African nations through independence and to stability," Tom Shachtman wrote in *Airlift to America*.[20]

Mboya had a vision that he had been nursing for years. What he wanted to do was create an educational airlift of Africa's best and brightest students, an airplane that would transport these students to the doors of American colleges and universities. All he needed was the help of his American friends. Riding the swell of his popularity, Mboya reconnected in New York with businessman William X. Scheinman, president of Arnav Aircraft Associates, and George Houser, the executive director ACOA, whom he had met on his first trip. Scheinman and Mboya had exchanged countless letters about specific students in particular and a possible scholarship program in general over the years. Now they were ready to take action, and the specific shape of an airlift began to emerge.

Together, they formed the African American Students Foundation (AASF) and assembled an impressive board of prominent African Americans, including Theodore W. Kheel, a nationally known labor lawyer and president of the National Urban League, and Jackie Robinson, the former baseball star. By the end of Mboya's five-week visit, the group had received pledges of more than fifty scholarships and had collected

$35,000, according to the AASF.[21] Though Scheinman became consumed with business interests in later years, he remained fascinated with Africa for the rest of his life. After his death in 1999, he was buried on Rusinga Island next to Tom Mboya's grave.

Mboya headed back to Kenya to start making arrangements for an aircraft. So began the first phase of one of the greatest achievements of his career. The airlift, which would turn out to be a series of flights, not only greatly enhanced Mboya's stature back home but it also produced a generation that would help shape the independent nation of Kenya. They were not large in number. At the time of independence, there were fewer than five hundred Kenyans with university degrees from overseas, one of the most poignant legacies of the colonial era.[22] But the scope of their achievement made up for their diminutive ranks. Over the next quarter of a century the graduates would make up half of Kenya's parliaments and cabinet ministries and would dominate the highest ranks of business. Today, they continue to comprise a select, albeit graying group with a unique collective memory of their country's historic formation.

Ever since the name Barack Obama first filtered into the American political lexicon in 2004, it has been said that his father was one of the students on the famous first airlift. President Obama declared it while campaigning in 2007, and it has been repeated many times since he became president. But Obama Sr. was not a member of the student airlift. Obama, in fact, was turned down for the much-coveted seat. And the man who rejected him was an enthusiastic young American named Robert F. Stephens.

From 1957 to 1959 Stephens was the cultural affairs officer at the U.S. Information Service (USIS) in Nairobi. An amiable Michigan native, Stephens counted among his many responsibilities the task of interviewing students to determine if they met the criteria for the airlift. Despite being a *mzungu* with a significant degree of power, Stephens was well liked by the African nationalists. Not only was he conversant in Swahili, he was an avid supporter of the drive for African education and did much to facilitate the students' success.

Stephens and others in the U.S. Consulate in Nairobi had long objected to the U.S. requirement that a Kenyan student have two years of additional schooling after high school in order to be eligible for a U.S. scholarship.

He reasoned that Americans needed only a high school degree to get into college, so why should the bar be higher for Africans? He was the one who helped convince Washington officials to drop the requirement so that Kenyans needed only a Cambridge School Certificate, the equivalent of a high school diploma, in order to apply.

A thirty-four-year-old father of three at the time he interviewed Obama, Stephens became an unofficial mentor for many Kenyan students eager for a chance to travel to America. Young men and women stood for hours outside his second-floor office on Government Road waiting to hear his advice. While interviewing them to determine their eligibility, Stephens often had to raise his voice to be heard above the buses and bodies churning outside his open window.

Stephens maintained a library of more than six hundred American college catalogues. Students—Obama among them—were constantly dropping in to thumb through their well-worn pages, never mind that they had never heard of either the schools or the cities in which they were located. Stephens also held some informal orientation sessions on American ways for prospective students. A chief subject was gender relations and sexual mores, which differed vastly from African habits. In the category of hygiene, clean socks were high on the agenda. "I told them they must always remember to change their socks and to wash them out," recalled Stephens, now retired in Marblehead, Massachusetts.

When Mboya arrived back in Nairobi, the exhausting process of selecting the eighty-one students who would fill the first charter plane began. Mboya, Kiano, Njiiri, and Stephens formed the selection committee. Often the four men would pour over the student lists long into the night in the living room of the Stephens's Muthaiga home, trying to make the difficult choice of who would get to go. The chance of boarding the Britannia aircraft that had been chartered for the trip had become a dream that infected young people from the shores of Lake Victoria to the rough-hewn docks of Mombasa. "Going to America was *the* thing to do," said Philip Ochieng, one of Kenya's most prominent journalists and a drinking pal of Obama's in later years. "If you didn't have an education, you'd never rise higher than a senior clerk."

Obama was determined to be one of the chosen ones. He talked about it constantly, sometimes comparing notes with other applicants. Thinking his friendship with Mboya was his ace in the hole, Obama headed into his interview with Stephens bristling with certainty.

Stephens recalls his meeting with Barack Obama well, not because he was so impressed with him but because he was not. Dapper in suit and tie, Obama appeared in Stephens's office one morning with his paperwork in hand. Stephens was put off by the younger man's manner from the start. Obama seemed cocksure, far more confident than his résumé merited. Concerned about Obama's abrupt separation from the Maseno School, Stephens asked him what had happened. "He really prevaricated about his school record," recalled Stephens. "He reassured me that he had gotten all the proper certification that he needed, that there was no problem."

But as Stephens examined Obama's file, he found that there was indeed a problem. Obama had somehow managed to get a Cambridge School Certificate, the British examination certificate required in order to pursue higher education, but he had earned only a third-division pass, the lowest score possible. Why he did so poorly is difficult to understand given Obama's obvious intellectual gifts. Perhaps he took his performance for granted and failed to apply himself as he had often done as a younger student. In any case, acceptance in an American institution of higher learning required a Cambridge certificate with a first-division pass. In some cases a second-division pass was acceptable, but almost never a third division.[23] Stephens told Obama he was sorry, but he could not recommend him for consideration for the airlift. "He was a very good talker and he tried to talk me out of it, but there was nothing I could do," explained Stephens. "He just did not have the grade. I explained that to him and he got up and left. When I heard later that he'd made it to America another way, I was pretty surprised."

For Obama, the news was devastating. Despite his difficulties at Maseno, he had never for a moment thought he would get turned down for the airlift. Adding to his humiliation was the fact that many of his friends were already rejoicing over their acceptances. Ochieng, an Alliance School graduate who had met Obama in Mboya's office when they checked on the status of their applications, was headed to Roosevelt University in Chicago. Jackson Isigie, who had spent years saving the 7,000 shillings he needed for his first year abroad, had been accepted at Wisconsin State College in Steven's Point, Wisconsin. And Pamela Odede, the daughter of a Nairobi politician and the woman who would eventually marry Tom Mboya, was going to Western College for Women in Oxford, Ohio. The list was growing steadily. Obama complained bitterly to Kezia and a handful of others that he was being unfairly denied this golden opportunity. "Barack was crushed that he was not to be on the airlift," recalled Olara A. Otunnu, president of the Uganda People's Congress party and formerly Uganda's Minister for Foreign Affairs as well as a close family friend of Obama's. "He wanted this very much and he was not used to being turned down. It was embarrassing to him."

Some who had not made the cut refused to accept the news. They wanted to go so badly that they would hover hopefully at the airport right up until the plane took off. As Gordon Hagberg, director of the USIS office and later the director of the Nairobi office of the Institute of International Education, wrote of the students who were turned down for some of the later airlifts: "They were unsuccessful candidates who nevertheless persisted in standing around hoping for a last minute change of fortune. Their tearful vigils were sometimes punctuated by more dramatic pleas, such as that of one boy who got down on his knees and begged to be allowed to go."[24]

Obama was not about to get down on his knees, but he tried everything else he could think of to reverse Stephens's decision. Even Obama's connection with Mboya, however, could not overcome his poor test score. Obama would have to find another way to get to the United States or likely be destined for a lackluster job in a back office for the rest of his life.

Once again, Mooney stepped in. She knew he was smart enough. Where many others had been put off by Obama's sometimes overbearing demeanor, Mooney resolutely kept her faith. But she also realized that he was going to need to change his attitude if he was going to overcome his lack of high school education. As a young man Obama's intelligence had allowed him to cut some academic corners, and because of this, he rarely had to immerse himself fully in his work. But with the prospect of an American degree before him, Obama agreed to buckle down and commit himself in earnest.

Mooney showed him what to do. She knew well from her own experience the difference a little encouragement and support could make. As a young woman, her two older brothers had paid for her to attend the

Maryland State Normal School for teaching in Towson, Maryland. Later, she lived with her brothers while all three attended George Washington University and supported one another. And so when she decided to help Obama in early 1959, she turned to her brother Mark, a mechanical engineer living in Pomona, California, and asked if he would send some books that Obama could use to prepare. "An African here is preparing to take an entrance exam for admission in an American college," she typed on her blue airmail stationary. "He has been out of school for some years, so he needs to do some reviewing. He can get books here but they are not slanted to American schools."[25]

Mooney asked for the gamut. She wanted books in "European History (any period), general science, biology and chemistry, English literature, English grammar or rhetoric." She suggested that her brother get "outline" course books, the kind that students use to cram for exams. Paperbacks would be best, as they could be sent more quickly. Mooney also wondered if he could track down a book that she had taken to India for teaching purposes, "a condensed course in Math prepared for the Army" that was stored somewhere in her belongings. If it was not too heavy, perhaps he could send that along as well. If not, Obama could manage with the math books on hand.[26]

Time was of the essence. Surface mail, she added would take too long. "There is a special rate for books by air," she wrote. "I am willing to spend as much as $25 for the books including the postage."

As the proposed airlift to America was increasingly the talk of Nairobi, Mooney too felt the frustration of the countless numbers who were not even in the running. She concluded her letter to her brother: "Really the eagerness of Africans for education is heartbreaking. There are so few opportunities for them here. Out of 5,000 who qualified for high school there were places for 800. There is no way for the others to study. Many are going to the USA, but it is rather expensive to go for high school."

The books arrived in February. Mooney wrote her sister-in-law a thank-you note and assured her that she would "give the books to the young man in a few days and I know he will be thrilled."[27]

Obama got to work. For the first time in his life, he worked relentlessly. Every evening after work and during much of his spare time, the elder Obama pored over his American books, running over his lessons time and again. He was so inspired by his own progress that he began to renew his visits to the Old Man in Muthaiga to show him that he had buckled down and was now working in earnest.

Onyango was generally a solemn presence in the Hagberg house, striding through the elegant home barefoot and clad in his kanzu. At night, he would retreat to the servants' quarters and read the Koran by candlelight. Despite the Hagbergs' request, the landlord had refused to put electricity in the Africans' living areas, saying there was no need. His grave demeanor considerably lightened, however, when his boisterous son showed up at the door. The Hagberg's twelve-year-old daughter, Paula, noticed that, on seeing Obama, Onyango even broke into a broad smile, something he did not often do.

Onyango was impressed by his son's perseverance, and relations between the two warmed considerably. "Barack would be dressed to the teeth, very natty, very full of himself," recalled Paula Schramm, sixty-four and living in Enosburg Falls, Vermont. "He'd ring the bell and announce, 'I have come to see the Old Man! Where is he?' And Onyango would be very pleased."

After a few months of determined study, Obama and Mooney decided he was ready to take the college entrance examination even though he was still short a few high school credits. He waited anxiously for the results, growing thin with worry. At last, notice of his score arrived. Mama Sarah did not see him open it, but when he told her about it later, "he was still shouting out with happiness. And I laughed along with him, for it was just as things had been so many years before, when he used to come home after school to boast about his marks."[28]

Obama had scored well enough to apply to a U.S. college. Now he just had to find a school that would accept him. Mooney and Roberts described the variety of schools in the United States, schools on the different coasts, urban schools that specialized in engineering, and southern schools that emphasized the Greek letter traditions. When someone from home sent an installment of magazines and newspapers, they scoured the pages for articles about colleges that might help him make some choices. Mooney and Obama were both struck by a 1958 piece in the *Saturday Evening Post* about the University of Hawaii, which it described as "one of the most unusual and colorful campuses on American soil."[29]

The "color" stemmed from the wide variety of races represented among the student body, a rich blend of Chinese, Japanese, Polynesian, Korean, Filipino, Hawaiian, and Caucasian heritages. In fact, according to the piece, the school had found that there were so many students of mixed races that it created a special category for mixed-race students called, "Cosmopolitan." Better still, the campus was home to so many beautiful women, the student yearbook recognized not just one beauty queen but seven in order to honor each of the seven different racial groups on campus. Last but not least, the school was flexible. Each year the University of Hawaii accepted a group of students from further south in the Pacific who were lacking a few high school credits, just as Obama was. All things considered, it would be hard to imagine a campus more fitting for Obama.

In the end, Obama wrote a personal letter to the presidents of thirty universities, among them Morgan State, San Francisco State, the University of Hawaii, and Santa Barbara Junior College. Attached to several of them was a letter of recommendation from Mooney, in which she explained Obama's truncated transcript and made the case for Kenyan students' urgent need for education. "Given Mr. O'Bama's desire to be of service to his country, he should be given a chance, perhaps on a one year basis," she concluded.[30]

And then it was time to wait again.

With a few days break from classes for the Easter 1959 holiday, Mooney and Helen Roberts used the opportunity to travel. During the almost two years she had been in Kenya, the primers had been completed in four languages and the Literacy Center had settled into a smooth routine. Mooney was beginning to think about what she was going to do when her contract expired in the fall. Although she was considering seeking a PhD or working in television, neither seemed quite right. And so she and Roberts packed up the blue Volkswagen and headed for the Murchison Falls National Park in Uganda for some adventure in the bush.

Maneuvering up the Nile River in a launch, both women were thrilled to see crocodiles and hippopotamuses lolling in the water. One day, when Mooney ventured close to an elephant in the park in order to take a photograph, their guide began to shriek, "'Kubwa! Kubwa sana!' (big, very big.) Then more urgently, 'Pita! Pita!' (pass! pass!) for the elephant had lifted his huge ears and started towards us," Roberts wrote in her memoir, *The*

Unfolding Trail. "So, I went full speed ahead. After that we usually took our pictures from a safe distance."[31]

By the time they got home, letters from two schools had arrived in the mail. Once again, the news was good. "You will be glad to know that the boy you sent the books for has received admission both to San Francisco State College and Hawaii University," Mooney wrote her sister-in-law. "He'll probably go to Hawaii as there is an engineering college there."[32]

Obama told everybody of his triumph, proudly waving his acceptance papers for them to see. Many, who had never heard of Hawaii, wondered where it was exactly. "I had never heard of the place, but Barack told me it was very good indeed," recalled Richard Muga, the friend with whom Obama lived briefly. "He told me all about the beaches and the wonderful weather. He was very overjoyed to be going there. And he said that he hoped I would be making it to America, too."

Word traveled swiftly to the shores of Lake Victoria, and the celebrations in Kanyadhiang and Alego stretched far into the night. Barack had *done* it; he was going to be one of the Big Men, one of the men in gleaming cars with silver-tipped fins and his very own office in one of the tall buildings on Victoria Street. His achievement meant not only that he would be the first of his clan to go to college; it meant that the doors at last were opening for all of them, that the dusty red road led not only to the next village but also to magnificent places far beyond. Many from home would admire Obama for this achievement regardless of what else he did with his life. Dozens of chickens were slaughtered that day, and bottles of *busaa* were raised to the heavens.

Not everyone shared in the celebration. Kezia, for one, had decidedly mixed feelings about Barack's news. His triumph was hers to share, for a degree from the United States would surely guarantee him a position in the country's critical years ahead and thus elevate her own status; in a way, it already had. But Kezia had also recently learned that she was pregnant with her second child. With Barack away, she would have to live between Alego and Kendu Bay, relying largely on both of their families to support her and her children. She knew the wait would be many years long.

Then there was the Old Man, who had retired to Alego earlier in the year. He was oddly heartbroken at the news. Although he had long been among the fiercest proponents of the importance of education for his children in general and Barack in particular, Hussein felt that Barack should remain in Kenya to take care of his wife and child. He also worried about how he could support Barack in the United States and still pay for school fees for the rest of his children.[33] But mostly he feared that his headstrong bird of a son would be won over by the temptations of America and lost to him forever. "*Winyo piny kiborne*," he sighed to his children. For the bird, the world is never too far. The bird was taking flight once again.

All the bird had to do was find the money to pay for it all.

For the gathering mass of students preparing to go to America in the fall of 1959, there was a grab bag of funding possibilities. Some students were lucky enough to earn full scholarships that covered the approximately $1,000 cost of board and tuition. Others were awarded scholarships that Mboya, Kiano, or another benefactor had secured, so they only had to cobble together money for room and board. A great many of them accumulated funds through years of hard work and family sacrifices, such as the sale of livestock or personal belongings. There were many *harambees*, community events such as teas or dances held by a student's clan or tribe to raise money for their expenses.

For the average student the cost was phenomenal. The American Consulate required that students, in addition to arranging for their tuition, also have $300 to cover incidental expenses and be able to prove that they could cover their own support during their first year in the United States. Whereas the chartered aircraft took care of the approximate $600 cost of the flight for the airlift students, Obama had that expense to cover as well.[34]

Obama went into action. In July his name was included in a list of students appearing in the Luo newspaper, *Ramogi*, who had been admitted to schools abroad but still needed funds. The item, which appeared under the heading, "Migosi Barack H. Obama," read in Luo: "*Wuod Alego (CN) dwaro Shs. 6,000 kuom konye e thuolo moyudo Hawaii (U.S.A.) mar dhiyo nyime gi puonjruok. En wuod Jaduong Hussein ma Luo mathot ong'eyo.*" (Son of Alego needs Ksh 6,000 to help him continue his education at Hawaii (U.S.A.) where he has secured admission. He is the son of Mr. Hussein who is well known among the Luo.)[35]

Over the next few months Obama contacted nearly a dozen organizations that supported African interests, including some in Hawaii, and made numerous personal appeals. The process was one he would get to know all too well, for while he was in the United States, Obama was constantly trying to drum up money, right up to his final weeks.

In the end he wound up with a smattering of contributors toward the first leg of his journey. The African-American Institute provided his airfare and some additional support, and the African American Students Foundation agreed to provide a modest amount of expense money. The *Ramogi* notice generated a few hundred shillings. But it was not enough—not by a long shot. Obama still did not have the money to pay for his tuition or even all of his expenses. Again, Mooney had a plan, one especially tailored for Obama.

Although Mooney felt Obama would ultimately get a scholarship or could earn his tuition himself, she decided that she herself would pay the $200 for his first year's tuition. Given her salary, this was clearly not an easy thing to do. But Mooney believed deeply in Obama's potential, and she did not want mere financial concerns to distract him. As she wrote to Laubach in March, "He is extremely intelligent and his English is excellent so I have no doubt that he will do well and for that reason I am willing to help him.[36] But given that he was still short a few credits and had not been in school for several years, she felt he needed to concentrate exclusively on his work.

Mooney, however, was concerned about giving him hundreds of dollars for expenses for fear that it was more than Obama could manage or that he would spend it before the year was out. In her letter to Laubach, Mooney explained, "I do not like to turn much cash over to Barack because my experience with Africans shows they are not very good at managing money—probably because they haven't had a chance to do so or much money to manage!"

So she devised a plan to protect Obama from himself. She asked Laubach in her letter if she could send him the $400 to cover Obama's second-semester room and board that Laubach would then hold for him. Laubach could then issue a statement saying that Obama had been awarded a $400 grant that could be presented to the university as proof that he could pay. That money would be made available to Obama in January of 1960 to cover his expenses. And one last thing: Could he possibly not send the money right away but perhaps the following January so that she could deduct it from her 1960 income tax? Given that Mooney's annual salary was $6,355, her gift to Obama was extraordinary. Although she would help many other young Kenyans with her guidance and incidental financial contributions, Obama was one of only a small number of students who so moved her that she committed significant amounts of her personal resources, including her time and money, toward furthering their ambitions. "I have the money in the bank for Barack so there is not doubt that it will be paid," she wrote. "I won't touch it but in the meantime it can be drawing interest."[37]

Laubach consented, as he often did with Mooney's requests. And so, at last, Obama had both a school that wanted him and the money to pay for it. He was on the brink of a step that promised to radically alter the trajectory of his life and foist him onto the front pages of Kenya's unfolding story. Deeply grateful to Mooney, Obama would visit her in the United States, and the two would remain in touch well beyond his return to Kenya. In July he wrote his own letter to Laubach saying that when he received the $400, "believe me, it is because of this that my hopes started to grow that I would come to America one of these days. I could not believe my eyes when I read the letter and was overjoyed."[38]

Obama was to land in early August in New York, where he planned to stay for a few days and hoped to meet with his ebullient benefactor. Although he never managed to do so, the two men stayed in touch and Laubach would provide substantial support for Obama during his time in Hawaii.

Obama's departure came at a crucial moment in Kenya's tumultuous drive toward independence. By the middle of the year the Emergency was still in place and there was still no succinct timetable for when Kenyatta would be released. Political leaders were growing increasingly restive. Throughout the rainy months the African members of LEGCO had struggled to form a multiracial party, convinced that the colonial government would soon permit the formation of political parties on a nationwide level. But their talks ultimately led to a stalemate. Their intramural quarreling resulted in a radical split in the ranks of the African nationalists. Although some LEGCO members, including Daniel T. arap Moi of the Rift Valley and Ronald G. Ngala of the Coast endorsed a multiethnic party idea, Mboya argued that such a party formation was a way to bar Africans from real power, and Odinga and Kiano soon fell in step with him.[39] The sharply drawn lines between the two African groups would be reflected in the formation of Kenya's two major political parties in the following year.

Continuing pressure from the nationalists ultimately triggered a series of decisions in London in the months to come that would vastly accelerate the move toward independence. The fall elections marked the replacement of colonial secretary Alan Lennox-Boyd by Iain Macleod, one of the most liberal of the Conservative party's young men. Keenly aware that the gradual pace of decolonization once favored in London was no longer acceptable, Macleod took action. He announced that in the coming year a constitutional conference would be held to design specific steps and a timetable for Kenyan independence. All members of the Kenya Legislative Council would be included. In one of his earliest speeches, Macleod dropped his bombshell: The state of emergency in Kenya would at last be lifted. When the announcement was made in Nairobi, the streets erupted in celebration and cheering.

For Obama, it must have been difficult to walk away from such seismic developments, with the prospect of self-government so tantalizingly near. He must have sensed that events were about to accelerate rapidly and that he would be absent from his country's long-awaited renaissance. But Obama had worked hard to shape his own destiny, and he was anxious to embark on the new path that lay before him.

With a one-way ticket to New York booked in August, Obama spent a hurried final month making preparations. He completed the last of the Otieno books and helped make a film strip about the work that the literacy office had achieved. Mooney was still fretting about what she would do next, eager for divine guidance, as her faith hit at low ebb. Homesick and troubled by a painful back, she wrote Laubach that she was tempted to take the next plane home. Making matters worse, her faithful Barack, who had done all her typing, was now gone. "Now I can't make the typewriter work," Mooney wrote to Laubach the day after Obama left the country.[40] She had no way of knowing that her own life would change radically in the next few months as well.

Obama did not linger long over his departure. He made a final visit to Alego and sat for a family photograph with the Old Man, Kezia, and his son in a local studio. Then he left his small family under the watchful eye of Sarah and the Old Man. Kezia, weeping, promised to wait for him.

On August 4, Obama flew out of Nairobi en route to the United States. Two years later to the day Barack Obama Jr. was born.

5

"WHO THE HELL IS *THAT*?"

L ess than two months before Barack Obama arrived in Honolulu, the bucolic, orchid-scented archipelago changed forever. On June 30, 1959, a cream and maroon Boeing 707 barreled toward the Honolulu Airport runway at 518 miles per hour. One of the Australian Qantas fleet, the plane didn't just break the record for the San Francisco-to-Hawaii run by one hour and fifty-nine minutes; it transformed the world's most isolated land mass into a destination resort. The Boeing's celebrated landing marked the arrival of the Jet Age on the Hawaiian Islands.

"4 hrs, 49 mins. *W-h-o-o-s-h!*" *The Honolulu Advertiser* headline proclaimed. With that, the once-sleepy paradise was now easily in reach of tourists the world over.[1]

The landing was one of a pair of momentous events that occurred in 1959, making it arguably the most transformative year in the history of the Polynesian island chain. Seven weeks later Hawaii officially became the fiftieth state admitted to the Union, ending a hard-fought battle by local civic and political leaders that had lasted for over a century. The celebration had swept through the islands months earlier when the statehood bill was approved by U.S. Congress, igniting a series of huge bonfires, impromptu parties in the streets, and a torrent of firecrackers. The party would continue until the end of the year.

Those twin events—the arrival of the Jet Age and the advent of statehood—would transform Hawaii into the bustling tourist mecca that it is today. During the three years that Obama lived in Honolulu, a construction boom would start to redefine the shoreline, perching dozens of hotels and office towers at the water's edge and drastically altering the rhythm of island life and culture. As thousands of visitors poured onto the airport tarmac, tourism soon became one of the largest industries in Hawaii along with sugar, for better or worse. Even on the languid University of Hawaii campus, where some students still spoke a local creole language known as "pidgin" when their professors weren't paying attention, the zeitgeist of optimism that pervaded the new state was palpable.

"It was a very exciting time because you felt that the whole world was opening up to you," recalls George Ikeda, a classmate of Obama's. "I was nineteen years old and before statehood I had never thought of going to graduate school or even going to the mainland. But suddenly there were opportunities everywhere, and people were reaching out to get Hawaiian people to participate because we were the new state. It was a great time to be from Hawaii."

When Obama first stepped onto the cool cement floors of the old Honolulu Airport that August, change was already sweeping across the islands on the gentle trade winds. Obama and Hawaii were both on the cusp of a new epoch, each embarking on a journey of growth and redefinition. Obama embraced the significance of the moment, no doubt noting that just as his own homeland was about to be liberated from an imperial power's long domination, his new home had at long last shed the second-class status of a territory and now reveled in the full standing of statehood.

As with Hawaii, a newfound sense of mission motivated Obama during his time there. With the difficult years in Nairobi behind him, he now found himself the subject of intense curiosity and discussion. Thousands of miles away from the churning events in Kenya of which he so often spoke, Barack Obama was a manifestation of the uprising of oppressed peoples round the world, the spokesman for the Africans' need—no, their *demand*—for self-determination. Although he worked hard in his undergraduate years, he could not resist preening in front of such a fascinated audience of students and assorted groups who invited him to address the situation in Kenya. If there were some students who found his passionate oratory about his beloved homeland annoying, others listened to his thundering paeans with tingling spines. When a teenage girl, with her own willful nature and a dreaminess that made her bold, smiled across the classroom at him, he was distracted from his central focus. But not for long. By the time he graduated Obama was prepared to do and say just about anything that would ensure that he achieved the academic degrees that he so craved. Hawaii was the first step in a destiny of his own making, and he was not to be diverted.

Like his new home, Obama was unhesitating in his willingness to turn his back on his past in his fervent pursuit of the man he wished to be. In Hawaii, statehood brought with it not only the blessed tourist dollar, but also an erosion of indigenous culture and natural beauty that would be almost impossible to reclaim. Similarly, when Obama headed to America, he left behind a pregnant wife and a young son, all of whom seemed to vanish into the parched red dust of Africa. Obama neither spoke of them nor acknowledged them to school or immigration officials, until, that is, he deemed them an asset to his résumé. In his recasting of himself during his years in America, he would marry one white woman, propose to another, and seduce many more. Polygamy was surely an aspect of the culture from which Obama sprang, but in the Luo tradition a husband makes his home with all of his wives. Obama did just the opposite: moving from one to the next, ultimately betraying not just the women he left in his wake but also the children he sired but little fathered.

But in the heady days of 1959, much of that was yet to come. It was time for Obama and Hawaii to get to know one another.

What Obama had read in the *Saturday Evening Post* was true. Then as now, the defining cultural feature of the islands was its varied ethnic makeup. Hawaii claimed the honor of being not just the last state to be admitted to the union, but it was also the only state with a nonwhite majority. The bulk of its citizens sprung from a host of ethnic groups, dominated by Japanese and Chinese, who had come to work in the sugar and pineapple plantations a generation earlier. There were also substantial numbers of Filipinos and Hawaiians. Caucasians, called *haoles*, accounted for about one-third of the population in 1959, and blacks represented less than 1 percent of the island's 632,000 residents.[2] Although the ethnic groups tended to stay largely among themselves rather than meld into the cliché melting pot, the encompassing spirit of aloha had enabled them to peacefully coexist.

In part, this diversity is what had drawn Obama to the Pacific. But although nonwhites were in the majority, a black face was still something of an event on the streets of Honolulu. Obama was not only the first

African student on the University of Hawaii campus; he was the first black person that many students had ever seen in their lives.

That his color marked him as unique among the student body was only the start. Obama differed in almost every respect from the campus norm, starting with his imperious baritone, right down to the cuffs of his neatly pressed trousers. The UH campus, like Hawaii itself, was strictly casual. Students wore brightly colored Aloha shirts and floral muumuus and baggy shorts. Sandals, or flip flops known as slippahs, were the footwear of choice—or no shoes at all.

Obama wanted nothing to do with such informality. For him, education was a serious business and he dressed the part. His uniform was unvarying—an ensemble that put as much distance as possible between himself and his goat-herding days on the dusty paths of Alego. It consisted of a white, button-down, long-sleeve shirt; dark, pressed gabardine pants; and stylish lace-up shoes, usually black. On occasion, he even sported an elegant silk tie. Whereas most students carried their books in a loose jumble, Obama chose a trim black leather briefcase. With his purposeful expression and classic attire, he was an intimidating figure striding between the nodding palms. And that was before he opened his mouth.

"He was the first real black person I had ever met. And he was not just black but a deep dark purple," recalled Pake Zane, a UH freshman and a member of Obama's closest circle of friends. "He'd walk into a room and say, 'Good Evening,' in a voice that was more resonant than James Earl Jones's, and it had just that bit of an Oxford clip to it. You'd think, who the hell is *that*?"

So when Obama walked between the neoclassical pillars of Hawaii Hall on a brilliant September morning for the first time, many eyes were on him. Barack Obama was exotic fruit. That fall, he was the subject of three newspaper stories, each more breathless than the last over this extraordinary being.

The campus newspaper, *Ka Leo O Hawaii*, which means "The Voice of Hawaii," noted that the arrival of the "tall well-built African" marks the end "of a long two year struggle through rigid British correspondence courses while working as a clerk for several private firms."[3] The *Honolulu Advertiser* exclaimed that the first African student on campus was "delighted with the hula girls, whose swiveling and swaying is akin to the owalo, a sort of seldom seen African hula."[4] In another story in the *Star Bulletin*, Obama expressed delight with the pace of his adopted home, saying, "I think people here are so much more relaxed. You don't see them hurrying around to do things as in New York City or London." Featured in a companion photograph showing him hard at work at his typewriter, Obama added that he found the lack of racial prejudice on the island "unique." Most surprising, he said, was "the inter-racial attitude where no one seems to be conscious of color."[5]

But paradise was not perfect. In the interview with *Ka Leo O Hawaii*, Obama confessed to some disappointment. Hawaii was supposed to have been much grander, a metropolis of the Pacific dotted with skyscrapers and star-studded nightlife. Then there was the staggering cost of living, far higher than he'd expected, with food costing three times as much as it did in Kenya. In a prediction that proved all too true, he added only partly in jest: "My money was supposed to have lasted a year and a half but it looks as if I will be working to supplement my income next semester."

Obama then went on to explain "the political turmoil that is now prevalent all over the Dark Continent." When people have asked him whether Kenyans are ready for self-government, he responded, "To these people I say, 'Nobody is competent enough to judge whether a country is fit to rule itself or not.' If the people cannot rule themselves, let them misrule themselves. They should be provided with the opportunity."[6]

In his first few months Obama settled into a monastic room in the YMCA's Charles H. Atherton House, a handsome building with a commanding view of Diamond Head, the iconic volcanic cinder cone that looms over Waikiki. Just across University Avenue from the UH campus, Atherton was one of the first university residence houses for males, and its ground-floor lounge was a popular hangout spot for the increasing numbers of international students who arrived on campus in the years after statehood.

Just as Obama was disappointed in Honolulu's size, however, he quickly grew bored with the university's tempo. When foreign students began to come to the school's new international graduate program on campus during his second year, Obama would complain that the undergraduates were slackers, certainly not able to hold their own in the kind of sophisticated conversation to which he was drawn.

On his latter complaint, he was not entirely off. Half a century after its founding in 1907, the university was home to predominantly local students, and the flavor on campus was distinctly parochial. The student body was heavily Asian, with a handful of haoles from the mainland in search of adventure and good climate. Students, however, tended to congregate less according to their ethnic group than with the classmates with whom they attended high school. Although they were required to speak English in the classroom, students often lapsed into pidgin as soon as they were in the corridors. University administrators struggled to stem the use of pidgin well into the 1960s, and students were routinely examined to ensure that they spoke proper English before they graduated. Nor did the chickens squawking at the College of Agriculture on the east side of campus lend the place a particularly sophisticated air.

A land grant university, the University of Hawaii had overcome some stiff local resistance in its formative years. Obama would have appreciated that just as the British colonists had severely limited educational opportunities for Kenyans in the interest of preserving a malleable workforce, members of the local sugar industry had likewise expressed alarm that a public college would have a negative impact on their labor supply and increase their tax burden.[7] Their resistance was ultimately overcome, however, and the Manoa campus opened its doors to a steady stream of plantation workers' offspring.

The compact campus just a couple of miles north of the city's pearly beaches presented a vivid array of tropical flora that adorned its classic beige architecture. Monkey pod trees hovered at the walkways edge, towering palms shaded the graceful stairs to Hawaii Hall, and banks of orange hibiscus and scarlet flame bean nestled against the base of Hemenway Hall. But in the decade's last year, the Manoa campus was a quiet place, a commuter campus of 6,923 students, of which only 172 came from other countries.[8] When the sun went down, the students largely went with it, for the majority lived in apartments in downtown Honolulu or in family homes in the lush Manoa Valley.

At the time, the campus activism and protests that would manifest in the late 1960s were unthinkable. Instead, discussion of whether ROTC participation should be compulsory dominated the *Ka Leo* headlines. Furthermore, there was debate in the paper about a proposed new international center that would promote discussion between the East and West as well as some lengthy observations about the candidates in the annual spring beauty contest sponsored by *Ka Palapala*, the student yearbook.

Even inside the classroom, a certain plantation mentality held sway. With students teethed on the plantation's hierarchical structure, the classroom gestalt was one of deference. Few dared to raise their hand, much less be so bold as to actually challenge a teacher. As one mainland professor lamenting the student body's complacency said to the *Saturday Evening Post* in May 1958, "Whatever you say is accepted as gospel, because it comes from the professor."[9]

Obama, not surprisingly, took just the opposite tack. From the moment he arrived, Obama was poised to engage, argue, and debate. Obama had learned his debate lessons well at the Maseno School. Although he held passionate opinions on most any subject, he delighted in arguing the opposite point of view and could do so persuasively at the drop of a hat. Part of the appeal for him was the intellectual challenge, and part of it was his characteristic showiness.

At twenty-three, he was also somewhat older than most undergraduate students and considered himself a more mature intellect. In class he could invariably be counted on to challenge a student or cross a professor. If some students grumbled that he was a know-it-all with his rhetorical flourish and perennial commentary, others breathed a sigh of relief. "Barack grabbed the spotlight during classroom discussions because he liked to talk," recalled George Ikeda, who took a political science class with Obama and went on to become a researcher in the travel industry management department at UH. "And most of us were willing to let him . . . because that saved us from having to recite anything in class. In those days local students didn't speak very much in class and we tended to accept whatever the professor said."

Nor was the classroom the only place he offered his opinion. When the latest edition of the campus literary magazine, *Asterisk*, was released, Obama would routinely drop into the magazine's tiny office under the staircase in Hemenway Hall with the new issue tucked under his arm to offer an opinion or two. Praise was rarely on his mind. "He'd pull out the magazine and point to a piece of writing and say, 'This guy doesn't know what the hell he is talking about.' And then he'd jab a finger at a poem and say, 'This poem, this poem isn't worth a *damn*.' He was very critical," recalled Dietrich Varez, then the magazine's editor. "You know, some people were afraid of him, the voice, the opinions, the black shoes, I mean, goddamned black tie shoes. We just weren't like that. Some people just went around him."

Varez, an English major, had little interest in international affairs and even less in politics. But he had come to Hawaii by a circuitous route himself and was drawn to Obama's story. Born in wartime Germany, Varez says his father had been a member of the Nazi party. When his mother divorced him, she married a Portuguese soldier who adopted Varez and brought the family to Hawaii after the war. Varez liked Obama's blunt manner and the forceful way he talked. The two would often continue an evaluation of the magazine over lunch at the Snack Bar, a popular eating place housed in an old military barracks on campus. Their meal of choice was unvarying: tuna sandwich on white bread for 25 cents. Varez found Obama extremely private, even a bit remote. But one thing Obama commented freely on was other students' behavior and appearance. And Obama did not like those bare feet, perhaps because they reminded him of the days when he ran barefoot to the Ng'iya School in his tattered brown pants. Now a college student being groomed for a higher calling, Obama did not want to be reminded of a childhood in which shoes were a precious commodity. "He'd say about the bare feet, 'You are walking in the *spit* of another man. Doesn't that bother you?'" exclaimed Varez, now a popular printmaker and painter living on Hawaii's Big Island. "He thought it was unclean, really, not a cool thing to do."

In the afternoons Obama was often a common sight outside Hemenway Hall, standing under the long arms of the sweeping bayur tree. Usually he was in deep debate about the prospects for the Pan-Africanism movement or the latest news from the emerging civil rights front or the proposed campus expansion. His ubiquitous pipe was used more for theatrical point than something to actually smoke.

A curiosity to the larger community as well, Obama was invited to speak on the situation in Africa at several downtown locations, including local churches, the NAACP, and clubs such as Rotary and Kiwanis. And when the *Star-Bulletin* wrote an editorial predicting mass violence in the aftermath of the Belgian colonial government's withdrawal from the Congo, Obama wrote a stinging response. In his letter to the editor he objected to the writer's description of the Belgian colonials as being both efficient and sympathetic, saying that he had seen with his own eyes "how the Africans there were whipped and put to jail for as petty offenses as walking on the wrong side of the street. It struck me that maybe you needed more first-hand information before you spoke about their efficiency and sympathy."[10]

Even UH administrators, eager to attract students from farther reaches of the globe, drew him out. Only two months after he arrived Obama was one of a handful of foreign students invited to discuss a proposed international program to be called the East-West Center with university president Laurence H. Snyder. A photograph of Obama, dressed in crisp, white Oxford shirt and a dark bow tie, sharing cocktails with Snyder and other faculty members, was featured on the front page of *Ka Leo*.[11]

Though Obama's worldly ways and his polished shoes set him apart from the rank and file on the UH campus, he nonetheless found a gang he could call his own. They were more varied than the candidates in the Ka Palapala beauty contest. First came Peter Gilpin, California iconoclast, renaissance man, and jazz aficionado. Owner of a collection of blues and jazz records that held them all in awe, he was their cultural guide. Neil Abercrombie was the politician of the group, a refugee from the bitter Schenectady winters where he had been an undergraduate. Fondly known as No-Neck Neil for his muscular physique, he alternately circulated petitions and worked as a sociology teaching assistant. Andy Zane was the local boy. Born to Chinese parents on Maui, he was a freshman with a burning desire to travel around the world. Somewhat surprised to find himself hanging out with some up-and-coming *haoles*, Zane would soon change his first name to Pake, Hawaiian for Chinese. There were a few others, like Abercrombie's younger brother, Hal, who came to Honolulu with his wife and enrolled at UH for a year, and Kimo Gerald, a Hilo native studying psychology and looking for a reason to drop out. Each of them found something different in Obama in the year or two they knew him. But Abercrombie and Zane would forge much longer-term relationships with him and would follow him to Kenya years later, when they would find him a very different man.

The Stardust Cocktail Lounge on South Beretania Street was their hangout, their home, "their union hall," as Zane dubbed it. A small working-class bar west of the campus, they had chosen it largely because of the generous pupu platters, an assorted appetizer tray that might include spareribs, Chinese eggrolls, and wontons. For students on a budget, as most of them were, pupus could serve as their primary meal of the day. "We'd go to class at nine and then head for the Stardust," explained Zane. "If you got there before 10 a.m., the pupus were for free. And then people would drift in and out all day, depending on your schedule. We had lunch there, we did our homework there, and then we might wind up having pitchers of beer at midnight."

Sometimes they branched out to the George's Inn, a beloved local restaurant nearby, or the Forbidden City, a popular nightclub famous for its striptease and topless go-go dancers. But by far the more popular alternate retreat was Gilpin's apartment, where they listened to Sonny Terry and Brownie McGhee and the best of the Delta bluesmen. One of the guys who had a car would pick up Obama at Atherton House and drive him to Gilpin's. They ate pizza and talked, and then talked some more. "We were all, 'counter-culture people': we hated authoritarian personalities of any sort and were anti-war and anti-A&H Bombs," as Gilpin described the group in an e-mail. "We actively worked against these horrors. We read Kafka, Nathaniel West, Bertrand Russell, John Dos Passos & many others. . . . We were also students of Daruma and Dogen, Zen masters."

For the group, Obama was many things: a provocateur, a source of entertainment, and a living, breathing manifestation of the struggle against imperialism that had landed in their lap. Obama's tales of the African bush and his lyrical accent mesmerized Zane in particular, for they gave a face to the wanderlust that had long simmered within him. He wrote Obama's address in his address book and vowed to go to Kenya to visit him, and a decade later he would do just that. "Meeting Obama, it was like here is someone I can go visit on the other side of the world," said Zane, who sells antiques at the Antique Alley cooperative in Honolulu. "It made my dream seem real. This was a place I could actually go to."

Abercrombie understood Obama the best. Deeply engaged with the unfolding social questions of the day, Abercrombie was drawn as much to Obama's political ambition as his connection to the seismic events unfolding on the other side of the globe. At the forefront of a host of campus issues and a well-known figure with his long, dark beard and thick black glasses, Abercrombie would go on to represent Hawaii in the U.S. Congress for two decades and was elected governor of Hawaii in 2010. Often he and Obama stayed up late at night discussing how things would work in a postcolonial world and assessing the similarities between the budding civil rights movement in the United States and the quest for independence in Africa.

That Obama had decided to become an economist was due only in part to his particular love of the field and his considerable aptitude. He was equally inclined to the profession because he believed that it would cast him as a catalyst in the unfolding drama of Kenya's independence, a Big Man in the tableau of movers and shakers just then coming to the fore. As an economist, someone knowledgeable about the philosophy of finance, econometrics, and foreign trade, he would be invaluable to an emerging country. It would be his hand that would help shape not only the country's financial underpinnings but also its very ideological framework.

Obama's passion for his country was visceral, and he readily launched into a discussion of events unfolding in Africa at any opportunity. In his discussions with Abercrombie, he described his particular interest in the concept of property and his conviction that the African notion of communalism could be squared with private ownership in a capitalist society. Ghanian president Kwame Nkrumah espoused some of the same themes in his writing about African socialism and his commitment to preserving traditional humanist values. Like him, Obama intuitively understood the value of Africa's traditions as well as the economic vulnerability his country would face as an independent nation.

Obama was fiercely passionate about Kenya in part because the Kenya of his moment was about men and women like him. Twenty-five years earlier he would likely have spent his life as a low-level administrator under colonial domination or, if he was lucky, as a teacher. But coming of age at the singular moment that he did opened a door to a completely different kind of a life for him. And he was not going to let anything get in his way. "He talked about ambition, his ambition for independence in Africa in general, and his own personal ambition to participate in the emerging nationalism in Kenya. He saw himself a key element," said Abercrombie.

"He was not obsessed, but it was the central focus of his life. He was full of such energy and purpose. We all had such high hopes for him, hopes that people like Barack would be the next leaders of Africa. He seemed completely capable of it."

But Obama also worried about the challenges of independence. From a budding economist's point of view, he well understood the difficulties of trying to wean the country from foreign capital and economic dependence. He also appreciated the challenge of trying to blend aspects of a capitalist economy with some of the more communal African traditions that he valued. Tribalism was also high on his list of concerns. Kenyatta's Kikuyu supporters were already a powerful and tight-knit group. Although some political differences among the country's different ethnic groups had been put aside in the determined drive toward independence, Obama predicted in his late-night conversations with Abercrombie that when the choke hold of British control—which had long suppressed those factions—was removed, the old tribal rivalries would reappear. In this, Obama was prophetic.

At a time when many linked Africa's rejection of colonialism to American blacks' escalating demand for equal treatment, Obama's passion was infectious. But he was also conversant on a range of other issues as well. Abercrombie, for one, admired Obama's intellectual reach. "He was brilliant," he said. "He did not have to cultivate the image. His grasp of the subject matter was total, and part of the reason for that was his willingness to get the information. He was an absolute bear for work."

Africa was Obama's singular burning focus, but he understood that America's own evolving political situation had global implications. Aware that as a foreign student—and a highly visible one at that—his activities did not go unnoticed, he often declined to get involved in some of the more public events in which his friends were engaged. But Obama could not resist taking to the podium on occasion. In May 1962, for example, he addressed a Mother's Day peace rally in Ala Moana Park, declaring that, "Anything which relieves military spending will help us. . . . Peace will release great resources."

On the subject of civil rights, Obama's engagement was complete. He was a voracious reader of newspapers and would pepper other students about the history of repression of blacks in the United States. The idea of protest, so resonant of his own country's ongoing drama, appealed to him. And despite his general caution about engaging in political events, he at times jumped in. When Alabama governor John M. Patterson, an avowed enemy of integration, arrived in Honolulu for the National Governors' Conference in the summer of 1961, Obama was among a surging crowd demonstrating at the airport. He later participated in a picket at Patterson's hotel. "This was the first real civil rights demonstration in Hawaii," said Hal Abercrombie. "There were Chinese, Japanese, haoles, and Barack there. He was the only black person. He was surrounding the governor's car with everyone else calling for an end to segregation."

Obama's participation came at a price. Few could measure up to his level of commitment, and he treated with respect only the small inner circle of those who did. He had no patience for other people's shortcomings and grew visibly exasperated with those he perceived as having lesser abilities than his own. If he was not interested in what someone else was saying, he would talk right over them. And if he felt their point was not well articulated, he bluntly told them so. If others were not so intimidated by his verbal onslaught and jabbing pipe, they might have given it right back to him. "He did not lack for a sense of self-importance. We forgave him for that because he was so genuine. But he was a very daunting personality," sighed Abercrombie. "He just could not contain his irritation with people who were not as facile as he, and he did not hesitate to say so."

Few experienced the force of that personality more fully than a musicologist visiting from the university from South Africa. The man, who was white, was scheduled to address the students over the course of days, but Obama and another student had a different agenda. On the first night, when the man approached the podium in Orvis Auditorium, Obama leapt to his feet before the other man could open his mouth. What right did the white South African government have to deprive Africans of citizenship? When the man attempted to answer, the other student, strategically positioned on the opposite side of the auditorium, would jump to his feet and fire off more aggressive questions at the musicologist. On and on it went. Their verbal battering made it virtually impossible for the man to respond, and finally he surrendered and walked off the stage. Some students joined in the questioning and applauded when the speaker left. But a few in the audience, even those who were opposed to apartheid, were left feeling ambivalent about the ambush. "It just went on and on and the poor guy finally gave up," recalled Kimo Gerald, now the house manager at Carnegie Hall in New York. "I had mixed feelings at the time because his delivery and body language sent the message to me that he was not an apologist for apartheid. But here he was forced in his position to represent the South African government in Hawaii."

Another place that regarded Obama with some consternation was the university's international student office. Administrators there repeatedly asked Obama to come into the office and complete some routine paperwork in his file, but he never showed up. His record was incomplete and vague, and the university could not fathom why. They were also becoming concerned about reports of Obama's dating habits; the international student office was the first to raise the questions about his womanizing and uncertain marital status. Every time he was asked about his family, Obama had a different answer depending on what served him the best. Sometimes he had a wife in Kenya, sometimes he did not. When he met his second wife, he claimed to have divorced the first. Later, he decided he had not. Mostly, he tried not to answer the question. Even so, such questions would dog him throughout his stay and would eventually culminate in disastrous results.

Immigration officials struggled to get to the truth of the matter. Sumi McCabe, UH's foreign student adviser, brought the issue to their attention during Obama's second summer in Hawaii, when she reported that Obama "has been running around with several girls since he first arrived here," according to a 1961 memo written by Lyle H. Dahling, an administrator with the Immigration and Naturalization Service's Honolulu office.

Dahling's memo is one of dozens of communications regarding Obama that the INS maintained in his alien file, known internally as an "A" file. Although Obama was likely unaware of it, such files are kept on any non-U.S. citizen in the country who has ongoing communication with federal immigration agencies. The correspondence includes Obama's applications to extend his period of admission to the country, requests for permission to work, as well as numerous related school documents and memos. McCabe told Dahling in an April 1961 phone conversation that during the previous year she had "cautioned him about his playboy ways. Subject

[Obama] replied that he would 'try' to stay away from the girls," according to Dahling's memo.[12]

He didn't try very hard. Early on, Obama gained a reputation as a party man who liked his whiskey straight up. Although he worked diligently, he was also a regular at gatherings at Atherton House and the Pacific House, another hangout popular with international students. Obama would grab a guitar and entertain the crowd by crooning his favorite Kenyan lullabies. And at private gatherings, he would drink. By his early twenties Obama already had a legendary capacity for his beloved Johnnie Walker, and he would regularly down half a dozen drinks as his jokes grew increasingly raucous and his come-ons to women more overt. At such moments no one had the faintest idea that he was married with two small children back at home. "He was a real ladies' man," recalled Dorothy Heckman Gregor, a graduate student at the time. "He was always ready to engage you as a woman beyond the normal conversation, you know, to take it one step further. Today you'd call it 'coming on.' Part of the attraction was his intellect. He was just a really smart guy. But he was also a very good conversationalist. Women were really attracted to him."

In the fall of 1959 Juditha Clark Murashige was fresh back from several months at a work-study program in Tanganyika and Kenya, and she immediately noticed a striking African man walking across the UH campus. When the attractive freshman with the cascade of blonde hair approached him, Obama leapt to his favorite topic and the two had a series of coffee dates over the next few months. One night they ventured down to Waikiki beach and dropped into Don the Beachcomber's, a trendy nightclub soon to become a tourist hot spot. They did not sit long. As the throbbing music grew louder, Obama spun around on his toes and twirled Murashige across the dance floor, her hair streaming behind her. Watching as their bodies glided toward one another, almost pressing together before they swung apart again, patrons at the bar grew silent. An ambitious African student was one thing, but a sweaty black man handling a pale co-ed in public was something else entirely. "This was a fairly upper-crust kind of crowd, and we were laughing and having fun," recalled Murashige. "People were watching us, of course, and that made it even more fun. I think some people didn't know what to think."

Although Obama cultivated an active social life, he devoted much of his energy to his work. Early on, he decided he would try to complete his coursework as swiftly as he could, partly to hasten his return to Kenya but also to reduce his tuition. By his second semester Obama was already running out of money and took a job that paid $5 a day as a dishwasher at the Ink Blot Coffee Shop downtown. During his first summer he worked for the Dole Corporation doing odd jobs for $1.33 an hour.[13] Money would be a perennial problem throughout his years in the United States, and Obama was constantly under pressure to come up with the following year's tuition.

Ultimately, he would complete his undergraduate work in three years rather than the standard four, but to do so he assumed an increasingly large course load. In his first semester Obama was registered in the College of Business Administration and signed up for a standard lineup of classes. These included Business Calculations, English Composition, Introduction to Government, World Civilization, Personal Hygiene, and Public Speaking. His first year grades were good, but not stellar. In all he earned mostly A's, with a smattering of B's. He got a single C in his Introduction to American History course during the summer session.[14]

One of the B's was for a class in Public Speaking, taught by James C. McCroskey, a young teacher from South Dakota who would remain in Hawaii for a single year. At the time, each speaking class selected its strongest student who would then compete against one another in hopes of winning a spot on the school's debate team. McCroskey remembers Obama trying out for a spot on the team, but he was not impressed with the young African: "He had a good voice, but he did not have very much to say. I remember him being loud more than anything, and not very distinct. But he was very open and friendly."

Ed Hasegawa, who had been raised by second generation Japanese parents on a sugar plantation on the Big Island, was a student in public speaking as well. Because he had been in the armed services for three years, he was, like Obama, somewhat older than the rest of the class, and the two often had lunch together. They chose the Snack Bar, where prices were significantly lower than the cafeteria in Hemenway Hall. As with Varez, they too had the same thing to eat for every lunch. "We'd get the sandwich made out of the heels of the bread because it was the cheapest, ten cents a sandwich," said Hasagawa. "And on the inside were tiny bits of minced ham, you know, the leftover pieces that they crushed together. It was okay. It was really the only thing we could afford, that sandwich and a drink."

By the end of his first year Obama had had it with public speaking. He decided he would focus more on his calling, the economics and statistics classes that would be of practical use. He also had a language requirement to satisfy. Obama had an abiding interest in the Soviet Union, largely due to his admiration for Oginga Odinga, the Luo politician who had secured a number of scholarships from there for young Kenyans. Despite the simmering hostilities of the Cold War, one of the more popular language courses on the UH campus was Russian. Ever since the Soviet Union had successfully launched the Sputnik satellite a few years earlier, the course had been in such great demand that the school had retained a second Russian teacher. Obama decided to add Introductory Russian to his lengthening course load in the fall of his second year.

That class was where he would meet a seventeen-year-old from Seattle with an appetite for the unconventional. Her name was Stanley Ann Dunham.

IN AUGUST 1960 PRESIDENT EISENHOWER signed an appropriations bill that would have a strong ripple effect thousands of miles away on the UH campus. The bill included an allocation of $10 million to establish an international exchange center at the university, officially called the Center for Cultural and Technical Interchange Between East and West. The aim of the project was to improve relations between Asia and the United States by creating a place where intellectuals from around the world could gather and share ideas.

Months after the bill was signed, construction began on the center's new buildings on the east end of campus near the Manoa River where the College of Tropical Agriculture's chickens used to roost. It was another triumph for Hawaii. The East West Center, as it came to called, was not only an added jewel in the crown of statehood, but it also meant that Honolulu might soon become recognized as the "Geneva of the Pacific," as it had long envisioned itself.

As the Center's new students began to trickle in from Burma, Japan, the Philippines, and farther afield, the flavor of the campus began to grow decidedly more varied. In Atherton House in particular, where some of the new grantees were housed while their dormitories were being built, discussions about global affairs and the realpolitik of the Cold War were commonplace. Downstairs, the meals students prepared in the small kitchen emitted an array of exotic scents. Bored with the docile under graduate students and their humdrum concerns, Obama welcomed his new housemates with enthusiasm. Early on, he warned them that the intellectual caliber of the school was disappointing. Not only did the students not study very hard, but the professors themselves were not particularly stimulating. Obama gravitated to the older, more sophisticated crowd from the start, and when the Center was completed the following year, he dined there a couple of times a week. "When I came in for dinner, he would be surrounded by people at the table, sort of holding court. He was in charge of the table and I had a feeling that was what he wanted," said Gregor, an East West student for two years. "He had a very authoritative air about him and he told us about Africa. But mostly he would ask questions. He really wanted to know about America."

Obama grew close to several of the newcomers whom he felt were his intellectual equal. One was Naranhkiri Tith, a worldly student of economics and the son of the former prime minister of Cambodia, Khim Tith. Another was a young American bound for the Foreign Service named Robert M. Ruenitz. The three took an economics course together and spent many hours discussing geopolitics—the role of communism in the developing world was their primary topic—over beers and pupus. Tith, a voluble debater, volunteered the three of them to speak on the subject at a local church, and soon they found themselves invited to appear at a number of local venues.

Each fell to their debate position by virtue of their life experience. Tith, who had observed the Hungarian Revolution and the Algerian War for independence while living in France in the mid-1950s, was a firm opponent of communism. Obama, who was drawn to the aspects of communism that he believed reflected African communalism, took the opposite side. Ruenitz, the diplomat, stayed the middle course. In time, Ruenitz dropped out, but the Obama-versus-Tith show found its way to several neighboring islands to appear before professional associations, municipal groups, and churches. "Obama and I were on opposite poles," said Tith, who went on to be a senior manager with the International Monetary Fund and an adjunct professor in international economics at Johns Hopkins University. "I did not believe communism could save the world. It was too good to be true and I gave examples of what I had seen. Obama senior was the opposite. He was always glorying about how communism had liberated Africa and Cuba. He had no idea what communism was all about. For him, communism was going to save the world. Capitalism was going to collapse."

The East West crowd also partied together. One of their friends was Arnold Nachmanoff, a naval officer stationed at Pearl Harbor who often opened his home so they could listen to records and drink beer. Or they gathered round the worn rattan furniture at Atherton House and drank coffee. Obama particularly loved to socialize with the East West crowd, as international affairs largely dominated the conversation. But with a whiskey in hand, soon followed by one or two more, Obama would lapse into other topics as well, running the gamut from literature, African music and dance, and the latest news. Although he rarely brought a date, Obama was famously flirtatious and could always be counted on to leap to the dance floor when the music began. Tith found Obama highly entertaining but difficult to know. "He was detached. He never talked about his personal life or anything to do with home or his tribe," recalled Tith. "So you only got so far. He never opened himself up, so you did not know him well. I liked him though. I was impressed by his intelligence. A very impressive guy."

Less impressive was Obama's drinking. Some nights he drank so much whiskey he passed out in the middle of the party or slumped onto the dining table while still sitting in his chair. Other students, accustomed to the sight, would carefully step around his sleeping form or talk right over him. And when the party wound to a close, they would slap his cheeks and pull him to his feet. Although mildly embarrassed, Obama was unapologetic. "People talked about it, sure," said Tith. "But sort of jokingly. I never mentioned it to him. It was none of my business."

Propelled by the simmering discussion of communism, Obama entered his first class in Russian language in the fall of 1960 with enthusiasm. Introductory Russian was taught by Ella Wiswell in Room 209 of the new Physical Science Building, and she had established the Russian undergraduate program several years earlier. One of his classmates was a slender young woman with expressive brown eyes who had recently graduated from Mercer Island High School in Seattle. Although Russian might hardly have been the expected choice for a girl freshly minted by the Seattle suburbs, Stanley Ann Dunham was never one for the predictable. The only child of a furniture salesman and a bank officer, Dunham had seen some of the world by the time she landed in Wiswell's classroom. Born in Wichita, Kansas, her ever-wandering father had moved his small family to California then to Oklahoma and with a foray into Texas before they wound up in Seattle in the mid-1950s. Her father, Stanley Dunham, a talkative dreamer, again decided to pick up stakes after his daughter graduated in June of 1960 to move to Honolulu, where he had been promised, as always, a bigger, better job that somehow always turned out to be somewhere else.

By then, Stanley Ann, as she was called as a girl, had grown succinct in explaining her unusual name. "My name is Stanley," she would say. "My father wanted a boy, and that's that." By the time Dunham arrived in Honolulu, she had dropped the Stanley. It wasn't cute anymore. Her name was Ann Dunham now, and she was a young woman. Although shy, Dunham had nonetheless asserted herself as an iconoclast, an independent thinker with decidedly liberal views. Like many self-respecting teenagers of the time, she abhorred the deadly conformity of the suburbs. She was an atheist who sported a campaign button for Democratic presidential candidate Adlai Stevenson and liked foreign movies and jazz. Although she was known for being a good and patient listener, she would not hesitate to roll her huge brown eyes in exaggerated disbelief at something she considered pompous or untrue. A dreamer like her father, she had a tendency to romanticize that enabled her to glide over human failings and foibles.

Dunham was also exceptionally bright. With a vast vocabulary and an intellect to match, she could hold her own on most any subject. And she didn't hesitate to challenge the sacred cows of her era. What was so good about democracy? What's so bad about communism? And why was capitalism so great?

She was a young woman who was quite clear that she wanted a life of the mind. No marriage for her, at least not yet. Even as a teenager, Dunham was already fascinated with other cultures and declared that she would be an anthropologist. "You have to remember this was the era of June Cleaver," explained Susan Botkin Blake, a classmate and close friend of Dunham's. "In the advertisements all the women cleaned their houses wearing high heels and girdles. So Stanley says she is going to be an anthropologist. What the hell is that? I didn't even know what an anthropologist was. I had to look it up in the dictionary."

At the time she graduated high school, Dunham had been accepted at the University of Chicago and was eager to go. But her father put his foot down, saying she was too young. Nor would he permit her to enroll at the University of Washington, known as "U-Dub," as many of her friends intended to do. Instead, Dunham and her parents headed for Honolulu a few days after commencement. Dunham was angry at her father, with whom she already had a prickly relationship. Annoyed at his protectiveness, Dunham declared to her friend, "Who ever heard of the University of Hawaii?"[15]

But within weeks of starting school Dunham had changed her tune. Her classes were interesting, she wrote Blake. While her old classmates were tucked into nylons and girdles, she was wearing shorts and muumuus to class. And one other thing, she added: She was dating "a very interesting fellow in my Russian class. An African from Kenya."

Many years later Dunham would describe to her son, Barack Jr., her first date with his father. Obama Sr. had asked her to meet him at one o'clock in front of the university library. She arrived before Obama and soon fell asleep in the warm sun. He got there an hour late. She awoke to find him peering down at her with a couple of his friends, saying, "serious as can be, 'You see, gentlemen, I told you that she was a fine girl, and that she would wait for me.'"[16]

He called her Anna, and their courtship was as swift as it was intense. In his book Obama ruminates about his mother's attraction to his father that warm day. He tells of going with his mother years later to see the movie *Black Orpheus*, a 1950s film remarkable because of its predominantly black and brown Brazilian cast, and it tells the tale of a pair of ill-fated lovers. When Dunham first saw it as a teenager, it was her first foreign film and she loved it. Obama Jr. suggests that the film's "depiction of childlike blacks . . . was what my mother had carried with her to Hawaii all those years before, a reflection of the simple fantasies that had been forbidden to a white middle-class girl from Kansas, the promise of another life: warm, sensual, exotic, different."[17]

Dunham could not wait to tell her friends about her new boyfriend. In a Christmas card to Blake, Dunham wrote excitedly, "I'm in love with the African! I'm in love with the African." Blake adds, "She always called him 'the African,' and I remember writing her, 'Does he have a name, this African?'"

Obama, however, said nothing of his new girlfriend to most of his friends on campus. This was hardly surprising because, despite all his talking, he was silent on the topic of personal matters. But he did take her to an occasional party with the friends with whom he hung out at the Stardust. She was the only girl Obama ever brought to their gatherings. Sitting quietly beside Obama, she spoke little herself and instead listened closely as the men—and it was mostly men at their gatherings—argued and laughed. Six years his junior and a head shorter, she was obviously smitten with her handsome beau. "Any female in his life, she was in *his* life, he was not particularly in [hers]," Abercrombie observed. "He was much more in love with his intellect than with a woman. And he did not change his ways at all to accommodate her. She was just with him. He was always the center of attention."

Dunham became pregnant around the time she wrote Blake. Now she faced some hard choices. As much as Dunham loved her boyfriend of a few months, the decision to get married could not have been an easy one. Although mixed marriage was far more common in Hawaii than most anywhere else in the United States, accounting for 36 percent of the 5,298 marriages that occurred there in 1961,[18] unions between black and white were still rare, in large part because the number of blacks on the islands was so small.

Outside of Hawaii, the impediments facing mixed marriage were even greater. At the time miscegenation, or marriage between different races, was a felony in most of the twenty-two states in which it was banned.[19] Even in states where it was legal, many still regarded intermarriage as a shocking violation of the natural order of things.

When the young couple told their parents they intended to get married, the fireworks erupted as loudly on the shores of the Pacific as they did on the banks of Lake Victoria. Stanley and Madelyn Dunham had been cordial to Obama when their daughter introduced him. They had both experienced racism firsthand during a one-year stint in Texas in 1951, during which, on one unforgettable day, Madelyn arrived home to find a group of children taunting her ten-year-old daughter and a friend who were sitting on the front lawn, with the children shouting, "Nigger lover!" and "Dirty Yankee!" Stanley Ann and her friend, who was black, were lying under a tree pretending to read a book, immobilized by fear.

Stanley saw himself as a bohemian. He liked jazz, read poetry, and counted among his closest friends a number of Jews. Madelyn too resisted conformist thinking and liked to come to a point of view on her own, all of which led their grandson to describe them as "vaguely liberal" in his book. They would have been inclined to welcome their daughter's new friend, he reasoned. But the Dunhams were furious when they learned she intended to marry Obama, worried about the vast cultural differences between the two.

There was also the small matter of Kezia, Obama's first wife in Kenya. That he also had two children, one of them only a year old, was a detail that he apparently neglected to mention to either Dunham or her parents. Obama had told school administrators that, according to Luo tradition, a man need only tell his wife that he wished to get a divorce in order to separate. And that he claimed to have done.[20] However, divorce was extremely rare in the Luo culture. According to tribal customary law, a couple who wished to separate was required to appear before a council of village elders who would determine if a divorce was necessary. If it was deemed so, then the committee would assess the number of cows to be returned, a process known in Dholuo as *waro dhok*. Obama and Kezia had not been separated in such a way and were thus still fully married, according to Luo marital custom. All he seems to have told the Dunhams was that he was divorced.

Even after he married Dunham, Obama clearly considered Kezia to still be his wife and wrote letters in which he referred to her as such. To Obama, coming from a polygamous culture in which multiple wives were the norm, taking another wife would have been the predictable, even laudable thing to do. Indeed, he wrote to his family explaining that he was going to take a second wife. Kezia, still waiting for him back home, was disappointed but says she wasn't particularly surprised. But Obama showed no desire to tell the Dunhams that he had a wife and two children waiting for him. Well aware of marital customs in the United States, Obama surely knew that Dunham's parents would not have permitted her to marry a man who already had a wife. What Dunham would have done if she had known the whole story, however, is another matter.

Madelyn was skeptical. More practical than her dreamer husband, she would say later that she had never particularly trusted Obama Sr.'s stories. "I am a little dubious of the things that people from foreign countries tell me," she said in a rare 2004 interview. Obama, she added, "was . . . straaaaaange."[21]

When Hussein Onyango learned of the impending nuptials, he penned an angry letter to Stanley opposing the marriage, declaring he did not want "the Obama blood sullied by a white woman."[22] He also wrote to his son, sternly reminding him that he had a family back home. Hussein, well aware of the white man's ways, got right to the point. Would Obama's intended "accept that you already have a wife and children?" he asked. "I have not heard of white people understanding such things. Their women are jealous and used to being pampered."[23]

The Dunhams were also alarmed that, because Obama had been married to his first wife according to traditional law, there was no document showing that he had been divorced. All they had was his say so. Madelyn Dunham was nearly hysterical over reports of the ongoing Mau Mau violence in Kenya, convinced that her only daughter would be beheaded in the wilds of Africa. The final straw came when Hussein threatened to have his son's visa revoked if he did not drop his plan. As the parents ranted and pounded the proverbial tables, Obama and Dunham decided to elope, just as her parents had done several decades earlier.

They chose for the site of their union the island of Maui, one of the most popular of the Hawaiian Islands, with its sweeping beaches and lofty volcanic peaks, long a favorite among honeymooners. Some would later speculate that the couple chose the location to avoid possible scrutiny in bustling downtown Honolulu. Others saw the choice of locale as endearingly romantic. After all, Obama and Dunham would have had to spend on costly airline tickets and a hotel at a time when neither of them had much money.

Obama and Dunham were married, according to their divorce decree, in the picturesque town of Wailuku on February 2, 1961, in the week-long break between final exams and spring registration at UH. Wailuku, which means "water of destruction" in Hawaiian, was a charming municipality of trim storefronts and inviting lawns, veiled in the scent of burning sugar cane from the Wailuku Sugar Company mill. The couple apparently had a quiet civil ceremony with neither of their families in attendance nor the symbolic markers of a cake or ring. She was eighteen; he was twenty-four. On their return to Honolulu a few days later, however, they had a small reception. Anna, now a married lady, was ecstatic. "Big news!" she wrote to Blake. "I married the African. I am now Mrs. Barack Obama and we are expecting a baby in the summer. My parents are dealing with it quite well."[24]

For Obama, who would begin his final year at UH when the baby arrived, the situation was infinitely more complex. As usual he told none of his friends that he had gotten married or was expecting a baby. He was already under a significant amount of pressure with his schoolwork and the specter of graduate school looming. That spring he was taking a particularly heavy load, including Public Finance, International Trade Finance, and Problems in International Relations. Nor could he vent his anxiety by talking to people about the prospect of becoming a father, yet again. To the Stardust crowd, at least, he remained a single, unencumbered guy with dazzling prospects.[25]

Once again, Obama faced the perennial problem of how to raise money. Although he had little contact with Mooney since he left Kenya, Obama turned to his old patron for help. Mooney herself had surprising matrimonial news, although Obama did not reciprocate with his own story. After returning to the United States a few months after Obama left Kenya, Mooney had struck up a correspondence with an old friend from her Koinonia days, a man named Elmer Kirk. A recently widowed electrical engineer, Kirk shared her spiritual devotion as well as her love of travel. He and his family had taken teaching classes at Koininia in the mid-1950s in hopes of traveling to Africa before his wife had fallen sick. After he and Mooney realized that their friendship was much more than that, they married in 1960 and she moved to his home in Tulsa, Oklahoma, with plans to travel. Mooney assumed her husband's name and now had three stepchildren to think about.

With the financial demands of running a household, Mooney was unable to offer Obama additional support. But she sent letters to many members of her sprawling family to see if others might be willing to help. Indeed, one of her uncles, Roy M. Clark, a retired mailman in El Cajon, California, agreed to contribute $10 each month for his niece's African friend. But Obama was still chronically short.

Obama managed to find alternate funding, but he had to work hard for it. During his second year he received a $190 scholarship from UH and $1,000 from the African American Institute in New York toward his room and board. But he needed another $1,000 to cover his expenses. In the spring of 1961 he was approved for $900 in funds from the Laubach Literacy Fund, which would be doled out to him in monthly increments. He also got approval from INS to work twenty-five hours part time, so he began looking for a job. Still short, the prospect of shouldering the cost of an infant must have been daunting.

Pressed by both academic and financial concerns in the spring after he was married, Obama also needed to apply once again to the INS for an extension of his stay. Although a largely routine matter, the process entailed an examination of his academic record and general behavior. With his extension due to expire in four months, Obama would have been anxious to present a case that would impress immigration authorities. A bigamist with a mixed-race baby, if that is how authorities chose to see him, was not likely to be the strongest of candidates. And so Obama decided to rewrite his story. In the new version there would be no baby.

Within two months of his marriage to Dunham, Obama told Sumi McCabe, UH's foreign student adviser, that his wife was making arrangements to give their unborn baby up for adoption. According to the INS memo concerning her April conversation with Dahling, the INS administrator, "Subject [Obama] got his USC [United States citizen] wife 'Hapai' [pidgin for pregnant] and although they were married they do not live together and Miss Dunham is making arrangements with the Salvation Army to give the baby away."[26]

Whether Dunham ever took steps to put her baby up for adoption is unclear. It is possible that Obama Sr., not always entirely beholden to the truth, simply lied about the matter. Salvation Army officials, who might have a record of any conversation they had with Dunham if one had taken place, declined to discuss the matter, citing privacy regulations. In an interview, Robert Gibbs, White House Press Secretary at the time, said that President Obama has never heard that either of his parents considered putting him up for adoption nor has he seen the INS memo. Obama declined to be interviewed on the subject "because of the very personal nature of the request," according to a White House spokesman. McCabe, eighty-nine and living in a retirement community in Honolulu, remembers Obama well. But she does not recall any conversation about his having a baby or about giving it up.

Interestingly, in his book *Dreams* Obama himself raised the possibility that his mother might have considered adoption. So reviled were relationships between blacks and whites when his parents were married, wrote Obama, that "the hostile stares, the whispers, might have driven a woman in my mother's predicament into a back-alley abortion—or at the very least to a distant convent that could arrange for adoption."[27]

Even without the baby in the picture, immigration officials were sufficiently concerned about Obama's marital status that they considered taking deportation measures against him. In his memo Dahling noted that Obama was already married to a Kenyan woman and thus possibly a bigamist. Obama told McCabe that he had divorced his wife, giving her the same explanation he had given the Dunhams. Immigration officials mulled over whether he could be deported if he were convicted of bigamy but decided against pursuing it. Instead, they decided that Obama should be "closely questioned before another extension is granted—and denial be considered. If his USC wife tries to petition for him, make sure an investigation is conducted as to the bona-fide of the marriage."[28]

Why Obama claimed that his son was to be given up for adoption is unclear. Perhaps his words were simply a rash response to a crisis situation, one that threatened to collapse his cherished dream. Clearly, Obama was deeply fond of Dunham, so much so that he was willing to marry her. But he also knew that his chance to be a big man in the Kenyan political sphere depended heavily on his success in America. Denial of his request for an extension of his stay—meaning an abrupt termination of his American education and a return back home—would be an unacceptable humiliation, a painful repetition of the Maseno experience, in which he might find himself punished not for any academic failure but because of the interference of a meddling bureaucrat.

Perhaps Ann Dunham, a frightened eighteen-year-old who was months away from giving birth to a child that many in America would disdain due to his mixed parentage, took the first faltering steps toward putting her baby up for adoption before changing her mind. After all, who in 1961 would adopt a mixed-race infant, particularly in Hawaii, where a black person was regarded as an oddity?

If she did consider it, she did not mention it to her friends back in Seattle or those whom she had gotten to know in Honolulu. Nor do those friends think it likely that she would have done so, as she appeared to be so thrilled about having a baby. Dunham's pregnancy continued uneventfully, and on August 4, 1961, she gave birth to Barack Hussein Obama II at 7:24 p.m. at Kapiʻolani Medical Center for Women and Children in Honolulu.[29] Births to blacks at the hospital were so rare that Obama Sr.'s race is described as African on his son's Certification of Live Birth issued by the State Health Department and publicly released by Obama's presidential campaign. Dunham's race is described as Caucasian.

The Salvation Army never came for the baby.

A birth announcement in the Sunday *Advertiser* that ran over a week later listed the couple's address as 6085 Kalanianaʻole Highway, a few miles east of the UH campus. But the announcement was inaccurate in one respect: At the time of Barack II's birth, they were already living separately. According to the INS record, Dunham lived with her parents, while Obama lived on the steep slope of Allencaster Street near downtown. Obama had left Atherton House after several months and lived at half a dozen different addresses around the city. But in the first year of Barack Jr.'s life, he would remain on Allencaster Street.

Dunham's plan for her future in the months following her baby's birth was unclear. An INS memo dated August 31, 1961, summarizes the couple's intentions this way: "USC spouse to go to Wash State University next semester. When finished school here plans to go to a mainland school for a Doctor Degree in Economics—after that to return to Kenya. They have one child born Honolulu on 8/4/1961, Barack Obama II."[30]

But at the same time, Dunham wrote Blake a note announcing that she was coming through Seattle at the end of August on her way to Boston to look into job possibilities for herself. Her husband, she added, had been accepted into graduate school there and they would likely move there the following year. Dunham would, in fact, enroll at U-Dub the following spring, but she made no mention of that. Blake remembers sitting with Dunham and her three-week-old baby on her mother's porch in the hot August sun sipping lemonade and eating sugar cookies. Dunham was as entranced by her baby boy as she was with his father. "She was wildly in love with Barack Obama, oh, so in love with him," Blake recalls. "She was excited about her future with this man, who was the rising hope of Africa, which was just about to emerge from under British rule. It was all so romantic. She was going to go to Boston and set up a beachhead for them there and get a job because they needed money. Then, she was going to be his helpmate and raise his children. I remember thinking, wow, that is just incredibly brave. I mean, she was eighteen years old."

As they were talking, Dunham nursed her baby and cradled him close to her chest. Blake was admiring his long, dark eyelashes when the baby suddenly soiled his diaper. Dunham wrinkled up her nose and thrust Barack Jr. in front of her body, her arms outstretched.

"How about you do it?" she implored.

"Your mother's been changing him up to now, hasn't she?" Blake asked. "You know, you've really got to learn to do it."

Dunham left later that afternoon, promising to stay in touch. But Blake and Dunham lost contact in the flurry of their young lives and never spoke again. On her return to Honolulu, Obama and Dunham resumed their life as before, still living separately but now with a baby to manage. Obama was working hard to finish his final semester. He was also trying to get used to the turned heads that followed him when he walked down the street with his wife and child, one of the first times he'd been made to feel uncomfortable about the color of his skin while in the United States. One night, at a friend's party, he finally met someone with whom he could frankly discuss his unusual marriage.

His name was Alonzo DeMello, a Lousiana native who had served in the 82nd Airborne Division and one of the few black people that Obama met in Hawaii. DeMello also married a white woman in 1961. A decade older than Obama, he was long accustomed to what he described as the "terrible discrimination against blacks" in Hawaii. And so when Obama asked him if people stared at him when he walked down the street with his wife, DeMello knew exactly what he was talking about. "I said, 'Sure, they stare. I stare right back at them,'" said DeMello, eighty-seven. "I mean, my wife was blonde, so people stared all the time. I told him he'd get used to it."

Of all the people he met in Honolulu, the group with whom Obama was most able to let down his guard was the Stardust crowd, so every now and then he took his new wife and baby to their gatherings. Abercrombie and the others never asked much about the couple's marriage or what their plans were, as Obama had known they would not. This was Hawaii, after all, and there was this beautiful cooing baby at their party to celebrate. Abercrombie recalls Obama balancing Barack Jr. on his knee one night, enthusiastically pointing out his son's dark hair and long fingers to the group. "He was overjoyed," said Abercrombie. "After all, there was another Obama in the world. Maybe he would take after him."

But Obama was still enthralled with developments halfway around the world, with his future and his soul utterly committed elsewhere. Listening to him talk in the months after Barack Jr. was born, Abercrombie began to doubt that the marriage would survive. Obama, he knew, was not about to give up his dream. And Dunham, clearly ambitious herself, was not likely to subordinate herself to his plans. "Obama had gotten into this so far, but his commitment to Kenya was far more powerful than the vagaries of a marriage literally made on the fly," said Abercrombie. "I always thought that the principal reason that Ann did not go with him was his utter and total dedication to independence. I think she began to think, Did she really want to go into this patriarchal world where she would play a secondary role?"

Just months after Barack Jr. was born, Dunham struck out on her own, at least for a while. Sometime in the fall of 1961 she moved back to Seattle with her baby and enrolled at U-Dub. She rented a one-room apartment on the first floor of one of the stately old homes of Capitol Hill. Dunham got in touch with a few of her friends from Mercer Island who were living in the city and explained that she was eventually going to Boston.

Her babysitter was a young woman named Mary Toutonghi, who lived in the basement and managed the building with her husband. Toutonghi, who had a toddler of her own and was pregnant, often stuck around after Dunham returned, and the two talked about their babies and their plans for the future. Dunham told Toutonghi that her husband was still in school in Hawaii and eventually they were going to go to Africa, but she did not explain why they were apart. "The thing that struck me was that she was very much in love with her husband," recalled Toutonghi, who later became a speech pathologist and moved to Alaska. "She talked about him very positively."

But the situation was complicated. Dunham told her babysitter that when she and her husband returned to Kenya, he would have to marry a full-blooded Kenyan woman in order to father purely African children, which was necessary for him to secure his place in his tribe and establish Kenyan heirs. Dunham, for all her intelligence and budding cultural savvy, bought the unlikely story. Obama had manufactured the scenario, either angling to ensure that he could take a third wife on his return home or to dissuade her from following him to Kenya when he returned as he knew he would eventually. He had also advised Dunham that their son might encounter a negative reception from his relatives, given his mixed race. But if Obama had been trying to dissuade his wife from accompanying him to Kenya with such stories, Dunham was undeterred. She told Toutonghi that she had discussed this predicament with both her parents and her husband at length and that she was willing to travel to Kenya. Obama was her husband, and she could handle any of the cultural challenges that lay ahead. "I wondered why she wasn't upset about this," recalled Toutonghi. "My feeling was that I could not have done it. But she was accepting of the situation, and that is what made me feel she obviously loved him a great deal."

AS THE CONSTRUCTION CREWS on campus were gearing up for a busy building season in the spring of 1962, Obama was finalizing plans for the next chapter of his American education.

Months earlier he had asked Mooney if she would help him prepare his résumé that would accompany his applications for financial assistance. From her dining room table in Tulsa, Mooney continued the job she had started three years earlier, now with the help of her husband. She and Obama could be proud of the accomplishments they typed on his résumé. In three years he had not only completed the coursework for a BA with a grade point average of 3.6, but he had also been named Phi Beta Kappa as well. He declared his goal to be "government work in economic development in East Africa."

Mooney sent the résumé to Tom Mboya, recently named Kenya's Minister for Labor and married not so long ago himself, and asked in a letter if he could help Obama secure a financial backer for his graduate studies. "As a fellow Luo I am sure you will be pleased with his accomplishments," she wrote. "And it will be an even greater honor if he can work for his PhD at Harvard. He has the opportunity and the brains. Now surely someone has the money."[31]

As Obama sought to tailor his résumé for the college admissions staff, his ever-changing marital status changed yet again. Suddenly, Kezia was back in the picture. Obama described his family on his résumé as "a wife and two children in Kenya." He made no mention of Dunham or Barack Jr., nor would he ever tell the Kirks about his Hawaiian family. If Obama was going to be competitive on the Ivy League circuit, claiming a proper African family would be a better bet than an interracial one of questionable legitimacy.

With talented Africans much sought after on campuses across the country, Obama, now twenty-five, was in the catbird seat—as long as no one probed his marital status. He submitted applications to Harvard, Yale, the University of California at Berkeley, and the New School in New York, and he sought financial assistance from them all. When his letters returned, he again had a choice. The New School offered a complete scholarship, including not only tuition and board but also a campus job that would enable him to support Dunham and his son. Harvard offered a scholarship too, but only enough to cover tuition.

There was no discussion. Barack Obama never entertained the possibility of compromise. If he had, he might have considered enrolling at a highly competitive school in New York that would have enabled him to keep his small family together. But Obama was meant for the best, and that meant Harvard. With only tuition covered, Dunham and the baby would be excluded. Years later Dunham would describe the moment to her son. "Barack was such a stubborn bastard, he had to go to Harvard. 'How can I refuse the best education?' he told me," Dunham said to Obama Jr. "That's all he could think about, proving that he was the best."[32]

Even before he left Hawaii, Obama was looking homeward. In a letter he wrote to Tom Mboya weeks before he headed to the mainland, Obama said he planned to write his dissertation on the economics of underdeveloped areas and hoped to complete his PhD in two years. Although he had enjoyed his stay in Hawaii, he added, "I will be accelerating my coming home as much as I can." Obama reminded Mboya that his wife was living in Nairobi and added, "I would really appreciate any help that you can give her."[33]

Mboya was irked. Although he was pleased with Obama's achievement and was keeping his eye on his maturation as an economist in hopes of putting him to work in the government upon his return, he was also annoyed with Obama's request. He did not feel that Obama was taking sufficient responsibility for supporting his wife and children in Kenya. Whether Mboya was aware of Obama's family in Hawaii is unclear. Mboya considered himself a family-oriented man, and he was concerned about Kezia and the children. He wrote back chiding Obama for "not taking better care of his family," said Susan Mboya, Tom Mboya's daughter. "It was all very well to further your career, but only if you know how to take care of your responsibilities."

Prodded by Mboya's words, Obama did not alter his plans, but instead he took steps to make sure that Kezia and his two children were being properly taken care of. For this he turned to Helen Roberts, the Palo Alto woman who had worked closely with Betty Mooney at the Literacy Center in Nairobi and had returned to Kenya earlier in the year. Obama had already asked Roberts if she would help Kezia find a school she might attend in Nairobi and keep an eye on his small family. Roberts, a straight-laced Methodist who had taken a number of students under her wing, promptly took action.

Within a month Kezia was in Nairobi taking courses at the Church Army school six hours a day and two hours at night while her children stayed behind in Kogelo with Obama's parents. Although working as a volunteer at the literacy center and dependent upon the small social security check that was virtually her sole source of income, Roberts took it upon herself to buy Kezia some sorely needed glasses and several bolts of material with which to make clothes. Impressed by Kezia's desire to improve herself, Roberts wrote to a fellow literacy worker named Alice Sanderson in May that she was prepared to support Kezia as long as she was in Nairobi. "I got her material for three dresses and will keep her supplied with necessary funds while I am here," Roberts wrote. "She is learning fast and is very anxious to be a suitable wife for Barack when he returns."[34]

By July Kezia had become settled in her urban life and was beginning to think about bringing her children to the city as well. But Roberts was concerned about not only who would support them but also where they would live. "Then the children will also be my responsibility and their transportation and room, etc.," Roberts wrote her friend. "I don't know what they'll do after I leave. I hope Barack can get enough work to look after them once he gets started in school again. Kezia is very nice and does many things for herself. She can make her own clothes and those for the children, she can knit too. . . . So I think Barack will notice quite a difference in her when he at last returns."[35]

But Obama was not pleased with his children's living arrangements. He did not want the children living with his parents and wrote to Kezia saying so. Nor did his and Kezia's family members feel that living alone in Nairobi with the children was safe. Although Kezia's brother was living in the city, he did not have enough room for her to move in. As no one seemed quite sure where she should go, Kezia returned to Kendu Bay to be with her children during their school vacation. When both children became sick at the end of the month, Roberts gave Kezia more money for their medical care. But she also wrote a stern letter to Obama suggesting that he should be ready "to make some sacrifice for his family," as she wrote Sanderson. "Barack has never even seen the little girl but he must have known about it before he left Kenya."[36]

Obama urged Kezia to remain with her parents in Kendu Bay, and in the end she stayed alternately at both their parents' homes. But by late August Obama had already turned his attention elsewhere. The bird was ready to fly again. *Barack, otenga piny kiborne*, as his old Alego neighbors liked to say in their own variation of Hussein Onyango's pakruok: For Barack, the bush hawk, no distance is too far.

As he headed east toward Cambridge, leaving in his wake two young families who had no idea whether he would be sending them support, Obama made several stops to visit friends and see some of the country along the way. He paused to catch up with Hal Abercrombie, Neil's brother and one of the original Stardust gang, who lived with his wife, Shirley, in San Francisco. Obama wanted to take the couple out for an elegant dinner, and he chose the Blue Fox, a city landmark renowned for its extensive wine cellar and haute cuisine. They were going to celebrate their good fortune of being young and at large in one of the most cosmopolitan cities in the world. And they would toast Obama's departure to Cambridge the following day, thus launching the next chapter of his educational career.

But things did not turn out exactly as they had planned. As the threesome stepped onto the restaurant's plush red carpet, the maître d' took a close look at the young blonde couple and their black companion. Although there were several empty tables in the front of the restaurant, the maître d' directed them to a table in the rear just a few feet from the kitchen door and largely obscured from the rest of the room, apparently in an effort to conceal their dark-skinned guest.

The three of them sat in stunned silence for a moment, unable to quite believe what had just happened to them. They decided to ask for a different table and waited for their server to return. And then they waited some more. Not only were they exiled to the rear of the restaurant, no one, it seemed, was in any hurry to take their order. "We all knew it was race, even in San Francisco," said Abercrombie. "And Obama was livid. I don't think anything like that had ever happened to him before."

Hawaii was already feeling far away. The spirit of aloha, it seemed, did not travel far.

6

THE WORLD'S GREATEST UNIVERSITY

The worn asphalt paths that wind about the campus of Harvard University have felt the tread of generations of aspiring students, some of whom have gone on to greatness and glory, some of whom have not. Two of the men who have walked briskly along those vaunted avenues, supremely confident that they would be among the former category, were both named Barack Hussein Obama.

The first to arrive found a home in the Littauer Center, a formidable granite structure with an imposing six-columned portico and the last of the Harvard buildings constructed in the imperial tradition. That he had made his way from a barefoot childhood on the parched African earth not far from the equator to the nation's oldest and most prestigious center of learning was a monumental achievement.

Barack Obama II, his son, would earn distinction nearly three decades later in the university's far more modest Gannett House, a three-story Greek Revival structure built in 1838. Just a few hundred yards away from the stolid Littauer, Gannett was the home of the illustrious *Harvard Law Review*. There, second-year law student Barack Obama II was named the first black president of the 103-year-old journal, a position considered to be the highest honor a student can attain at Harvard Law School. That victory earned him his first taste of national media attention and positioned him on the path that led ultimately to the presidency.

In a way Harvard was as close as the Obama father and son would come to each other. Although they of course never met on the Harvard campus, their presence there represented a pinnacle of achievement that linked them far more than the awkward month they spent together in a Honolulu high-rise. What had brought them to Cambridge in the first place were the very characteristics that they shared: well-honed intellects, fierce ambition, and the daring to aspire far beyond the circumstances to which each was born. If they had met on the gently curving walkway that leads from Littauer to Gannett, paralleling bustling Cambridge Street, each might have recognized strokes of himself in the other.

One cannot help but wonder how the two Obama men might have regarded each other. Did Obama the younger dwell much on his elusive father during his years at Harvard? During the long hours that he toiled over legal articles on the third floor of Gannett, did he peer through the window at Littauer and imagine his father loping up the granite stairs, his books held close to his pressed white shirt? How deeply did he resent that his father had chosen Littauer and all that it represented—Harvard, career, his own future in Kenya—over his infant son in Hawaii? The subject clearly weighed heavily on his mind, for during the busy months after his election as president of the law review, Obama signed a contract to write his memoir, *Dreams from My Father*, a heartfelt rumination on his relationship with his absent father and his painful discovery of all that he was not. That a twenty-nine-year-old Harvard student felt his life even worthy of a memoir suggests a robust measure of self-confidence, one reminiscent of that exhibited by a certain young Kenyan in his twenties as he interviewed for a seat on the airlift to the United States.

And what about Obama Sr.? What would he have said to the slender young man in tattered blue jeans and leather jacket, his very American second son? Would he have indulged in a rare moment of paternal pride or admonished his namesake to work harder at his studies, as he had done decades earlier? Or would he have cringed in remorse at the decision he had made as an equally ambitious young man himself to abandon his small family in Hawaii in order to pursue his own dream? Perhaps he would have tried to explain the many years that they had been apart.

For both young men, their time at Harvard was a richly formative period: for the son, the law; for the father, the critical shift in economic thinking underway that would make him of singular value on his return to Kenya. For both, their Harvard pedigree would ultimately become an aspect central to their identity, although in sharply contrasting ways.

On his arrival in Cambridge in the fall of 1962, Obama must surely have thrilled at the sight of the venerable ivy-shrouded brick buildings that flank Harvard Yard, feeling the weight of more than three centuries of academic ritual. For a man instilled with a deep reverence for the power of the mind and the practical virtues of an education, a man who had walked miles as a child just to get to a tin-roofed schoolhouse where he had had to share the tattered and dusty primers, Harvard must have felt other-worldly. This was no second-rate state university where students stepped around chicken poop in their flips-flops. This was the epicenter of learning in America— some would say the world—a monument to the potential of the human mind. But as Obama pointedly noted, even Harvard wasn't perfect.

"I find Harvard a very stimulating place at least intellectually," he wrote in December to Sylvia Baldwin, a friend in Hawaii who had hosted a number of international students for meals with her family in her home. "It sort of reminds me of Cambridge University, but rather artificially. Nonetheless, I do think this is a very good institution and I will stay here at least for two years to three years depending on when I am able to finish my dissertation."[1]

Obama's years on the Charles River would coincide with a momentous period not only in American political life but also in that of the University as well. In 1962 the aroma of the placid 1950s still lingered heavily. Students still wore ties at meals and women were forbidden in upper-classmen's dorm rooms after midnight.[2] But the issues that would so luridly dominate the later part of the decade—civil rights, drugs, the women's movement—were already beginning to percolate. Harvard psychology lecturer Timothy Leary and assistant professor Richard Alpert, who would soon be known as Ram Dass, openly promoted the use of hallucinatory drugs like LSD and psilocybin to students, saying they were no more harmful than "psychoanalysis or a four year enrollment at Harvard College," until the college sent them packing in 1963.[3]

Harvard and Radcliffe students were becoming closely attuned to burgeoning issues of race. They picketed Howard Johnson's restaurants throughout Boston in protest of the chain's segregation policies in the South and contested the complete absence of any tenured black professors at their own schools. Black nationalist Malcolm X would draw increasingly large crowds during three visits to the campus between 1961 and

1964 and had already prompted soul searching among the handful of black students there. Weeks after Obama arrived, Dr. Martin Luther King Jr. addressed the future of integration at the Harvard Law School and urged Negroes to take a greater role of leadership in the fight for equality. If necessary, he said, the Negro should be prepared to die in their quest for fair treatment, but to "die quietly."[4]

But the biggest news on campus early in the decade was a Harvard man named Jack. Just one year earlier John F. Kennedy, Harvard class of 1940 and one of a host of Kennedy family members to boast a Harvard degree, had reached heights barely imaginable even at University Hall when he claimed the U.S. presidency. A resident of Winthrop House and a member of the varsity swim team during his student days, Kennedy had richly marbled ties to the school. As Kennedy assembled the team that would march into the New Frontier behind him, he cherry-picked from Harvard's ranks.

On the stately quadrangle that runs from Grays to Holworthy Halls in Harvard Yard, the mood was ecstatic. In the weeks after the election, speculation on who would be summoned to Washington, DC, and for what post was widespread and in some cases the subject of a wager or two. In the end more than fifty Harvardians would get the call, including the brilliant and charismatic McGeorge Bundy, who left his post as the dean of arts and sciences to become National Security Adviser; the eloquent John Kenneth Galbraith, who set off from the Economics Department to become envoy to India; and the erudite Arthur M. Schlesinger Jr., who became a special assistant in the White House as well as resident historian. No less than four Harvard men assumed positions in the president's Cabinet.[5] The raid on Harvard prompted much commentary in the media, such as the *New York Times* columnist James Reston's notorious quip that soon there "will be nothing left at Harvard but Radcliffe."[6]

The campus newspaper, the *Harvard Crimson*, kept breathless watch of the comings and goings of key players during the two and a half years that Kennedy was president and took close note of the doings of other Kennedy family members as well. When newly elected Senator Edward Kennedy (class of '54) gave his first speech in Washington, DC, it was front-page news. So too when the undergraduate humor magazine, the *Harvard Lampoon*, voted Caroline Kennedy "Little Girl of the Year" in 1963, the news appeared on page one. And during the spring of that same year the paper exulted in the announcement that the university's Board of Overseers, of which Kennedy was a member, would hold its spring meeting in Washington, DC, and would dine at the White House—for the president's convenience, of course.[7]

Much has been written about the intimate—some would say incestuous—relationship between Harvard University and the Kennedy administration. But Richard Norton Smith summed up the relationship perhaps most succinctly when he wrote in his book *The Harvard Century* that "Under John Kennedy, the University sometimes imagined itself to be the fourth branch of government, an impression JFK did little to dispel."[8] It was an intoxicating example of how academic brilliance could position a person next to the ultimate seat of power, and as such it held a magnetic allure for Barack Obama. Indeed, he applied himself to his studies at Harvard with greater determination than ever before, confident that the same kind of elevation that Kennedy had offered his contemporaries would be proffered to him once he returned to Kenya and Tom Mboya's potent inner circle. Destiny, it seemed, had determined that Obama should join the elect.

Obama arrived at Harvard at a time when the campus was swathed as never before in a self-confidence bordering on hubris. Part of that was due also to significant changes in the cast of the student body that had occurred in recent years. Harvard had worked hard since World War II to broaden its mandate so that by the early 1960s it was no longer the parochial arena of the Brahmin gentry alone but instead home to a much broader swath of backgrounds and intellectual potential. As the pool of applicants knocking at Harvard's door steadily grew, the number of Harvard alumnae offspring admitted had declined, to the consternation of the school's admissions officers. Increasingly, the school had its pick. The result was a more sophisticated and academically talented pool of candidates. To say that the students who ultimately selected were supremely self-assured, many of whom were prize winners, Merit Scholars, or just plain-old first in their class, doesn't begin to do them justice. As Smith describes the students of the time: "Their view of Harvard's significance roughly matched their own self-estimate, and neither was notably modest. . . . At their best, they were remorseless in their precocity, stimulating in their company, and challenging in their conversation. At worst, they were neurotic, opinionated grade hounds. Onlookers noted a syndrome called 'Valedictorian's Ego,' wherein over-achievers were thrown together, forced into mortal combat to justify their well-worn halos."[9] In short, they were a lot like Obama.

In most other respects the first-year graduate student from Kenya was a curiosity, just as he had been in Hawaii. Part of it was due to his dark skin. Although Harvard had steadily increased its international community, most students from overseas were from Europe or Asia. In 1962 there were a total of 81 African students enrolled school-wide, of which one dozen were in the Graduate School of Arts and Sciences.[10] Blacks accounted for only about 1 percent of the 13,668 students, which, added to the African students, made for a total of just over 200 black faces on campus.[11] Because they were so small in number, Harvard's black students, whether foreign or homegrown, invariably knew one another. So when Azinna Nwafor, class of '64 and a native of Nigeria, saw a lean black man in horn rims whom he did not know striding in front of Leverett House that fall, he promptly introduced himself. "Obama walked with confidence," noted Nwafor, who went on to become an assistant professor of what was then called Afro-American studies at Harvard. "Like, this is someone who is very sure of himself. He held his head high and his shoulders back. It was quite unlike how we saw African Americans at the time who walked around looking so defeated."

Soon afterward Nwafor invited Obama and a few other African students to his dorm room and the conversation immediately turned into a passionate debate over the relative merits of Hegel and Marx. Obama, as the eldest student among the group, dominated the discussion. But Nwafor, a math major, was bored. He showed one of the other students where he kept the drinks and headed out for a walk. "I came back three hours later and they had just left," Nwafor recalls, erupting into laughter.

Although black students on campus found common cause on a host of fronts, they also faced a number of cultural hurdles. Many black students had been raised not as African Americans but as American Negroes, as they were still called in some quarters. Not only had their parents discouraged them from embracing their African roots but in some cases advised them to disdain their ethnic lineage entirely. To them, Africa was the past, a place of unwashed feet and barbaric habits. To the astonishment of some

African students, hair straightening was still practiced among some black Americans, and the question of how best to uncoil nappy hair was a common one. It would not be until a couple of years later that many African Americans embraced their African heritage, and the untamed Afro hairstyle became a popular means of defining black identity.

In fact, for many African students the state of black America in the early1960s came as something of a shock. Not only did many of the African students come from prominent political families, but like Obama, they had been among the highest academic achievers in their country and they carried themselves with great pride. That African Americans were routinely treated as second-class citizens and in some cases appeared to regard themselves as such was difficult for the Africans to grasp. And when the African students actually found themselves the victims of racial discrimination—when time after time an apartment said to be available over the phone was suddenly no longer available when they showed up in person to take a look at it—some were tempted to head for home.

Obama himself was the subject of some pointed racial hostility, although he likely never knew it. When he first arrived in Cambridge, Obama lived on the edge of campus on the first floor of one of New England's less appealing architectural standbys known as a "triple decker," a three-story wooden apartment building with one unit stacked on top of another. Within months he moved to a spacious third-floor apartment a short distance from the Charles River on the top floor of a home owned by Reverend Arthur J. Metaxas, the priest at the nearby Saints Constantine and Helen Greek Orthodox Church and a Harvard chaplain. Harvard president Nathan Pusey himself had asked Metaxas if he were able to put up some African students. But when Obama and his roommate, a graduate student from Nigeria, moved into the Metaxas's house on Magazine Street, a neighbor marched to the front door and strenuously objected. "They said we had *ruined* the neighborhood," recalled his wife Georgia Metaxas. "They were very annoyed at us for renting to these black boys, and I don't think they ever talked to us again. But my husband being a priest and all we did not think that way. Those boys were from a good college and I respected that. Whenever we made cookies, I would send some up to them."

Then there was the incident at the Hayes Bickford cafeteria in Harvard Square, a popular student eatery fondly known as "The Bick." Uchenna C. Nwosu, a Harvard undergraduate from Nigeria along with a Nigerian graduate student from M.I.T. had just sat down to eat when they noticed that their tray was dirty. When they asked the manager for another tray he declared, "You don't get such good things in your home country." The students persisted, saying they were entitled to good service as members of the public, to which the manager retorted, "You don't belong to the public." Making matters worse, when Nwosu called the police, the officers asked no questions but promptly charged the African students with trespassing and disturbing the peace and jailed them overnight. Although Harvard provided a lawyer to defend them and the two students were ultimately acquitted, the incident left a deep impression on the young men.[12] Nwosu, who went on to become a doctor of obstetrics and gynecology at East Tennessee State University, ultimately wrote a memoir that describes his years at Harvard. "You know, I was not from Mars. Civil rights matters were on television all the time, so I knew what was going on," said Nwosu. "But being put in jail for no good reason and standing up all night, it was very upsetting."

By the spring of 1963 black students at Harvard realized they had much in common with each other and came together to form a club of their own on campus in an effort to promote mutual understanding and provide themselves a voice. The idea, as one student described it to the *Crimson*, was to end the "artificial alienation" between African and Negro students that many felt was largely fostered by whites who saw the two groups as largely unrelated.[13] But the plan ran into trouble immediately.

The proposed Association of African and Afro-American Students (AAAAS) was to be open only to African and Afro-American students currently enrolled at Harvard and Radcliffe. The University found this membership clause discriminatory and refused to recognize the group unless it reworded the clause, and students, both black and white, hotly debated the issue. After months of wrangling the Association agreed to remove the offending language from its membership clause and received official sanction, prompting a collective sigh of relief. The change, however, had little effect on the group's intent to exclude whites. Organizers had deliberately worded the new clause to stipulate that membership was to be "open to Harvard and Radcliffe students and shall be by invitation only," meaning they could let in whomever they wanted. But the struggle between the AAAAS and Harvard was not over. Weeks later the Association was again admonished when, in January 1964, it tried to institute a sliding scale for admission to hear its first speaker, James Baldwin, the African American author of the influential *Notes of a Native Son* and *The Fire Next Time*. The Association proposed a charge of 50 cents for members of civil rights organizations and residents of the depressed neighborhoods of Roxbury and Dorchester, and $1 for all others. But the University insisted on a single charge for all.[14]

Obama stayed aloof from much of these civil rights doings on campus. As a graduate student he had little time for extracurricular activities. Although many African undergraduates routinely flocked to the speeches of Malcolm X and Martin Luther King Jr. and leapt into the Association fray, graduate students were more circumspect in their political activities for fear that engagement might create problems around their routine applications to the Immigration and Naturalization Service for an extension of their stay. Obama was supported by three fellowships, one for $1,500 from Harvard and two for $1,000 each from the Laubach Literacy Fund and the Phelps Stokes Fund, and he would have been mindful not to offend his supporters through any engagement in potentially controversial activities.[15] "We were on student visas and we did not want to attract attention. We had come to study, not play politics and that would have been the interpretation if we had been involved," said Sylvester E. Ugoh, a Nigerian graduate student in economics in the early 1960s. "But we were very interested in what was going on and we read everything that was written. We read it all."

Although Harvard's traditions and intellectual reach clearly impressed Obama, it was not an environment he found easy to embrace. By then he had been away from Africa for three years, he must have found the fiercely competitive landscape and the predominantly WASP culture on campus challenging at best. Like the acclaimed African American scholar and civil rights activist W. E. B. DuBois, who arrived at Harvard in 1888, Obama chose to hold himself apart from the white-dominated mainstream. As DuBois wrote in his memoir, "I was in Harvard, but not of it, and realized all the irony of my singing 'Fair Harvard.' I sang it because I liked the music, and not from any pride in the Pilgrims."[16]

Obama instead largely kept company with the African students on campus, among whom he found the conversation, not to mention the music, more to his liking. One of a loose-knit group of African students who socialized together on weekends, Obama attended gatherings in students' apartments and at the International Student Association on Garden Street in Harvard Square, a few blocks away from the Cambridge Common, which often hosted live bands and drew foreign students from other campuses in Boston. Few among the group could afford the prices at the pubs and restaurants off campus, so they created their own alternatives.

Those lucky enough to have a friend with a car would also head to New York on summer weekends to meet up with other African students from around the country, members of the Kenya Students Union, at International House on Riverside Drive. The students, many of whom would not return home for several years while they pursued their education, eagerly traded political news, talked soccer, and swapped the latest music from their native country.

There was much to discuss about the situation back home. The colonial forces were in retreat, and the liberated African nations at long last claimed their own governments and institutions. Almost all French and Belgian former colonies became independent in 1960, including the giant Congo, followed by Nigeria, and in the following years Tanzania and Uganda. Finally, on December 12, 1963, Kenya triumphantly raised her brilliant new flag of black, red, and green stripes with the traditional African shield and spears set in the center, thus ending more than sixty years of colonial rule. Even as much of America was consumed with grief over the assassination of President Kennedy three weeks earlier, the African students celebrated with parties and impassioned speeches. On a hot summer night or two at the West End Bar on Broadway, Obama could be found tossing down a few whiskeys over a spirited assessment of Kenya's first president, Jomo Kenyatta. "Most Kenyans at the table talked about the positions they wanted to hold when they got back, but Obama was a bit more of an intellectual," recalls Fred Okatcha, a Kenyan who attended Yale University and got his PhD in educational psychology from Michigan State University before returning to teach psychology at Kenyatta University in Nairobi. "I did not know him to be critical of Kenyatta, but he was very forthright."

As a Kenyan enrolled in graduate economic studies, Obama was keenly aware of the jockeying already beginning among the handful of his countrymen passing through Cambridge and with whom he would compete head-on upon their return to Nairobi, armed with their dueling Harvard diplomas. Hilary Ng'weno, who received a BA from Harvard the year before Obama arrived, would become one of Kenya's most prominent political journalists and would document the nation's impending political turmoil in the pages of his *Weekly Review*. Philip Ndegwa, a soft-spoken Kikuyu who attended Harvard's Graduate School of Public Administration for one year starting in the fall of 1962—although he did not get a degree— would go shoulder to shoulder with Obama for the job of planning officer in the Ministry of Economic Planning and Development in 1964. Ndegwa would become one of Kenya's most accomplished economists and would serve as permanent secretary in several ministries, a highly regarded leader for decades on the Kenyan scene. There was also Washington Jalang'o Okumu, who graduated from Harvard College in 1962, another Kenyan graduate student in economics who would become an international mediator of note, but long before that he would be Obama's chief competitor for an economist's job in the country's new tourism development office in the late 1960s. For each of the Kenyans, Harvard would add an incomparable luster to their résumé that family members back in their villages would revere but, for the most part, could not begin to comprehend. "Barack was from Harvard. He was the big voice from Harvard and he let you know that," said Peter Aringo, a close friend of Obama's and a six-term member of the Kenyan Parliament. "Harvard was a big thing here. Who here could begin to imagine going to Harvard?"

With some intuition of what lay ahead, Obama immersed himself in his studies in earnest with a focus on the development economics that he hoped would prepare him for a career with either the United Nations or the Kenyan government. In a way, his timing could not have been better. Obama arrived at the imposing gray fortress of the Littauer Center at a time when the field of economics was undergoing a seismic transition that would change the practice forever, transforming its core from one focused primarily on institutions, empirical measurement, and social-historical context to a much more abstract field rooted in a mathematically defined model of equilibrium.

In the same way that John Maynard Keynes's book *The General Theory of Employment, Interest and Money* had revolutionized economics two decades earlier and established the bedrock of modern macroeconomic thought, the postwar introduction of sophisticated and complex mathematical models into the field was radically changing not only what economists did but also how they thought. In place of narrative construction based on observed realities, mathematical models and the logic of formulae were the new modus operandi. Transfixed by the success of physics in the natural sciences, these new economists believed economic production and exchange could potentially be modeled with an analogous exactness. And by the late 1950s, with computers growing in size, number, and computational speed, the time it took to do complex data analysis fell from days or even weeks to mere hours. Never mind that you had to write the computer program yourself—it was a heady time to be entering the field. Being a young economist in the early 1960s, as Obama's classmate Roger Noll described it, "was like being the first person walking in the peach orchard and all the fruit is hanging low. This was a whole new way of doing business and if you could embrace it as a twenty-five-year-old economist, you could do something that no one else could do."

All you had to do was figure out the math. For Obama, his training occurred at a time when he could make practical use of instruction in linear programming and econometric techniques that would help redefine the field rather than focus on the older style practices that were quickly growing obsolete. On the down side, some of what was being taught was so new and so dependent on relatively advanced math that many students who had not been well versed in the field in general and differential calculus or complex regression analysis in particular floundered.

Not only was the subject matter itself singularly taxing, Obama's classmates included a formidable group of brainiacs who would go on to make major contributions to the field. They were white, male, and angling for No. 1, even if they would not openly admit it. Among the thirty-five graduate students who entered the PhD program with Obama in 1962 were Lester Thurow, who would be the first to complete the program and go on to become one of the nation's best-known economists, a prolific author, and eventually the dean of MIT's Sloan School of Management; Sam Bowles, the son of Chester Bowles, who served as the undersecretary of state in the Kennedy Administration and a rigorous critic of free market economic theory from professorial posts first at Harvard and then the University of Massachusetts at Amherst; and Richard Zeckhauser, who for a few summers was one of the youngest "whiz kids" summoned by U.S. Defense Secretary Robert McNamara to critique military strategy and later a noted pioneer in policy analysis. Obama, clearly, was no longer the smartest guy in the room. If a few of his classmates privately suspected that the Africans on campus were second-rate students, however, they did not show it. "There was a feeling they weren't particularly good, I don't know why," recalled Lars Gunnarsson Sandberg, a graduate student in economics and later a professor of economics emeritus at Ohio State University. "There was a lot of snobbery, but it was intellectual snobbery. There were hot shots from all the schools in the country. We thought we were God's gift to the world."

Under the chairmanship of John Dunlop, an avuncular and politically connected labor economist famed for his bow ties, the economics department was a microcosm of Harvard's legendary decentralization. Professors zealously pursued their own endeavors, many of which took them outside the university, all the while keeping a benign eye on their students. Some students formed close relationships with a particular faculty member. Wassily Leontief, the prominent Russian economist whose input-output analysis would later win him the Nobel Prize, would occasionally take a favored student fly-fishing on the Charles River, despite its polluted waters.[17] So too the silver-haired economic historian, Alexander Gerschenkron, who kept a rifle by the couch in his office, would reward a student who piqued his interest with a glass of the Dry Sack sherry or Remy Martin cognac he kept on a silvery tray on his desk.[18] But, more commonly, students struggled to get time with their prominent and often quite preoccupied professors.

Not everyone made it through the rigorous and highly competitive program. More than a few who found the heavy emphasis on math in the early 1960s not what they had expected cut their losses after two years and fled with a master's degree, widely considered by those left behind to be a consolation prize. Professor James Duesenberry regularly greeted his opening class in Money and Finance with the chilling observation: "In every entering class there are just so many *geniuses*," he would say, taking a long, slow look at the students listening intently to him. "I just don't know where they all go."[19]

The first year was a slog of must-dos. There was economic theory with Ed Chamberlin, a department fixture who had made his name in the early 1930s with the publication of his theory of monopolistic competition, and macroeconomics taught by Robert Dorfman, a stern figure who was one of the department's earliest proponents of the mathematical trend. Statistics and economic history were also de rigueur. In their second year students were free to branch into areas of their own particular interest, with the realization that whatever they chose they would have to make a comprehensive presentation of several subject areas for their oral exams at the end of the year. If they passed their exams, they could then move on to pursue their dissertation.

Like the majority of his classmates, Obama had taken only a modest amount of math in his undergraduate years and was largely unprepared for the rigors of macroeconomics as it was being taught. He was an admirer of some of the pioneers of the emerging field, such as MIT's legendary Paul Samuelson, author of the largest-selling economics textbooks of its time, *Economics: An Introductory Analysis*, and Kenneth Arrow, who had coproduced a transformative mathematical proof of a general equilibrium, and Obama read their work closely. Although he managed to pass the department's math test in the first few months, he struggled to keep up with the weight of his coursework. In his letter to Sylvia Baldwin, his friend in Hawaii, Obama uncharacteristically conceded that things were getting "pretty rough." "The competition here is just maddening," Obama wrote. "In fact I have to read at least 12 books a week plus monographs, periodicals and professional journals, let alone the routine of school, the papers required and my own research on the theory I am trying to build. It really does keep me busy."[20]

Obama was so busy, in fact, that he had no time for either the public speaking or campus socializing that he had dallied in while in Honolulu. A month after Obama arrived, Dr. Ralph Bunche, who in 1950 was the first African American to win the Nobel Peace Prize and was an active supporter of the civil rights movement, spoke on campus and declared that not only was the Congo unprepared for independence, but also that many of the new African states were not ready for such a step. The same

Barack H. Obama as a student in Hawaii. He was one of an elite group of young Kenyan men and women educated in America and charged with shaping the new Kenyan nation after independence was achieved in 1963.

The gravesite of Obama Opiyo, the great grandfather of President Barack Obama. The grave is located in Kanyadhiang where the president's father, Barack Hussein Obama, was born in 1936.

3

Kezia Obama, the first of Barack Obama's four wives, standing with their children Malik and Auma in the 1960s. Kezia now lives in Bracknell, England, while Malik and Auma live in Nairobi.

4

Barack H. Obama was recognized as an exceptionally bright student while still a young boy. Although he was accepted at the prestigious Maseno School in Western Kenya and studied there for several years, the principal grew annoyed at his challenging behavior and would not allow Obama to complete his studies.

Arthur Reuben Owino, a classmate and childhood friend of Obama's. Reuben recalls that Obama would often say, "You don't know what you are talking about. I am telling you what I know. 'And then you would be arguing with him endlessly, endlessly.'"

Elizabeth "Betty" Mooney was an American literacy worker in Kenya in the late 1950s. In this photograph—one of her favorites—she visits a Masai tribal community in 1959.

Mooney with Helen Roberts, an American literacy volunteer from California, standing near their car in Kenya. Mooney hired Obama as her secretary in 1958 and later paid for his first year's tuition at the University of Hawaii.

Obama and Mooney worked closely together for nearly two years, and she took many photographs of him. Here, he poses in front of the radio in her home in Nairobi.

8

The primer writing committee hard at work. While working for Mooney in the Kenya Adult Literacy Program, Obama wrote three primers in the Luo language for new literates on health, agriculture, and citizenship. The first book was called *Otieno Jarieko: The Wise Man.*

10

Barack Obama in a photograph taken by Betty Mooney.

11

The Obama family on a picnic in Kenya with Betty Mooney in 1958. From the left: Kezia and baby Malik, Betty Mooney, Barack Obama, and George Wanyee, another worker in the literacy office.

12

Barack Obama studying at the YMCA in Honolulu. He was the first African student on the University of Hawaii campus, and his crisp attire stood out among the more casual clothing favored by other students.

During his years at the University of Hawaii, Barack Obama was hard to miss. He frequently spoke in public on topics related to Africa and debated other students on the subject of communism versus democracy.

Nearly a decade after he graduated Phi Beta Kappa from UH, Obama returned to Honolulu in 1971 in a far more somber mood. During that visit, the only time that he saw his son, Barack Obama II, his third wife was in court back in Nairobi seeking a divorce.

Although Obama was an undergraduate at UH, he often spent his time with a diverse group of graduate students at the university's East-West Center. Here he attends a party of international students in Honolulu in 1961.

Obama attends a peace rally in Ala Moana Park in May of 1962. In brief remarks to the crowd, Obama called for a reduction in military spending. "Peace will release great resources," he said.

Fellow UH student Pake Zane was a friend of Obama's on campus and later traveled to Kenya to visit him. Obama told Zane that he had received death threats as a result of his testimony in Tom Mboya's murder trial.

Tom Mboya, the popular Kenyan nationalist leader, in London for the 1960 Kenya Conference. Mboya, a fellow Luo, was a mentor to Obama, and the two spoke on a Nairobi street corner a short time before Mboya was assassinated in July of 1969.

19

Jomo Kenyatta, president and founding father of Kenya, attends a 1964 ceremony in Nairobi. Obama was openly critical of Kenyatta's economic policies and the tight-knit group of Kikuyu with which he surrounded himself.

20

Omar Okech Obama, Barack Obama's half brother, attended the Browne & Nichols School in Cambridge, Massachusetts, from 1963 to 1965. Omar Obama, third from the left in the back row, played varsity soccer and was a member of the school's Debate Club and Newspaper Club.

21

Ruth Beatrice Baker, graduating from Simmons College in Boston, in 1958. Baker dated Obama for several weeks in Cambridge and then followed him to Nairobi where she became his third wife on Christmas Eve, 1964.

22

Obama and his growing family lived in the Woodley Estate section of Nairobi in the late 1960s and early 1970s. Neighbors could often hear his booming baritone over the fence and were well aware that the Obama marriage was a troubled one.

The two Barack H. Obamas pose for a photo that was apparently taken in Honolulu in 1971. The Christmas visit was the only time the two were together after the elder Obama left his small family in Hawaii to attend Harvard University in 1962.

Hawa Auma Obama, the sister of the elder Barack Obama and president Obama's aunt, standing outside her home in Oyugis, Kenya. Auma sells coal by the roadside for a living.

The Kaloleni Public Bar, a favored Luo watering hole on Nairobi's southeast side. Obama retired to the Kaloleni almost daily after work and passed his final hours drinking there with friends before he died in November of 1982.

Habiba Akumu, Barack Obama's mother, sits mournfully beside her son's coffin in 1982.

The gravesite of Barack H. Obama on the Obama family compound in Alego. The gravesite of his father, Hussein Onyango Obama, is a short distance behind it.

Mark Ndesandjo, one of President Obama's six siblings on his father's side, is interviewed in Guangzhou, China, in 2009. Ndesandjo wrote what he calls a semi-autobiographical novel in which the father is described as physically abusive and a heavy drinker.

The second oldest of President Obama's siblings, Auma Obama, published her autobiography, *Das Leben kommt immer dazwischen,* or Life Always Comes in Between, in 2010. Auma Obama, who studied in Germany, writes that she found it hard to forgive her father for the breakup of their family and years of neglect.

The youngest brother. Born six months before his father died, George Hussein Onyango Obama never knew the father that he shares with the U.S. president. A resident of the Nairobi slum of Huruma, George penned his own memoir, *Homeland: An Extraordinary Story of Hope and Survival,* in 2010.

Barack Obama's oldest son, Malik Obama, made headlines of his own in the fall of 2010 when he took his third wife, a nineteen-year-old still in secondary school. Malik, 53, lives in Alego next to his grandmother, Mama Sarah.

The first of Barack Obama's four wives, Kezia Obama, maintains that she never divorced her late husband and that he continued to father children with her, even after he married two American women.

argument had provoked Obama to loud fury two years earlier in Hawaii, but this time he said not a word in public. No admonishing letter to the *Crimson*. No pontificating on the granite steps above Cambridge Street. Nor was Obama one of the regulars at the coffee shop on the mezzanine at Littauer, where some of the heavyweights in the class like Thurow and Bowles regularly hung around noodling over multiple regression analysis and linear programming, not to mention debating the Vietnam War and the racial turbulence in the South. More often than not, Obama was in his cramped study carrel in the Littauer basement bent over the calculus problems that bedeviled him. The coffee klatch was a telling measure of the changes transforming the study of economics. The things that were cutting edge—structural imbalance, econometric forecasting models, game theory—were not so much in the textbooks as they were in the air. "The guys you saw there every day had a higher batting average, they just did better than the others," explained Roger Noll, then a classmate and later a professor of economics at Stanford University. "The up-to-date conversation was going on in the lounge. That's where you were talking the new stuff. That's what kids do if you want to be at the forefront. You don't want to be Ken Galbraith, you want to be Ken Arrow."

Noll, who had earned a BS with honors in mathematics from the California Institute of Technology, was one of the math guys. With his West Coast openness and affable manner, he was also an approachable sort. So he was the one Obama stopped one day in the lounge and asked if he would give him a hand with a class on calculus that was at the heart of the program. "Obama was saying, boy, this is hard, this is really hard. This is not what I thought economics was," recalled Noll, who worked with Obama on several occasions. "But he did not complain. He was just reacting to a different kind of economics than he had studied as an undergraduate. He was not at all unusual for the twenty-five or so other students who were completely underwater. There were a lot of students who were in worse shape than he. The disparity of preparation in the class was immense and it made it an extremely difficult group to teach."

Obama managed to master the new techniques and would ultimately pass both his general and oral exams in the spring of his second year at Harvard. But in the version of his Harvard experience that he recounted when he got back home, the story line went quite differently. By his account, Obama was not the one who needed tutoring in math but rather Philip Ndegwa, his budding rival. And the man to whom Ndegwa turned for help was none other than Barack Obama. Obama, who clearly learned his stuff, likely did give Ndegwa a hand. Although Ndegwa had attended the prestigious Alliance High School in Kenya and Makerere University before he came to Harvard, he apparently struggled with some of the advanced math himself. Nor did he get a degree from Harvard, as he left after only one year. But for years afterward, as Ndegwa rose steadily higher, Obama would flaunt his tutelage and angrily denounce Ndegwa as unfit for his job. "Obama would slam his fist on the table and say that Philip knows *nothing*, he knows nothing about math or economics," recalled Francis Masakhalia, Obama's friend and a prominent Kenyan economist who served as Permanent Secretary of the Ministry of Finance and Economic Planning. "He would say, 'I am a much better economist than he can ever hope to be.'" In a particularly creative twist on his Harvard years, Obama claimed to have been taught there by Ken Arrow and recounted in detail to his superiors the classes he took with the famous economist.[21] But Arrow did not even arrive at Harvard until 1968, four years after Obama left.

Still, Obama loomed large to the growing number of young Kenyans arriving in Boston in the early 1960s, eagerly seeking a college degree and, in some cases, a high school diploma. They came with little money and less an idea of what to expect in the churning cities of America. What they did know was that Obama had already achieved many of the things to which they aspired. He had not only earned a college degree but had also been recognized as Phi Beta Kappa. Now at one of the world's most famous universities, he had a summer job at the International Marketing Institute in Cambridge, a small firm that offered programs in product marketing to business people from around the world, and this meant that he had a little extra cash. Just as impressive, he had a series of girlfriends who hovered over him and cooked rice and novel meats. And when the younger students came knocking at the door on Magazine Street, Obama welcomed them warmly and offered them not only a place to sleep but also all the advice they could absorb. "We looked upon him as a model. He really gave us inspiration," said George Saitoti, a former vice president of Kenya and later Minister for Internal Security. "This was a serious person who was very well respected and who was very approachable. We were just young boys, you know, and he spoke very firmly to us about education and what we needed to do. He sounded just like President Obama does now."

Saitoti, then eighteen and a senior at the Cambridge School of Weston was one of a half-dozen young men who made their way to Obama's apartment. Some would stay for only a night or two, while others spent an entire summer there while working odd jobs in the area after school. Brothers Moses and Otieno O. Wasonga, who were attending high schools north of Boston, routinely spent their weekends with Obama, who nicknamed them *wuod ruoth*, Luo for son of a chief. The Wasongas' father was, in fact, a chief and had known Hussein Onyango well, which drew them even closer to Obama.

Oyuko Onyango Mbeche was only fourteen when he arrived in Massachusetts on the second of Tom Mboya's airlifts in 1960 to attend Assumption Preparatory School in Worcester before going on to Assumption College. But Mbeche quickly found that conventional sources of guidance were not particularly helpful. When he sought assistance from the Kenyan Mission at the United Nations in New York to help find a job a few years later, he claims that simmering tribal hostilities between the Kikuyu and Luo had already poisoned the waters. For a Kenyan whose name began with an O, thus immediately identifying him as a Luo, no guidance would be available from the Kikuyu-dominated office. Mbeche asked around for help, and when he learned of an older student named Obama, he too headed for Magazine Street. Mbeche wound up not only spending the summer on Obama's floor while working as a technician at a nearby hospital at Obama's suggestion, but he also eventually changed his career objective as a result of Obama's influence. Obama, he recalled, frequently talked about the importance of advanced math and urged Mbeche to study calculus so that he could take on more sophisticated mathematic challenges. Intrigued, Mbeche enrolled in Harvard Summer School to study math and eventually abandoned his plans to go to medical school in order to become an engineer. "He was always saying that math is a language like any other and I began to understand what he was talking about," said Mbeche. "You get curious, you know."

At twenty-six years of age, Obama was the old man of the group. Some evenings, far from the cerebral intensity of the Littauer Center, he would

sit with his pipe jutting out of his mouth and riff with the young men staying with him. They listened to his favorite Lingala music or the innovative
jazz compositions of Tabu Ley Rochereau, an immensely popular Zairian
singer who popularized the "Independence Cha Cha."

Another favorite pastime drawn from Obama's childhood was an
exchange of *pakruoks*, a Luo game in which several people would trade
humorous or self-flattering phrases about those in attendance. Obama
would often raise his hand, call a halt to the music and declare of himself,
"*An wuod akumu nya Njoga, wuod nyar ber*," meaning, "I am the son of
Akumu, the daughter of Njoga, who was a beautiful woman." Or he might
say, "*An Obama wuod kogello, wuoyi madichol manyiri thone, wuoyi
mochamo buk ma musungu oyie*," meaning, "I am Obama, son of Kogelo, a
dark man who ladies die for, a man who has eaten books until the white
man acknowledged." The young men were accustomed to hearing the
admonishment, "*Wuoyi mariek somo kwano kendo ok dhi e miel*," meaning, "A smart man studies math and stays away from parties." The game
would devolve into a riotous play on personal characteristics or foibles
that would leave them all weak with laughter.[22]

When Obama was around there was always a steady stream of conversation that sometimes stretched into the early hours of the morning. The
situation back home was always high on the list. In the months after independence leading up to the declaration of the Republic in 1964, Kenya
bustled with activity as the real job of nation building got underway.
Already simmering differences between the political parties KANU and
KADU over critical issues of Africanization and the country's economic
structure were becoming more fraught. Obama's mentor, Tom Mboya, had
been named Minister for Justice and Constitutional Affairs, and Obama
was anxious to see that Mboya had increasingly aligned himself with
Kenyatta's more conservative supporters. Obama paid close attention to
such developments, and on his return would insert himself directly into
the evolving political debate over the country's future shape.

Although Obama clearly took pleasure in mentoring the young
Kenyans who flocked to his apartment, his thoughts were preoccupied
with his own brothers and sisters back home. As the eldest male, it fell to
Obama to provide financial assistance for school fees for his siblings and
to help out generally. What that really meant was that he needed to help

his brothers. In a Kenyan family of the early 1960s people generally thought that daughters would get married and be consumed by domesticity, and thus they would have no need for postsecondary education. Obama's older sister, Sarah, was just as clever and willful as her brother, and she often begged for advanced schooling, but Hussein Onyango would hear nothing of it. In the Obama family the next male in line after Barack was Omar Okech Obama, the first son born to Hussein Onyango and his wife, Sarah Ogwel. Omar was eleven years younger than his big brother in America, and it was his education that the family was now anxious to advance.[23]

Obama took his responsibility to heart, and in the little spare time he had he explored high schools in the area that might be suitable for his brother. As it happened, Obama had become friendly with a woman who had close ties to what was then called Browne & Nichols, a tony boy's preparatory school that had graduated many of Boston's preeminent politicians and businessmen and just happened to be located in a leafy Cambridge enclave a short distance from Harvard. Her name was Ellen Frost, a Radcliffe student with an interest in developing countries. Frost had gotten to know Obama at a party of African students, and the two had an occasional coffee together. Not only had Frost's brothers attended Browne & Nichols, but her father, a downtown investment banker, was a treasurer at the school. Perhaps her father could mention Omar to the school's admission officers, she suggested.

Frost's father agreed, and in the fall of 1963 a sturdy young man with a somber expression arrived in Cambridge eager to go to work. Omar had apparently been brought to the United States on Tom Mboya's 1963 airlift, as his name is included on one of the early student lists. According to a notation on that list, his brother, Barack, had put up $300 toward his brother's travel expenses.[24] "Omar was a tall, gangly good-natured adolescent," recalled Frost, who went on to have a varied career in international affairs in the U.S. government and in business. "He did not look much like his half brother. But his classmates were fascinated with this boy from the jungles of Africa."

Although Omar was apparently the only African student on campus, he seemed to fit in with the privileged prep school crowd in his trim blazer bearing the school's seal and his starched white shirt, which he wore daily just as his brother did. A good three years older than the rest of the members of the class of 1966, he entertained his fellow tenth graders with elaborate stories of wild animals roaming the bush and of the indomitable Mau Mau freedom fighters. Mesmerized by his arched British accent, other students hung on tales of a life that seemed vastly different and more exotic than their own tame suburban existence.

Omar Obama squeezed in with his brother and his roommate on Magazine Street at times during the first few years he lived in Boston. With Obama Sr. immersed in his own studies, the younger Omar must have lived a fairly independent life. Given the substantial age difference between them, the half-brothers often seemed to visitors more like an uncle and nephew than siblings. By his second year on campus Omar was deeply involved with both the campus newspaper and the school's debate team. But where he really excelled was on the soccer field. Soccer coach Stephen "Hummer" Holmes remembers the first day Omar headed out to play. He had on a T-shirt and shorts, but nothing else. No soccer cleats or shin-guards, not even a pair of socks. Like most any young soccer player in Kenya, Omar was accustomed to playing in his bare feet. And when Holmes insisted he wear something on his feet, Omar loudly objected. "'Coach,' he'd say," as Holmes recalls, "'I need to take off the shoes. Please coach. I can't feel the ball. When I kick the ball, I cannot direct it. Please coach.' And I'd answer, 'Omar, I wish I could help. But when we play the game here, we wear shoes. It's the rule.'"

Finding cleats that would fit him was no easy task. Omar's feet were not only extraordinarily wide but were also deeply layered with callous from his years of playing soccer in his bare feet or, as Holmes describes it, "as if he had sewn in shoe leather for soles." Custom cleats had to be made for Omar's extraordinary feet, and he then took weeks to adjust to them. But when he finally got back on the field, Omar quickly became one of the team's highest scorers with a unique kicking style that propelled the ball clean off the top of his foot. Although a far more talented player than others on the team, Omar readily volunteered to teach his teammates his skills. "He put his team first, his teammates second, and himself third," said Holmes. "A very humble guy."

Whether because of a lack of funds or poor grades, Omar did not graduate from the school. He withdrew after two years and enrolled in the public high school in nearby Newton in the fall of 1965.[25] By then Obama had gone back to Kenya and Omar was on his own, apparently struggling without his older brother's supervision. In his move to Newton, Omar was sponsored by John R. Williams, the amiable alumnae coordinator at the International Marketing Institute in Cambridge where Obama had worked years earlier and whose son was also enrolled in the Newton High School. For reasons that are unclear, Omar did not graduate from that school either but dropped out before the end of the year.[26]

Shortly afterward Omar changed his name to O. Onyango Obama, preferring his father's African name to his own.[27] He remained in Cambridge for several years, living in an apartment on Perry Street several blocks from his brother's old apartment, and his residence became a legendary meeting place and crash pad for visiting Kenyan students. When Barack Obama came to visit in the early 1970s, he too spent Sunday mornings exchanging pakruoks and listening to music over ugali and fish on the porch at Perry Street. Achola Pala Okeyo, a graduate student in anthropology at Harvard at the time, also recalls Obama's half-sister, Zeituni Onyango, who was visiting the United States and would periodically drop in for a visit. "Perry Street was a rite of passage, an initiation. If you were a Kenyan in Boston, you had to go there," recalled Okeyo. "We'd do praise names and dance until we dropped. It was a huge amount of fun."

Until their nephew became the president and the hordes of eager cameramen came in hot pursuit, Obama's aunt and uncle lived relatively quietly in the Boston area. Apparently, in the early 1990s the same "Uncle Omar" who the president wrote in *Dreams* had gone missing in Boston was the treasurer of a small convenience store called the Wells Market in Dorchester, Massachusetts, where he sometimes pitched in and worked as a clerk.[28] He was the one who was on duty when two men in black masks attacked the store one night in the summer of 1994, and he was beaten with a sawed-off rifle and robbed, according to press accounts. Now sharing a house with several other Kenyans in the western suburb of Framingham, Omar maintains his low profile and declined to be interviewed.

Zeituni, however, has had a hard time keeping out of the news. When British reporters went searching in the final weeks of Obama's presidential

campaign for the Aunt Zeituni, they found her living in a squat brick public housing complex in South Boston. A blunt and outspoken woman,
Zeituni, fifty-nine, worked as a computer programmer for Kenya Brew-
eries in the late 1980s before moving in 2000 to the United States. When
the press learned that her request for political asylum had been denied and
she had been ordered deported, her case instantly became a cause célèbre,
igniting the issue of illegal immigration. During much of President
Obama's first year in office, Zeituni, even by her own description, was seen
as a political liability as she put the immigration laws to the test in her own
battle to remain in the United States. Since her nephew's election, the dramatic Zeituni has made two colorful court appearances in Boston, each
trailed by a platoon of suited lawyers and dozens of reporters to whom she
exclaimed periodically, "Praise God." In the spring of 2010 an immigration judge astonished some observers by granting her political asylum,
which enables her to apply for a green card and, ultimately, citizenship.[29]

Like Omar, Zeituni looked up to her big brother. The second child of
Hussein Onyango and Mama Sarah, Zeituni was one of several family
members who lived for short periods with him in Nairobi in the 1960s. In
Dreams she says that Barack was her favorite dance partner when they
were young and describes the many dance contests they entered together.
In a brief interview Zeituni added that she was deeply indebted to the
elder Barack for helping her throughout her life and in particular for buying her a cherished pair of shoes as a child.[30]

DURING THE YEARS that Obama Sr. attended Harvard he lived largely
like any other student. He dutifully attended classes and bent over his textbooks late into the night. But Obama was also a man of Africa, and he had
certain personal appetites that he made little effort to curb. One of them
was for women. The gang holding court back at Littauer Center saw virtually nothing of this side of Obama; indeed, many do not recall him at all.
But those who knew him more intimately saw a man who often drank
heavily and aggressively pursued a succession of young women. And Harvard administrators soon noticed it too.

To Obama, women were there to be taken. Raised in a polygamous culture, he believed that a man should necessarily have multiple women as a
measure of his virility and mastery of the world. His own father, Hussein

Onyango, had at least four wives and countless other women in his life, and most Luo men traditionally had at least a few. So integral a part of the culture is this practice that a man's wives traditionally live on the same compound together, with the first wife having the highest status and overseeing the others. In fact, if Obama had married only his first wife Kezia and never married or had children with another woman, this would have been the subject of some note back home.

However, Obama's relentless pursuit of women—and sometimes more than one at a time—was something more than cultural habit. It was as if he had to engage sexually with any eligible women whom he encountered. Obama, to be sure, could be devastatingly charming and attentive to the women who wound up as his wives—when he chose to. But with a certain category of women he knew less well, he made no pretense of being interested in them for any reason other than their bodies, and he made not the slightest apology for it. It was an attitude that some American women found astonishing. Ellen Frost, who experienced Obama's charm firsthand, describes his aggressive come-on to women as a kind of compulsion. "As Obama saw it, it was natural for a man to collect many women. That was the natural order of things," said Frost. "In fact, he was very proud of his ability with women. You'd watch him at parties. He liked to dance and he was a very physical dancer. He'd dance in a very suggestive way, no subtlety. It was as though he gained some power in the conquest. He did not bother to come on intellectually to women. He used suggestive, provocative language, I would say overtly sexual. I liked Barack and found him interesting but I did not like it when he did that. It was a kind of God's gift to women thing."

One of the African students on campus while Obama was at Harvard was a Nigerian named Chukwuma Azikiwe. The son of the first president of Nigeria following independence, Azikiwe was an undergraduate in the class of 1963 and later earned an MBA at the Harvard Business School. Obama's earnest working habits impressed Azikiwe, but he was taken aback to find that when Obama was not at his books, he often imbibed heavily. Once, Azikiwe encountered an inebriated Obama aggressively propositioning a very uncomfortable young woman in a doorway and called him off. Another time, he ran into him at a party moments before Obama, again well into his cups, got into a fist fight with another guest.

Azikiwe began to avoid Obama when he saw him on campus. Obama, Azikiwe concluded in an interview, "was an unguided ballistic missile."

Over the course of his four marriages, Obama was selective about who he told about his wives and children and who he did not. Prodded by Frost's amiable questioning, Obama revealed that he had a son in Hawaii of whom he was very proud. But when he mentioned to Azinna Nwafor that he might be visiting Hawaii, he said he was going "because the weather is quite good there" and made no mention of a son. For the women he dated, such erratic revelations were, to put it mildly, problematic. Some became furious when they learned that not only was he married, but married to two women at once.

Nwafor recalls a Saturday evening when he was a sophomore and studying in his room when he suddenly heard a loud banging on his window. It was Obama's girlfriend at the time, a Radcliffe undergraduate, weeping and begging to be let in. As Nwafor consoled the young woman, who had apparently just learned that Obama was married, Obama himself abruptly appeared and snapped at Nwafor to leave her alone. "He was very angry with me, as he thought I was trying to take his girlfriend," Nwafor sighed. "But I never did that. I never had difficulty getting my own girlfriends. It was interesting that someone who was capable of having multiple affairs could jump to that conclusion. We didn't see each other much after that."

Back in Honolulu, Ann Dunham was also growing annoyed with Obama's dating habits. It wasn't that she wanted him back. By the end of 1963 Dunham had resigned herself to the fact that Obama would not be returning to her side nor would they be going to Africa together when he completed his studies. When he had left, however, Obama had agreed to send financial support for their son. But pressed by the burden of providing for his visiting family as well as by the genuine costs of being a student, Obama never provided as he had promised. When Dunham gleaned from his occasional letters that he was dating other women in Cambridge and presumably spending money on those dates, her seemingly inexhaustible patience at last ran out. In the beginning of 1964 she began divorce proceedings, and by the spring of that year the unlikely union that had been sealed on the sun-kissed island of Maui came to an end. Obama signed a postal notice indicating that he had received the certified divorce documents in Cambridge, but he did not make an appearance in the Honolulu courtroom where the divorce was finalized.

In the years to come Dunham confided to her closer friends that Obama had greatly upset her during his days in Cambridge when he had chosen to spend the little extra money he had on women rather than his young son. "She mentioned that he had girlfriends in Boston but she did not mind because she knew that in African society men often had more than one girl," said Alice G. Dewey, the chairperson of Dunham's doctoral committee at the University of Hawaii and later an anthropology professor emeritus. "But it did bother her that he was spending the money on them that he should have spent on Barry [Barack Jr.]. Somewhere along the way, 'This made sense,' shifted to 'Hey, you said you'd send me money,' to 'This is not going to work.' She figured Barry was a responsibility of Barack's that he was not living up to and it increasingly annoyed her."

A few months before the divorce became final in 1964, immigration authorities once again grew alarmed at Obama's interactions with women just as they had been during his Hawaii days. This time, Obama was dating a young Kenyan woman who had been brought to the United States under the auspices of the Unitarian Universalist Service Committee and was attending high school in Sudbury, Massachusetts. The girl was not only doing poorly in school but had also taken an unauthorized trip to London, which greatly disturbed UU officials. Obama, who was believed to be her boyfriend, was frantically trying to get her reinstated at school, according to his "A" file. In a memo describing the situation to J. A. Hamilton, then district director of Immigration and Naturalization Service's Boston office, Immigrant Inspector K. D. MacDonald concluded, "Obama is considered by [redacted by federal authorities] to be a slippery character."[31] Aware of Obama's track record in Hawaii, Hamilton was apparently troubled by Obama's involvement with yet another young woman who was having difficulties.

Concerned about the incident, immigration officials decided to look into Obama's status at Harvard. They also decided to hold up on his routine request for an extension of his stay, just for the moment. Officials contacted Harvard's International Office, but far from gaining clarity through their conversations with the staff there, more clouds began to gather. Obama had told immigration authorities he was married to someone in

Hawaii and intended to get a divorce. But Harvard officials, prompted by the INS call, had done a little digging into the matter and were concerned that Obama was married to two women; they just weren't sure if that made him a bigamist or a typical Luo. As immigration inspector M. F. McKeon wrote in a memo, "Harvard thinks he's married to someone in Kenya and someone in Honolulu, but that possibly he belongs to a tribe where multiple marriages are O.K." Harvard, which had apparently never before probed Obama's statement that he was married, as it had seen no need to, was distinctly not happy. David D. Henry, the director of Harvard's International Office, told INS that he would talk to Obama about his marital situation, but he would not do so until after Obama had taken his exams, according to the INS memo, "in case he might get upset and use that as an excuse for not passing. Harvard will call us with the results of the interview."[32]

Two days later Harvard's International Office was beside itself. After talking to some of Obama's acquaintants, the office now believed Obama was married to a third person, this one a woman in Cambridge whom he had been known to be dating. The school administrators were wrong; Obama was indeed dating someone, but they were not married. They also found that Obama had financial problems. Although Harvard had already signed off on the necessary immigration forms indicating that it expected Obama would be a full-time student the following year and would complete his dissertation, Henry was now considering whether Harvard wanted Obama back the next year at all.

The more Henry looked into Obama's personal record, the more disturbed he became. Henry was a Harvard man, a rock-jawed member of the class of 1941 and the former director of the school's admissions office. Four years earlier he had founded the African Scholarship Program of American Universities, which brought some of Africa's brightest students to the United States on full scholarship. Henry, a former prep school teacher, had a lot riding on the African students in the United States and he was apparently not inclined to tolerate Obama's behavior, never mind that Obama's actions would have seemed largely acceptable to many of his fellow Luos back home. They were not acceptable to David Henry in Boston. Three weeks after immigration officials contacted Harvard, Henry called them back and said that Obama would not be returning to Harvard. Henry explained that he had talked to the chairman of the economics department and one of the school's deans, and he learned that Obama had passed his general exams and was entitled to stay to complete his thesis. "However, they are going to try and cook something up to ease him out," M. F. McKeon wrote in an internal memo. "All three (Harvard administrators) will have to agree on this, however. They are planning on telling him that they will not give him any money and that he had better return to Kenya and prepare his thesis at home." Henry told McKeon that it would take about a month to "get all the details settled." But he made it clear that "Harvard does not plan on having Obama registered as a full time student during the academic year 1964–1965."[33]

The letter that Henry sent Obama on May 27, 1964, got right to the point. Although Harvard had provided scholarship money for Obama during his first two years, it would no longer do so. Henry wrote that "neither the Department of Economics nor the Graduate School of Arts, Letters, and Sciences has any further funds to support you in Cambridge. . . . We have, therefore, come to the conclusion that you should terminate your stay in the United States and return to Kenya to carry on your research and the writing of your thesis."[34] The letter was copied to R. H. Phelps, Associate Dean of the Graduate School, and John Dunlop, chairman of the Economics Department, the two men apparently complicit in the decision.

Obama was furious. With Harvard's withdrawal of support, the INS decided not to grant him an extension of his stay. Instead, Obama was abruptly informed that he must leave the country within thirty days. Frantic, Obama called the INS office and demanded he be told the specific reason for the denial of his request for an extension. An immigration officer told him firmly that the matter had been thoroughly reviewed and that his application had been denied based on Henry's letter. Despite Obama's repeated request for more information, the officer told him "that the decision made in his case was FINAL," according to an internal memo.[35] Obama called repeatedly, but he was unable to get anyone to explain what had happened.

Harvard's decision was disastrous for Obama. Over the past five years he had worked determinedly toward a single, overarching goal. He had left his country at its most critical historic juncture and repeatedly put aside family and personal concerns in order to obtain the PhD that would serve as the cornerstone of his life's achievement. In passing all his exams alone, he had attained heights that had eluded countless others. But now he had been abruptly kicked out of Harvard and ordered to leave the country without so much as a chance to appeal.

As Obama wrestled with immigration authorities, however, one thing lightened his burden immeasurably. Her name was Ruth Beatrice Baker. A tall twenty-seven-year-old with a crown of wavy blonde hair, Ruth had graduated from Simmons College in Boston several years earlier with a major in business and had a good head for numbers. A large-boned woman and the daughter of a Jewish salesman, Ruth had a tentative manner that bordered on shyness. But bored with several years of secretarial work and less than enthusiastic about her current job teaching elementary students, she was open to something different when she met Obama, wearing his crisp white shirt and pressed gabardine pants as he was bumping out a rhumba at a festive summer party of Nigerians. Ruth was swept into the gyrating line of dancers, and the attraction between them was instantaneous. This was different, all right. This was about as different as it got. The following day Obama came knocking at her door and asked her for a date.[36]

Over the next month they carried on a passionate affair. They went dancing at the hottest clubs around Cambridge. They spent languid summer afternoons in his apartment and ambled the banks of the Charles River. And slowly, Ruth Baker—an insecure Newton girl who had been a member of the Brookline High School's honor society in her graduating class of 1954 and an honor board representative in college, a girl who had always obligingly done what was expected of her—did the unexpected. She fell in love with an African man.

Although an enthusiastic lover, Obama was distracted by his battle with Harvard. With his orals and written exams now behind him, Obama was eager to get his dissertation launched. His topic, "An Econometric Model of Staple Theory of Development,"[37] would not only be germane to the agricultural issues now being debated in Kenya, but it would also allow him to practice the econometric skills he had so painstakingly learned at school. Obama telephoned the immigration office repeatedly in an effort to get it to reverse its decision, but neither INS nor Harvard would yield. Unwilling to abandon his dream of earning a Harvard PhD, Obama stalled and said he did not have enough money for an airplane ticket home. When INS insisted that he go, Obama came up with the funds and bought a one-way ticket to Kenya in early July. As he said a passionate farewell to a moist-eyed Ruth, he urged her to come visit him in Kenya. "Come," he whispered, kissing her hard. "We'll get married," he added. And she heard him.

Ruth knew that Obama had two young children back in Nairobi. He had told her that she would need to take care of them if she joined him. But she did not know then that Obama also had a toddler son in Hawaii or that he had made the same invitation to other girls he had met in the United States. All that would come later. What she knew was that the life that yawned before her in Boston seemed flat and uninteresting, a life of nine-to-five jobs and phones that did not ring and nights alone in front of the television set. So she considered what Obama had said. She weighed the pros and cons with her closest girlfriends. She tentatively mentioned it to her parents, who, horrified, contacted the INS and begged them to stop her.[38] In the end Ruth, who had not only never been outside the United States but who had also never before flown on an airplane, decided to follow her lover to Africa.

"I was in love with a capital L and that was it," she declared. "I knew that I did not have the strength to make something of myself in America, to make myself someone special. So, I thought if I went to Africa my life would turn out differently."

She was right. It did.

7

THE NAIROBI MEN

When Barack Obama returned to Nairobi, he found his homeland almost unrecognizable. In the five years that he had been gone, Kenya had been transformed from a beleaguered colony choked by imperial regulations and restrictions into a proudly independent nation churning with excitement as the transfer of political and financial power into African hands was finalized.

As Obama had foreseen, the Lancaster House conference of 1960 in London had proved to be a pivotal juncture in the country's march toward freedom. British authorities had stunned the Kenyan negotiating team with the announcement that they were abandoning their gradual plan of decolonization and intended instead to promulgate internal self-government and move swiftly toward independence. The White Man's Country was to be white no more.

The following year Jomo Kenyatta was released from detention and declared president of the Kenya African National Union (KANU), one of the two dominant political parties that would briefly wrestle for control in the country's first year of nationhood. In a series of conferences in London over the next two years, British and Kenyan negotiators gradually hammered out an independence constitution that was designed to establish a central governing authority as it also attempted to prevent the domination of any one regional or ethnic group. As the government began a gradual process of moving impoverished African families onto estates once owned by whites, many settlers who felt betrayed at the decisions being made back in London began to flee.

At midnight on December 12, 1963, just eight months before Obama returned, the transfer of power became official. Standing next to Prime Minister Kenyatta, the Duke of Edinburgh and Governor Malcolm MacDonald watched as the Union Jack was pulled down and the black, red, and green flag of Kenya was hoisted overhead to wild cheering and song. As more than half a century of colonial rule came to an end, thousands of Kenyans celebrated with dancing and fireworks that lasted until dawn. *Uhuru*, at last.

Kenyatta would embrace many of the principles of British rule, such as economic growth and privatization of land, but he also endorsed a number of highly symbolic changes that would gradually recast the face of the nation. The hated signs, for one thing, had to go immediately. Those signs, declaring, "No Africans or Dogs Allowed," had long hung at the doorways of many of the city's finest hotels and restaurants. But now they were nowhere to be seen. After six decades of being excluded from whites-only establishments, Africans were now permitted to pull up a chair at the table. The elegant housing estates to the west of the city center, once the exclusive province of the wealthiest colonists, were slowly dropping the color bar. Even the toniest social clubs, such iconic British retreats as the Muthaiga Club and the Nairobi Club, were grudgingly cracking their doors to admit a handful of the new African elite. And resentful settlers who had once named their dogs Kenyatta or Odinga now faced penalties for their insolence.

Even the city's streets were hard to recognize. As Nairobi had grown from a barely inhabited swampy outback to a modern metropolis bustling with human traffic, the imperial government had carved its identity on the city's soul with a series of street and place names that memorialized its own illustrious history. One of the first things that the uhuru leaders did in the wake of independence was to eliminate those names, peeling them off the city's face like a mottled scab, making way for the fresh, new skin underneath. The broad boulevard that splices the city's heart, long known as Delamere Avenue, was rechristened Kenyatta Avenue. The intersecting crossroad of Princess Elizabeth Way became Uhuru Highway, and Connaught Road was transformed into Parliament Road. Coronation Avenue, a tree-lined thoroughfare framed by some of the county's most important government offices, was crowned Harambee Avenue. So confusing were some of the changes even to those who had not been away from the city for years that the *Daily Nation* newspaper published a guide to the new street names, proclaiming, "There's no need to get lost!"[1]

When Obama stepped back on Kenyan soil in August of 1964, Kenyatta had already managed through the deft use of a series of constitutional amendments to eliminate some of the checks on his authority and was preparing to go even further in strengthening his political power base. In that same month he announced his intention to replace the constitution with a presidential republic, a structure that would provide him with sweeping executive powers. Less obvious, he had also made critical progress in vanquishing his political opposition and cementing the one-party structure that would enable him to rule nearly unchallenged for close to fifteen years. By the end of the year the Kenya African Democratic Union (KADU), which had formed in large part to counterbalance just such a highly centralized government, saw many of its members defect to Kenyatta's dominant KANU in response to the amendments and some political arm twisting. KADU ultimately disbanded. When the country celebrated the first anniversary of independence in December 1964, Kenyatta was named president of the new republic. He was the undisputed head not only of the nation and the new government but also of the dominant political party.

The next task was to put Africans in positions of power that whites had long dominated. "Africanization" was the mantra of the day, a potent slogan that Kenyatta had employed when promising to return the country to its people. What it meant was that the country's institutions—its economy, industry, and political structure—would be reclaimed from Europeans and Africans installed into every aspect of national life. At least that was the idea.

Obama was swept up into a surge of young men and women who returned from schooling overseas and were confronted with the task of creating a nation of their own. Although it would take years to alter some of the social and economic structures that were colonial legacies, thousands of the 56,000 Europeans who were in the country at the time of independence had already fled, apprehensive about how the new government might treat them. So too did a large portion of city's nearly 177,000 Asians, who had long dominated the local business scene.[2] It was an intoxicating moment, a time when seemingly only the breadth of one's ambition limited one's possibilities. With thousands of jobs in civil service and private industry that needed to be filled and only an estimated 600 Kenyans with college degrees from overseas qualified to fill them, getting a job was largely a matter of showing up.[3] "You could literally choose what job you wanted," recalled Hilary Ng'weno, a Harvard graduate from the class of '61 who was appointed the first Kenyan editor of the *Daily Nation* and later launched a journal of political news and analysis called the *Weekly Review*. "It was tremendously exciting and for any educated person particularly so."

Within weeks of his return, Obama landed a post as a management trainee in the finance department of Shell/BP on Harambee Avenue. Although Obama envisioned himself as a government economist, the Shell job was a plum opportunity that would provide him the kind of basic training he needed to assume a government post. Obama was one of many young Africans striding down the company's black linoleum floors, and within months he was promoted to the post of management accountant. His job was to provide financial reports on the company's performance and its information systems.[4] In the haste to "Africanize" in the post-independence years—or at least to appear to endorse that process—many corporations positioned Africans in jobs for which they were ill-prepared and would later be accused of using them as window dressing while giving them work of little substance. Shell's Nairobi office, however, had promoted a number of able Africans early on and was regarded as being largely cooperative in the process of nationalization.

For those blessed with a college degree, the possibilities were profound. Flush with the salaries their newfound corporate and civil service positions provided, many young Africans found their lives transformed. With directives from then Minister for Home Affairs Oginga Odinga lifting the color bar at many downtown establishments, many young professionals adopted an upscale urban lifestyle unimaginable in the Kenya of their youth. They drove elegant cars with thick white-walled tires. Their favorite vehicle of the day was the plump Peugeot 403 saloon car, nicknamed the "Nization" in honor of the Africanization of the roads. They shopped at the fine clothing stores on Government Road, where the shelves were heavy with lush Oriental silks and Egyptian cottons. And they clinked glasses of fine amber whiskey at the New Stanley and the Norfolk, two of the city's premiere hotels that had long refused them. So palpable was the change in the very feel of the city that one young British man teaching in Dar es Salaam was moved to ask a cab driver to what he attributed the lighter mood. "The driver said, 'Well, that's easy,'" recalled John M. Lonsdale, who later would become a professor of Modern African History at the University of Cambridge in England. "'You no longer call us baboons.'"

Nowhere did the members of this new urban tribe have a greater impact than when they left the capital. For when they wheeled their sleek automobiles down the dusty roads of their ancestral homes, where a car itself was an astonishing sight, the villagers gaped with open mouths. "We called them the Nairobi men," sighed Manasseh Oyucho, the principal of the Senator Barack Obama Primary School in Kogelo, still impressed by the memory. "They spoke English and they wore suits and they had beautiful cars. They were working in groups of very smart people and we all wanted to be just like them. We wanted to be just like Obama."

With college and immigration officials no longer keeping an eye on his doings, Obama reveled in the city's burgeoning social life as never before. Even among the Nairobi men, Obama stood out. Dressed in elegant silk ties and tailored suits from Peermohammed, one of the city's finest clothing shops, Obama was careful that no upcountry dust dull his perennially polished shoes. The Sportsman cigarettes of the old days had been replaced with the more refined Benson and Hedges, and Johnnie Walker Black was now his drink of choice. Obama made it no secret that he preferred the company of educated men, and he referred to those he considered inferior as "intellectual dwarfs," only partly in jest. If one dared to speak Swahili in his company, a swift reprimand would often be forthcoming. Only English—and proper English at that—would do. "You had to meet certain criteria," recalled Obama's childhood friend Peter Aringo, a former member of Parliament who served six terms. "Obama wanted you to rise up to his standards."

Obama's legendary baritone was now colored by his American years, a fact that elevated his status at the same time as made it difficult for some back home to understand his new accent. But his Luo grounding was as deep as ever, despite his elaborate airs and Western ways. On coming upon his Luo friends in the city, Obama would often greet them fondly with Luo nicknames, and he was a loyal supporter of several welfare societies supporting schools and causes back in Kogelo. As tribal divisions soon became manifest in ongoing political debates over the country's direction, Obama embraced his Luo roots ever more fiercely. "*Wuod Akumu N'yar Njoga*," or "the son of Akumu, the daughter of Njoga, we'd hail him when he showed up," recalled Wilson Ndolo Ayah, who received a master's degree from the University of Wisconsin and was a businessman who would go on to hold several high-ranking ministerial posts. "'What are you having to drink?' '*Jobungu*,' Obama would jokingly call back, using the Luo term for 'bushmen.' 'You must be paying then, I see.'"

Plunging into conversations about the latest government proclamation or political promotion, Obama often found a way to refer to his Harvard training. He insisted on being called *Dr.* Obama, despite his incomplete dissertation. Few were aware that Obama was a Dr. in his imagination alone. Anyway, it was more than sufficient that he had any Harvard degree at all. Only a handful of Kenyans could claim such a distinction, and Obama played it frequently, demanding, "Where were you when I was getting my training at *Harvard*?" He was, as Aringo recalls it, "the big voice from Harvard and he let everyone know that."

When he arrived at the dim bar at Brunner's Hotel or pulled up a chair at the trendy Sans Chique, where he was a regular, he routinely trumpeted his standard order. "A double round of *scotch*," he would say, lingering over a word he seemed to relish. He would then promptly order a chaser of another round of the same—two more shots of scotch. And thus did Obama earn himself the nickname, "Double-Double."[5] Even in Nairobi's hard-drinking culture of the time, Obama was at the head of the pack in his alcoholic intake. By the count of some of his bar mates, Obama could down four "double-doubles"—or sixteen shots—at a sitting and still walk out of the bar. Never a big eater, Obama would reluctantly put down his glass for a plate of ugali and roasted meat or, one of his preferred dishes, *sukuma wiki*, a mix of leafy greens and tomatoes. "We drank quite often together and we went home not in a very nice condition. Sometimes he had trouble getting home at all," recalled Philip Ochieng, then a columnist for the *Nation*. "Barack was always outspoken, very jocular. He liked people. But he was a lot about himself. He was arrogant but it was a very seductive arrogance. Not unpleasant at all. He had big ambitions, big unrealistic dreams. He just needed to dominate and that is what caused so many problems for him."

Obama did not join many of the private clubs in town, even those established expressly for the new urban elite such as the African Club, reserved for senior African civil servants, or the United Kenya Club, which had been founded as a multiracial club nearly two decades earlier. But he often dropped in to visit with his many colleagues, such as Fred Okatcha, a former board member at the UKC who had encountered Obama several times in New York during their college days. Obama never hesitated to speak his mind. "He was not a typical man," said Okatcha. "If you didn't know what you were talking about he would say so right to your face. He'd say, 'Man, you have no idea what you are saying.' If someone didn't know him, they might get annoyed or buy him another drink to placate him, but usually that only made it worse. But if you knew him, you knew that was just the way he was."

Once at a cocktail party of Europeans and well-to-do Africans, Obama happened to overhear an American professor commenting on Kenya's political situation. Not liking what he heard, "Barack went right up to him and said, 'You are ignorant on that subject and you should not talk about such a thing until you understand,'" recalled his friend Otieno O. Wasonga, a family friend who'd known Obama in Cambridge. "Well, it was probably the first time that professor had heard such a thing. But Barack would be the first to tell you to your face that you didn't have it right. He'd say, 'Take this fact and maybe it will improve your knowledge on the subject.'"

He was no less reluctant to point out the errors of his superiors in front of others. Obama, ever sure of his position, would marshal his evidence, quote a scholar or two, and declare the person flat out in the wrong, seemingly unaware that he was embarrassing or humiliating them. "You know, he was just being Barack, just being bold," said Arthur Reuben Owino, who attended the Ng'iya School with Obama and worked as a government information officer. "He didn't realize that someone in a high position might be very embarrassed at being corrected in such a way. After he'd said such things, he'd laugh and laugh and offer to buy everyone a drink. Most people you know they just thought, well, that's just Barack."

For some, the newly minted Obama was an acquired taste. Like many African men of the time, he did not traffic much in personal talk. Only a handful of his closest associates knew of his son in Hawaii or much about his children back in Kogelo. Although he craved social interaction, he held himself apart, as though unwilling to be known or to know too much. It was as though the booming interrogations and prideful claims were intended to set a listener back, to keep him from coming too close. But those who understood Obama's style knew that the thumping bravado and interrogatory dialogue was his particular way of engaging. And once the cross-examination was done, there were drinks for all. Obama was famously generous at the bar, and he frequently ordered rounds for everyone to be put on his tab, even in later years when he could ill-afford to do so. His favorite barroom prank was to send his bill to someone else at the bar, particularly if he spotted someone of high rank. Obama took particular pleasure in sending his tabs to Tom Mboya himself or to Mwai Kibaki. That his targets paid up was a good measure of the tolerant fondness with which many regarded him.

The city's beckoning barrooms were not the only new development that won Obama's attention. He was equally smitten with the sleek sedans cruising the city's streets, often available for bargain prices from departing colonists eager to shed their belongings. For a while after he returned, Obama proudly ferried a large green Mercedes from his Rosslyn home to Shell's downtown offices. Ed Benjamin, a Boston lawyer who had been impressed by Obama's sophisticated repartee when he met him at a Cambridge cocktail party in the spring of 1964, wound up in Nairobi on a business trip not long after Obama returned to Kenya. When Benjamin called him on the phone from his room in the posh New Stanley hotel, Obama promptly offered to give him a tour of the city. "He said he would be by in an hour and to look for him in a brand new Mercedes," recalled Benjamin. "He was obviously quite proud of that car. He drove us around, showed us the sights and told us where to have dinner. He was very gracious. Very charming. He was obviously an extremely bright and elegant guy."

But Obama's far more impressive vehicle was a huge blue Ford Fairlane emblazoned with wide, white racing stripes running down the sides. A few young boys who encountered that car decades ago still remember it vividly today. Taa O. Pala was ten years old when he and his older brother,

Francis, who was a friend of Obama's, nearly ran into the car on a sunny afternoon in 1966 as it swung around a corner just outside Kisumu. The elder Pala and Obama, who had not seen one another for years, each jumped from their vehicles and ran to greet one another. "I still remember that incredible car. I had really never seen anything like it in my life," recalled Pala, who would later become a captain with Rwanda Air. "Obama got out of the car smoking his pipe and then he reached into the car and pulled out a couple of cold beers and a pair of glasses. He put them on the bonnet and the two of them were talking and drinking. I mean, he was driving around with a bar in this incredible car. I was completely impressed. I think I remember it partly because it looked so much like a plane and I knew then I wanted to be a pilot."

Erastus Amondi Okul, a cousin of Obama's, was several years older than Pala when he first saw the car, but even at seventeen he was stunned when the vast blue machine purred into Kendu Bay. A grinning Obama swung open the passenger door and beckoned to several giggling children to jump in. That was the first time Okul had ever ridden in a car. "It was like an airplane! It flew," exclaimed Okul. "And when we got inside, it had air conditioning. I could not even imagine such a thing. He always encouraged us to go to school and on this day he said, 'If you do not go to school you cannot drive a car like this.' We all decided we would go to school just like Dr. Obama."

On his return to the villages of his childhood, Obama came laden with gifts. There was colored fabric, bags of potatoes and guavas, and, for the luckiest child of all, a pair of shoes. In the eyes of the villagers, Obama was one of the biggest men around, and they anticipated his visits with excitement. His message was always the same. "He always, always talked about education, that was the thing he valued most of all," said Ezra Obama, a first cousin whose own education Obama paid for in large part. "Later he would tell me, the best thing you can do for your children is get them an education. Don't save the money for them for later. Get them an education. If you give them that, you've given them everything."

And then the bird from Kanyadhiang, the *winyo* who had flown so high that he had obtained a Harvard degree and a car more magnificent than a jet airplane, added something even more stunning to his list of achievements. He was going to have a *mzungu* wife. Obama may not have entirely expected that his Cambridge girlfriend would follow him to Kenya, but only five weeks after he left Cambridge, Ruth Baker made up her mind to take him up on the invitation that he had laid before her.

Her decision was a most improbable act of faith. Since graduating from Simmons College as a business major in 1958, Ruth had trod a conventional path. As befitted her role as member of the school's honor board, she had always been keen on doing the right thing—or at least trying to figure out what that was. She had worked as a legal assistant for a Boston lawyer for a couple of years and then tried her hand teaching the sixth grade in a suburban school. A tall young woman with a straightforward manner, "Ruthie" was not a particularly adventurous sort as far as her friends were concerned. But she was nothing if not determined. Her doting parents in nearby Newton kept a close eye on their well-mannered daughter who lived with some girlfriends on tony Beacon Hill. And although she embarked on a number of blind dates, Ruth was neither a dreamer nor a romantic. And so when Ruth announced to her elementary school friend Judy Epstein that she was considering following her African lover to Nairobi, Epstein was shocked. But Epstein was just as much taken aback by Ruth's matter-of-fact manner. "She was very much in love with him, but she was pretty businesslike about it all," said Epstein. "She was thinking of going to Nairobi to check it out and see if she wanted to marry him. It was pretty factual."

Ignoring her parents' urgent remonstrations, Ruth packed a small bag of essentials. She could not stop thinking about Obama and the way he talked in such bold, declarative sentences, as though he knew exactly what was what. To a young woman struggling to find her way, his authority was as seductive as his full-lipped smile. "The truth was I had no self-esteem," Ruth said later. "People did not know that but I did not have the self-confidence I should have. And I was very innocent because I had led a very conservative life. Obama was just the opposite. He seemed to be very confident and he was very, very charming." At the end of her long solitary flight to Nairobi, Ruth walked expectantly into the waiting area of the Embakasi Airport, searching for her lover's face in the crowd. Obama was not there. Ruth took a deep breath and began to wander through the airport asking if anyone knew of a Barack Obama. Many people did, as Obama's name was widely known. A Luo woman took her hand and drove her to her house where they called Obama on the phone. He appeared, ebullient, an hour later. But it was not an auspicious beginning. "You know, I am not supersensitive so I was not hurt," said Ruth. "I probably thought what's wrong here, you know? But then he came and we were together. So, it didn't matter."

Obama was immensely proud of his bride-to-be. *Mzungu* wives were still rare, and in general only those of advanced education and means could claim such a trophy. He took her around town and dropped in on some of his most prominent associates to show her off. Visiting his old Kendu Bay friend Samuel O. Ayodo, a member of Mboya's inner circle who served as Minister of Natural Resources and Wildlife, Obama clapped him on the back and excitedly insisted, "'Tell Ruth that my father is a *king* and my family is very, *very* important.' We just laughed," recalled Ayodo's widow, Damaris Ayodo. "He really wanted to impress her."[6]

He also wanted to use her to impress other people. As with his Harvard degree, Obama did not hesitate to brandish his pretty white wife with the Boston accent. At times Obama jokingly refused to let a friend pull up a stool next to him at a bar, saying, "You can't sit next to me. Don't you know that I'm married to a *mzungu*, you stupid African." And when he encountered a colleague who was married to a white woman, Obama would throw his arm around his shoulders, exclaiming that he was "my in-law."[7]

Obama eventually took Ruth to the village that he considered home. Together, they drove the hundreds of kilometers from Nairobi to Kanyadhiang, past fields of maize and millet and scrub dotted with the traditional Luo homesteads of thatched dwellings and finally around the gentle curve of the Winam Gulf into Nyanza province. As Obama's azure automobile glided into the village amidst a cluster of scrappy huts, a crowd of dozens of Obama relatives peered excitedly into the car window eager for a glimpse. Men and women alike watched intently as the passenger door swung open, anxious to catch the first glimpse of the lady's legs. If her legs were small, she would surely have small, possibly weak children. But if her legs were big, she would deliver strong and robust offspring, or so the local wisdom would have it. Fortunately, Ruth's legs easily made the grade. "Ruth had the most beautiful legs of any white woman anywhere," declared Charles Oluoch, Obama's cousin. "People in the village still talk about them."[8]

With her direct manner and broad smile, Ruth won the villagers over easily. There is a black-and-white photograph of that day, a cherished family possession, perched on Oluoch's mantel. It shows a line of grinning Obama relatives posing in front of the dashing Fairlane with Obama and Ruth, who is wearing a short summer shift with her blonde hair cropped close as she is standing in the middle. But if Obama's family was impressed by her calves and her warmth, they had only seen the half of it. Sometime later, when Obama and Ruth visited Kogelo, the time came when some water was needed for cooking. It was Ruth herself, a *mzungu* with a college degree, who took the pot and headed down to the River Awach to collect it. Many in the village still shake their head at the memory. "He came and dragged me to his house so I could meet his white wife. He wanted to show me how he could talk to the white lady," said Dora Mumbo, ninety-two, a retired teacher from the Nyang'oma Primary School. "He was so proud of her. When I asked Barack why he had married her, he said she had agreed to cook for him. She agreed to so many things. She was a real lady that she could take that pot to the river and get water."

The couple moved into a stately home in Rosslyn, a predominantly white neighborhood in Nairobi that was lush with sprawling purple jacaranda trees and trim green hedges. Like many of the spacious estates located northwest of the city, Rosslyn had long been the exclusive province of Europeans. Now a handful of Africans were trickling in. Not all family members were so pleased with Obama's new domestic situation, however. Hussein Onyango stormed into the house one morning and adamantly insisted that Obama take his first wife Kezia into his home along with their two children. If his son could not respect his first wife in such a way, then at least he could establish a separate home for her as any good Luo would do.[9]

But Obama refused. Obama was an educated man now, and though he was eager to have his children join him, he told his friends he had no intention of living "like an African" with multiple wives at a time.[10] Although Ruth agreed to have the children live with them, as she had promised Obama she would back in Cambridge, she was horrified at the notion that his first wife would join them as well. She would just as soon not meet Kezia at all. But the proposal was only one of many aspects of life in Nairobi that she was finding difficult, as did more than a few other white women who had met their African husbands in the West.

These young women were quickly learning that husbands who had seemed highly Westernized back home soon reverted to deeply ingrained tribal customs when back on African soil. Kenyan men generally went out drinking at bars or nightclubs without their wives and were absent for long periods of time. They did little in the way of domestic chores, and many presumed broad sexual freedoms, taking mistresses or even second wives as due course. Young women, who had expected a position of some respect in their new marriages, suddenly found that they had quite lowly status. As Celia Nyamweru, a young British graduate student doing field research in Kenya in the mid-1960s, wrote in an essay on her experiences, "Often these young women received fairly rude awakenings when marital relationships that had started happily between graduate students or young professionals had to be renegotiated under circumstances where most of the power lay on the husband's side."[11]

Helga Kagumba, who met her Luo husband at Case Western Reserve University in Cleveland, Ohio, before moving to Nairobi, puts it more bluntly. "For some of the white woman here, it was hell," declared Kagumba, who socialized with Obama in the early 1970s and later moved to Achego with her husband. "You were not equal here. You were a commodity, a second-class citizen. You were not to ask your husband where he is going. So for a lot of the foreign wives who came here it was a disaster. When their husbands took other women, their marriages ended and they fled. We tried to help them, driving them to the airport and getting them fake passports so they could get out. They were afraid their husbands would track them down and kill them."

These young wives also ran headlong into the African tradition of extended families. Now that they were flush with a big job and a Nairobi home, many of the new African elite in Nairobi found a succession of siblings, cousins, and acquaintances showing up at their door, sometimes planning to stay for long periods. So it was in Obama's various households. His children, then called Roy and Rita, moved in soon after he returned. His sister Zeituni and cousin Ezra would live with the couple periodically while they attended schools in the city. Later, his mother's son from another marriage would move in. At the same time, a succession of other family members dropped in for shorter durations, many of whom Ruth could not begin to identify.

Nor were these young wives the only ones who found the situation stressful. For the Kenyan men, the demands of their new lives were also profound. On the one hand, they were urban professionals under pressure to provide for a vast extended network of family members back home who still had very little. But they were also still deeply rooted in the culture and ways of the bush, and what their role was in either locale or exactly how to bridge the gap was not always clear. Were they Kenyan villagers or downtown professionals? With one foot firmly placed in Luoland and another on Harambee Avenue, Obama in particular struggled to find his balance. Of the pressures facing this new and somewhat dislocated class of Kenyans, Andrew Hake, author of *African Metropolis: Nairobi's Self-Help City*, wrote, "It is no wonder that there were some, living lives of insecurity and tension, heavily mortgaged and uncertain which of their friends they could trust, who succumbed in one way or another to such intense stress."[12]

In their first few months together Obama and Ruth lived much as they had in Cambridge. Ruth got a job as a secretary at the *Nation* newspaper while Obama applied his new econometric skills to the job at Shell. After work, they often went dancing at the new Starlight nightclub, the city's hotspot, featuring Congolese music and an eclectic crowd reflecting Nairobi's increasingly diverse population. Well aware that his moves were electrifying, Obama could not resist twirling Ruth extravagantly across the center of the dance floor as a small crowd clapped in appreciation. Some nights the couple danced until the early hours of the following morning. So bleary-eyed was Ruth by the time she got to work that her bosses let her go after only three months. "We were out all night so I wasn't getting any sleep," sighed Ruth. "I was exhausted. Oh, God, I was in a mess you know. I could not focus on anything."

However, Ruth began quite quickly to notice changes in Obama. Some nights he drank so much he could barely make it to the car and Ruth was afraid to let him drive them home. As he worked increasingly long hours, he often did not come home from work until well after midnight, stumbling to the door reeking of whiskey and perfume. At times he shouted at her with rage, calling her slow and stupid. And one night he astonished her with the news that he not only had been married a second time, but had a young son in Hawaii. "He just said he had a little son there and he was very proud of him," said Ruth. "He had a little picture of him on his tricycle with a hat on his head. And he kept that picture in every house that we lived in. He loved his son. He never mentioned the wife, though. I knew nothing about her. But none of that bothered me. As I said, I was in love with a capital 'L' and that was that. I didn't know anything about anything."

Despite Ruth's growing misgivings and Obama's own ambivalence, which he shared only with a handful of friends, the couple decided to get married by the end of the year. Propelled by the turbulent currents of their love affair, for either one of them to turn back would have been difficult. Ruth could hardly face returning to America and the failure that would have signified. Nor could Obama easily surrender the wife who had given him such cachet. And, in at least some respects, they still shared the intense passion that had consumed them back in Cambridge. So on Christmas Eve of 1964 they stood before a justice of the peace in the city registrar's office as two of their friends looked on.[13] The service was strictly bare bones. There was no ring, no gifts. As she reached out to take Obama's hand before the ceremony began, Ruth hesitated for an instant. "I was thinking should I *really* marry this guy?" recalled Ruth. "I mean, how long was this going to last? I just had a feeling it was risky. But, you know, I went ahead with it."

AS THE OBAMAS BEGAN THEIR NEW LIFE together in the opening days of 1965, so Kenya also entered a critical new phase of development. Obama rode roughshod into both experiences. Within months he had thrust himself into the turbulent political debate of the day and assumed a public position that would put him at odds with the prevailing political powers for the better part of his career.

During the first year of independence Jomo Kenyatta had devoted himself primarily to centralizing his powers and ensuring that any potential political challenge was neutralized. The first Cabinet, dominated by Kikuyus and several of Kenyatta's own family members, had been put into place, which would color Kenyan politics for generations.[14] Although the popular Luo leader Oginga Odinga had been appointed vice president of the new republic, the post had been deliberately defined with severely limited powers that muted his ability to challenge the president or his policies. With the inauguration of the Republic on December 12, 1964, and the appointment of Kenyatta as president, Kenya's founding father had firmly asserted his personal authority by establishing a centralized executive authority, and this set the stage for his political dominance for years to come.

Almost as important as the political shape of the new nation was its economic mooring. In his conversations with the departing British administrators during the days leading up to the declaration of the republic, Kenyatta had already committed himself to a mixed economy that would leave many aspects of the European-established infrastructure largely unchanged. Growth rather than redistribution was his priority, as was the maintenance of ties with foreign investors and multinational corporations.[15] The African nationalists had also already endorsed the controversial notion of extending private land titles begun during the colonial era, continuing a shift from the African tradition of communal property holding.[16] The ongoing process of Africanization called for the installation of African employees throughout business and government and also the eventual shift in ownership of the nation's assets into the hands of Africans through a steady process of growth. But the question of exactly whose hands would control those assets was not settled. To resolve some of these issues and to implement the economic program he had in mind, Kenyatta turned to a core group of his highest-ranking deputies under the guidance of a lingering expatriate community.

The beating heart of the process was the new Ministry for Economic Planning and Development (MEPD) housed in the beige four-story Treasury Building on Harambee Avenue. Development planning—the notion that an infusion of resources paired with a workable program could provide self-sustaining growth—was all the rage in the underdeveloped world and in the West. Kenyatta had appointed Tom Mboya to be the office's new minister along with Mwai Kibaki as his deputy. Some speculated that Kenyatta, ever wary of Mboya's widespread political base, had given him the MEPD rather than a more prominent post such as the vice presidency or Ministry of Finance to undercut the power of his potential rival. But Mboya accepted the position with enthusiasm. As he saw it, the job presented an opportunity to shape the country's economic structure and to deal head on with some of the thorny issues of land allocation and foreign investment that some left-leaning members of the KANU party were beginning to question.[17]

In the opinion of many of the young economists fresh back from their overseas training, the MEPD was the place to be. Imbued with Mboya's intelligence and zeal, the Ministry operated far more efficiently than most other government agencies and attracted a cadre of highly trained economists and planners. Many of them were deeply passionate and committed to their homeland's potential for development, and they considered themselves a united force. Years later some of that close-knit club of junior economists, who have since gone gray, would fondly refer to the tired corridors of the MEPD as "home." In the final weeks of 1964 that team was being carefully assembled.

On a warm morning in December a genial Vermonter named Edgar O. Edwards sat in his second-floor office heavily scented by the scarlet bougainvillea just outside his window as he perused the résumé of a young economist he was about to interview for the job of planning officer. A professor at Rice University in Texas under contract with the Ford Foundation, Edwards was one of a number of expatriates who had been hired to provide technical and management expertise in the formative period of the *uhuru* government. Edwards was a sharp-minded economist, and due to his extremely close relationship with Mboya, he had been granted a wide range of responsibilities, including hiring.

Edwards liked what he read. The candidate, Barack Obama, had done graduate work at Harvard University and now worked at Shell/BP, just a few doors down the street. One of the outgoing British managers had recommended Obama to Edwards for a planner's job and, given the Ministry's sweeping mission, it was precisely the kind of job that Obama had long dreamed about.

When Obama arrived a few minutes later, Edwards was even more taken in. Not only was Obama well versed in econometrics and economic modeling, both of which the Ministry keenly needed, he was impeccably turned out in an elegantly cut suit and a royal blue silk tie. The only problem was that Edwards already had someone else in mind for the job, another young economist whom he had met at a wedding recently named

Philip Ndegwa. A graduate of Alliance High School and Makerere University, Ndegwa was a versatile and soft-spoken Kikuyu who had already been pegged for advancement by Kenyatta's inner circle. Edwards had no idea that the two men knew one another and decided to offer both of them a job as senior planning officers. In time, he reasoned, one of them would surely rise to the chief planning officer's job, which would also soon be available. "Obama was an impressive guy, no doubt about it," Edwards recalled in an interview in his home in Poultney, Vermont. "So I told him he could start as a planning officer and it was possible in six months or so we could make a decision about something more."

Obama was miffed. Here he was, up against Ndegwa already, a man *he* had helped to educate himself. But Obama restrained himself and said nothing about his rival; instead, he argued that he was well qualified for the chief planning officer's job and asked for that position instead. "He was adamant that he was up to the post," sighed Edwards. "But I did not feel I knew him well enough to give it to him. I gave him time to think about the planner's job, but in the end he turned it down."

A few days later Obama ran into Francis Masakhalia, his old Maseno School friend who had recently accepted a job with the Ministry himself, and he angrily railed against Edwards's offer. The specter of Ndegwa was only part of it. The job came with a salary of 2,000 Kenyan shillings. Masakhalia had accepted a position as an economist statistician at the same rate of pay, which he thought very reasonable. But Obama insisted it was not enough. "He said, 'They are paying *peanuts*. I am not going to take it,'" recalled Masakhalia. "He said, 'You bachelors, you don't know what it's like.' And we said, 'You with your foreign women and children. You always need more money.'"

Then there was Ndegwa—always Ndegwa—a step and then a mile ahead. The truth was that Ndegwa's difficulties with math were only part of what galled Obama about his rival's success. Ndegwa was a circumspect man, ruminative and cautious in his outlook—all things that Obama distinctly was not. He too was married to a white woman. And Obama did not like him. His annoyance turned to outright anger when Ndegwa was eventually given the chief planner's job, and just three years later he was promoted to Permanent Secretary of the Ministry. Ndegwa was only thirty years old when he was awarded the post, usually reserved for far more senior men. In time Ndegwa would hold some of the most prominent positions in Kenya's government and business arenas and would advise the nation's political leadership for generations. With each successive step he took, Obama resented him more deeply.

Nor was Ndegwa particularly fond of Obama. Several close to Ndegwa felt that for all his success, he was self-conscious about his earlier difficulties with math and the fact that he did not get the Harvard degree he had set out to achieve. When Obama frequently pointed that out and publicly declared his superiority over the other man, this served only to widen the gap between them. "We all knew Obama had tutored Philip. We knew the problems Philip had because he was being pushed by his fellow Kikuyus for these big jobs," explained Masakhalia. "But Obama could not let it alone. Every chance he got, he would say, 'Philip knows nothing.' And Barack was not going to take a job where he might have to work under him."

Obama's encounter with the Ministry darkly presaged what was to come, for he would repeat the same laments time and again in coming years: The money was never enough, he was employed below his abilities, or those above him were out of their league. Among the close community of economists in Nairobi, Obama was well liked and deeply respected for his considerable skills, at least in the early years after independence. Many who started out at the MEPD would rise steadily in government, including Ndegwa, Masakhalia, and Kibaki, and they would all cross paths time and again. But some of the key players in this close-knit group were dismayed to see that Obama's attitude was causing serious problems in the workplace, and by the decade's end his troublesome reputation would become widespread. When his effrontery became so flagrant that Kenyatta himself took note, Obama's predicament became another matter altogether. Some who had worked with him would reach out to try to help him. Others did not.

Part of Obama's difficulties clearly stemmed from his own public posturing and brazen disregard for the rules in later years. But it is also true that within the political culture of the time, criticism of or dissent from the ruling powers was increasingly forbidden. In a more forgiving political era, Obama's bluntness might have been overlooked, thereby allowing his career to span a different arc. But it quickly became clear in the months after independence that critics could expect to be dealt with unsparingly. The first in a succession of political assassinations inscribed in the Kenyan history books was that of Pio Gama Pinto, a journalist and avowed communist who was gunned down in his own driveway in 1965. Pinto was closely aligned to Odinga, the spokesman for the opposition, and many believed his death was directly attributable to Kenyatta's men.

Obama's own collision with the Kenyatta government extended over the course of four years, a simmering confrontation that spiked over several key events. It was triggered by the government's celebrated blueprint for economic development, called "Sessional Paper No. 10, African Socialism and Its Application to Planning in Kenya." The document, released by Mboya's office in May of 1965, was a broad summary of the country's philosophical underpinnings and specific programmatic plans.

The paper was intended to address a growing cleavage within the KANU ranks between Kenyatta's conservative supporters and a more radical group critical of some of his economic plans, rallying around the left-leaning Odinga. Kenyatta had never been an advocate of radical economic change of any kind, and in the early days of the new government's formation he had swiftly emerged as a friend to both the British political establishment and its financial interests. Alarmed by government strategies that left much of the country's pre-independence framework untouched, the radicals called for a more public-minded approach to land and economic policy on a number of fronts. They wanted less dependence on foreign capital, a quick end to emerging class divisions, and a redistribution of land that was being amassed in the hands of an emerging propertied elite.

They also called for more rapid Africanization. But finding Africans qualified for the jobs that needed filling was a more complicated process than had been expected: Most Africans had virtually no business experience other than small-scale shops and even less in the sphere of management. Those Kenyans who had worked in the city in pre-independence days, such as Hussein Onyango, had been employed largely as house servants for Europeans, and the very idea of a nine-to-five office job or something called credit was novel. Because of this, a substantial expatriate community remained in control of key positions for many years after independence. Of 1,690 of the highest-ranking professional jobs in Nairobi surveyed by the government's Directorate of Personnel in 1967, Europeans still held two-thirds of them, and Africans occupied virtually all of the jobs at the lower end of the scale.[18] Obama and many other

Kenyans found the continuation of white control infuriating, and racial tension in the workplace was not uncommon during the several years of the transition.

But Kenyatta was tired of debate over the country's direction. Sessional Paper No. 10 was designed to nip it all in the bud. Though declaring the government in favor of neither capitalism nor communism, the paper called for a form of socialism that would draw on the best of African tradition while pursuing a vigorous path of economic growth. Shrouded in a rhetorical embrace of socioeconomic equality, the document nonetheless heartily embraced a free market economy and kept the door open to foreign investment. In a personal note introducing the paper, Kenyatta made crystal clear that far from encouraging discussion of such issues, the paper was intended to close the door on debate once and for all. "When all is said and done we must settle down to the job of building the Kenyan nation," Kenyatta wrote. "Let this paper be used from now as the unifying voice of our people and let us all settle down to build our nation."[19]

A few objected openly. Dharam Ghai, a lecturer at Makerere University with a PhD in economics who went on to become the director of the United Nations Research Institute for Social Development, wrote in the June 1965 issue of the *East Africa Journal* that the plan was unlikely to increase the African stake in the economy and that it would exacerbate emerging inequities in wealth.[20] But his criticisms were milquetoast compared to Obama's.

Obama's critique, published in the following month's issue of the *East Africa Journal*, derided its authors first for failing to adequately define African socialism. He then moved on to warn that the government's proposal largely perpetuated an existing economic system that left Kenya dependent on foreign capital and did little to resolve economic and class disparities that the colonial government fostered. He took particular issue with the paper's endorsement of land titles and privatization over the African system of communal ownership, writing, "It is surprising that one of the best African traditions is not only being put aside in this paper but even the principle is not being recognized and enhanced."[21]

But Obama by no means embraced communal ownership for tradition's sake alone nor did he employ stale African clichés. Instead, he argued for a novel approach to land consolidation through the creation of clan cooperatives that could provide for the equitable distribution of any gains while avoiding excessive concentration of economic power. Although he did not go into detail about how such cooperatives might work, what he proposed was a creative blending of the opposing economic principles that were under debate. Why could land not be used as an asset even if it was held in collective hands? However, if individual ownership was to be the chosen route, he insisted that the size of farms should be restricted in size. And in a provocative shot at Kenyatta himself, he added, "This should apply to everybody from the President to the ordinary man."[22]

Sessional Paper No. 10 states that the country has no class divisions such as those in European society. But Obama bluntly—and accurately—declared, "This is to ignore the truth of the matter. One wonders whether the authors of the paper have not noticed a discernible class structure has emerged in Africa and particularly in Kenya."[23]

Although Obama accepted that foreign capital was vital to the country's growth, he called loudly for a wider distribution of the nation's assets and a greater commitment to genuine Africanization. Noting that it was not Kenyans but rather Europeans and Asians who controlled the bulk of the country's commercial enterprises, Obama argued that the government should focus less on how the country's resources could be used to make profits and more on how they could benefit society at large. "We have to give the African his place in his own country and we have to give him his economic power if he is going to develop," declared Obama. "The paper talks of fear of retarding growth if nationalization or purchases of these enterprises are made for Africans. But for whom do we want to grow? Is it the African who owns this country? If he does, then why should he not control the economic means of growth in this country? It is mainly in this country that one finds almost everything owned by the non-indigenous populace. The government must do something about this and soon."[24]

In conclusion, Obama sarcastically praised the government for producing a paper at all. "Maybe," he wrote, "it is better to have something perfunctorily done than none at all!"[25]

It was a courageous piece of writing, a blunt appraisal of the government's capitalist orientation and a heartfelt appeal on behalf of the common man. In eight pages Obama attempted to respond to a major position paper drafted by dozens of experts and resolve the complex issues confronting underdeveloped economies. It was also an extraordinarily risky public stand on several fronts. In defending such socialist concepts as nationalization and land cooperatives, Obama had put himself squarely in the Odinga camp of radicals, which was in ever-increasing disfavor with the government. That he had even gone so far as to publicly question Kenyatta's considerable accumulation of land, however indirectly, meant that he was a marked man. The paper likely also threw a shadow over his relationship with Tom Mboya, who was responsible for drafting the paper. Although Obama was seeking to reach a compromise position, he was nonetheless critical of his friend's handiwork.

David William Cohen, a Kenya expert and professor emeritus of anthropology and history at the University of Michigan, wrote a March 2010 paper analyzing Obama's article in which he describes it as shrewd in its maneuvering among the dominant political personalities of the time—and also prescient. The article, he wrote, "makes an almost forgotten case for the African state (and for good governance, progressive taxation, and effective regulation of private investment). The 1965 article is an improbable yet extraordinarily acute rehearsal of the best critiques of structural adjustment (and its privileging of the private sector against the state) in the 1980s and 1990s and of the failures of unregulated capital in our present decade."[26]

Cohen suggested that far from just criticizing the government, Obama was trying to establish common ground between the two political giants of Odinga and Mboya. He added, "In a sense, this argument goes, Obama Sr. sought to remake the political craft of Odinga by borrowing from Mboya's political style, while restaging some of the positions familiarly associated with Odinga's leftwards agenda."[27]

Either way, Cohen, coauthor with E. S. Atieno Odhiambo of *The Risks of Knowledge: Investigations into the Death of the Hon. Minister John Robert Ouko in Kenya, 1990*, said that the article would have borne personal consequences for its author. "It was brave and it was futile. Those close to Mboya would have wanted to distance themselves from Obama while Kenyatta would have surely heard of the article. If he had not already worried about Obama, he would have begun to by then."[28]

Far from ending the debate about Kenya's economic direction, the publication of Sessional Paper No. 10 generated continuing acrimony and contributed to the widening ideological gap between the left and conservative wings of the party. By the spring of 1966 the hostility between Odinga and Kenyatta had reached its zenith. In March Odinga resigned and set up his own opposition party called the Kenya People's Union (KPU). With his departure, he denounced Kenyatta for the "Kikuyization" of the government and declared in his resignation statement that an "invisible government" composed of foreign forces and external commercial interests was running the government. Of that government, he proclaimed, "Its guiding star has become personal gain."[29]

Odinga's departure now left Kenyatta with only token internal opposition. Although Mboya publicly remained one of his closest advisers, the aging oligarch now began to look askance at the articulate young Luo politician, convinced that he was now angling to succeed him. Following Odinga's resignation, Kenyatta and his coterie of Kiambu supporters were free to pursue a course of economic growth without apology. As Norman Miller and Rodger Yeager put it in *Kenya: The Quest for Prosperity*, the nation would be guided "on a capitalist course under the expert direction of a trusted civil service. In fact, the rapidly expanding bureaucracy remained loyal to the president because of the social status and material rewards conveyed by membership. African socialism soon became an empty vessel floating on a sea of pragmatism and ambition."[30] An autocracy of patronage was now firmly in place.

Odinga's resignation deeply disheartened Obama, but it was only one of many dark clouds that gathered overhead in the months after his marriage to Ruth. One of them engulfed him as he was driving a friend's new green Fiat just weeks after the publication of his paper. Obama was an exuberant driver when sober and a menace when he drank. His drinking pal, Philip Ochieng, likens him to Toad in *The Wind in the Willows*, saying, "He would get very excited behind the wheel and he'd zoom like Toad, completely out of control, his arms and legs flying. You did not want to be in the car with him."

One evening, after a night of hard drinking with a sweet-faced young man named Adede Abiero, Obama slammed the car headlong into another vehicle in a Nairobi suburb. Abiero, a twenty-six-year-old postal worker and the breadwinner for four brothers, was killed instantly.[31] Obama broke both of his legs as well as a number of other bones. Hospitalized at the Aga

Khan Hospital, Obama remained in traction for over four months as his legs healed. Despondent over Abiero's death, he had friends sneak bottles of whiskey into his room, and one night he fell out of bed drunk and broke yet another bone.[32] The accident with Abiero was the first of numerous car crashes involving alcohol that had a cumulative impact on Obama's legs and ultimately left him dependent on crutches or a cane.

Obama's mother, Habiba Akumu, often journeyed from Kendu Bay to Nairobi to help take care of him after his accidents and would sit by his bedside and talk to him. She was forever urging him to stop drinking and would frequently declare, "Alcohol will kill you," recalls one of her other sons, Razik Otieno Orinda. Obama would just laugh and promise her that he would stop.

During his long hospital stay two of Obama's wives had the unexpected pleasure of meeting one another for the first time. Not long after he returned to Kenya, Obama had spent a week with Kezia and his children in Alego. He told her that he was setting up a home in Nairobi and would come back when he was able. Although he had told Kezia of Ann and his young son in Hawaii, he never mentioned Ruth, let alone that she was coming to Nairobi soon. So Kezia waited, something she was well used to doing. By this point she had been waiting for her husband's return for five years. Having no phone with which to call Obama, Kezia followed up his visit with a letter inquiring when he might return, but she did not hear back. The next she heard of Obama was when her brother sent word saying that he had had a terrible car accident and was not expected to survive. Frantic with alarm, Kezia caught the overnight bus to Nairobi, and on her arrival she hurried directly to the hospital.[33]

As she entered, relatives engulfed her and told her the news. Barack, they reassured her, would be all right. But there was more. "They told me that he had an American woman from Boston and they were married. I could not believe it. How come? I had been waiting and waiting for all those years and he had gotten married," exclaimed Kezia. "It hurt me so badly. I was just saying, where do I go now? What do I do?"

The two women were ushered into a small waiting room where they exchanged a few awkward words. Ruth recalls virtually nothing of the encounter. But Kezia remembers wondering how much of Africa this white woman could take, even as she welcomed Ruth to Kenya. "I said, we shall see. We shall see," declared Kezia. "What I meant was, you think you know what it is like here. Well, we shall see."

Over the next few years Kezia caught an occasional glimpse of Ruth when she visited her children, but little more. Kezia was content that the children lived with their father because he paid for their private schooling that she could not begin to afford. But Ruth wanted nothing to do with Kezia and would often flee the house when she was expected. Kezia got a job working in a Mombasa restaurant shortly after the two women's encounter, so she visited less often. Although Obama apparently visited his first wife whenever he was in Mombasa on business, he apparently made no effort to bring the two women together. Kezia, in fact, was the only one who seemed to wish for closer relations.

Toward the end of the year alarming news found its way to the hospital. As Obama lay with his legs suspended in the air, he learned that his still-cherished hope of earning a PhD from Harvard was unlikely ever to happen. Months earlier Obama had written to Harvard asking if he might be able to return in order to present his dissertation titled, "An Econometric Model of Staple Theory of Development." But Harvard clearly did not want him back. In November the school registrar responded that he would not provide immigration authorization for Obama's return, noting that he had not registered the title of his thesis. That a student who had passed all of his exams would be blocked for failing to register the title of his dissertation, if indeed Obama had failed to do so, seems extreme, at best. But that is precisely what the registrar wrote. He advised Obama to inform the Economics department what faculty member he was working with, to explain how near he was to finishing, and to send to his department any completed chapters of his dissertation. When those conditions had been fulfilled, the registrar wrote, "we can then take up the question of the necessary immigration documents."[34]

Obama did not pursue the matter. Despondent at the news, he seemed to have put his dissertation aside. Then, mysteriously, it disappeared. One afternoon a few months later, when Obama and Ruth were not at home, burglars apparently broke into their house and took off with the television. They included in their haul Obama's thesis. Or so he told Ruth. "That is what he said," recalled Ruth. "I don't know. Maybe they took a briefcase with the papers in it or something. That's not impossible. But whatever happened, he was pretty upset about it because he never went back to it and he didn't have any copies. So, that's the end of the doctoral thesis."

Nor were things going particularly well for Ruth. Isolated and often left alone for long periods in the rambling Rosslyn house, Ruth initially went knocking on some neighbors' doors and introduced herself in an effort to make friends. But most of the neighbors were British and not particularly interested in a young American woman who was married to an African—and a loud one at that. Ruth tried other means of connecting and occasionally attended gatherings of a small group of expatriate wives who met regularly in one another's homes for coffee. But perhaps propelled by her own insecurities, Ruth found herself drawn more to the African women she encountered and she continued to feel miserably alone. Even the discovery early in 1965 that she was pregnant did not entirely dispel her mounting disappointment in the state of her marriage. By now Obama was making no secret of the fact that he was spending time with other women. He saw no reason why he should not. When Ruth insisted that he stop, he shouted at her to be quiet and abruptly walked out the door. Some afternoons, she cried for hours alone in the empty house wondering where her husband might be. "I cried for two years in Kenya," sighed Ruth. "I missed my mother and my father. I missed home."

Despite his extramarital dalliances, Obama was immensely pleased with Ruth's pregnancy. Another baby, hopefully a boy, would be an additional feather in his cap. Nor did he entirely disregard his wife's unhappiness. When he met a young Scottish woman at the African Club one night, Obama asked if she might come and visit his wife. She was, he said, a bit lonely. Touched by Obama's concern, Catherine Wilson, then working as a teacher in the town of Embu northeast of Nairobi, agreed. Wilson and Ruth, both young women in their twenties struggling to navigate Nairobi's complex social scene, took to one another, and Wilson was soon a regular weekend guest.

Observing the couple, Wilson was struck by Obama's aggressive manner of conversation. It was as though, she noted, "he did not really want to be understood. He was loud and bombastic and I felt he did that precisely so you would not understand him. He was a bit of a maverick in that he wanted not to be known. That seemed very threatening to him." But Wilson remembers her conversations with Ruth even more poignantly. Ruth confided in the younger woman the depth of her unhappiness, and she even admitted that she was thinking of going back to the United States. Now with a baby on the way, she was missing her family even more. "It just seemed to be a very painful situation for her and she was extremely lonely," said Wilson. "I think Ruth did not like to see the way that others saw through Barack's bluff and bluster. I have to say, I was very glad that I was not in her shoes. He seemed like he would be a hard man for a woman to have a relationship with, much less to be married to."

Toward the end of 1965 the outlook began to improve a bit in the Obama household. Ruth landed a spot as secretary to the general manager of Kenya's Nestlé office. Not only did she find the work stimulating, but her boss also became a close and supportive friend. Then, in November she gave birth to a baby boy named Mark Okoth. The boy was called by his Luo name Okoth, meaning "born while it is raining." Enchanted with her infant son, Ruth was temporarily distracted from her marital woes. She also had a young woman helping out with the baby who provided her with some much-needed company.

Obama's name also came up for a plum new job. In September of 1966 the new Central Bank of Kenya opened its doors in the old Army Records Office, a stately three-story colonial office building in the heart of the city, and it began a search for dozens of economists. Obama had been chafing in his Shell posting for months, disgruntled that he had not been given a second promotion and openly objecting that he had an education superior to many of those above him. Days before the new bank opened, Obama gave notice to Shell and reported for work at the Central Bank in what had been rechristened "Herufi House."[35] Hired as a graduate trainee, Obama was assigned to the research department conducting economic analysis of other banks in the country and developing performance prognoses of certain businesses.

He lasted nine months.

Obama's first complaint was that there were too many Europeans in the bank. In fact, of the bank's sixty employees, twenty-two were expatriates and most of them were in controlling positions.[36] Obama's own supervisor was an English economist on loan from the World Bank. Like many other Kenyans working there, Obama deeply resented the continuing British presence. Although most kept their resentment to themselves, Obama openly criticized his supervisors to anyone who would listen. "He complained they knew nothing at all," said Masakhalia, who was still working at the MEPD. "The truth was they were arrogant. Most of them thought we were black people who knew nothing and they knew everything. But it was our country now and we wanted them out. I'd say to Barack, 'My friend, play the fool. You must in order to survive.' But he could not. He didn't know how."

Instead, the junior trainee denigrated the credentials of economists many years his senior in both age and experience. And he often did so to their faces. "He always talked about his Harvard training," recalled Gladys Ogolah, the personal assistant to the bank's governor. "He'd say, 'You call yourself an economist and you haven't even been to Harvard? Where did you go to school? You have no idea what you are talking about. I happen to be one of the best economists in the country.' Well, anybody would take offense. Of course some people just ignored him because often he was drunk."

Then came the day when a Kenyan was made the first African governor of the bank in the spring of 1967. Here was another Ndegwa not up to the job, as Obama saw it. This one's name was Duncan Ndegwa, and he was a graduate of Makerere University and St. Andrew's University in Scotland. He was also one of Kenyatta's most trusted advisers, having served as secretary in the Office of the President as well as head of the government's Civil Service. Ndegwa had an impressive résumé by most any assessment, even Obama's. But he was also a Kikuyu, and Obama grumbled that tribalism had carved him a career path that he did not entirely deserve. Nonetheless, the two men got along well when they encountered one another at the bars they both favored, and Obama's intellectual and oratorical skills impressed Ndegwa. The man was clever all right. No discretion, mind you, but he was immensely entertaining.[37] Behind Ndegwa's back Obama continued to complain to friends that the new governor was not as well trained an economist as he. "He hadn't gone to Harvard, after all," laughed Otieno O. Wasonga. "He'd say, 'Why didn't they make *me* the governor?' Ndegwa hadn't been properly trained in an economics school as he had."

Obama clearly possessed some sophisticated economic skills, but he was beginning to have trouble managing some of the basic aspects of his life. Often he came to work late and was so hung over that he needed hours to pull himself together. Other days he was delayed by minor traffic accidents en route to work. What's more, his personal finances were in mounting disarray. Obama bounced several checks in his first months on the job, and his superiors were increasingly concerned. Yet when they admonished him for some of his behaviors, Obama told them exactly what he thought. Obama managed to do his job adequately, but the bank's managers found his personal excesses unacceptable and let him go the following summer.[38] "It was a pity, but he had no discipline," explained Ndegwa. "And a bank must have discipline."

Ndegwa was sorry to see him go. Establishing Kenya's primary banking institution was a critical component of building a nation, and Ndegwa was disappointed to see a Kenyan forced to quit that process. What's more, he had grown fond of Obama and worried where he would land. "I think Obama was too much of an intellectual force of his own. I always thought he should have been in an academic institution which would have suited him better than a professional environment," said Ndegwa. "I didn't see him succeeding much anywhere else because he had no sense of cooperation with people. He had a lot of compassion for people, but he was not good at cooperating."

Angry and dejected, Obama began to live up to his nickname in earnest. Unemployed for several months, he spent afternoons in a series of bars and was absent from home for long stretches of time. Word traveled fast in Nairobi's small professional circle, and most of Obama's colleagues were aware of what had happened, which made his humiliation greater. Nor did Obama make much attempt to shield his wife. Even when Ruth and the baby were by his side in public, he flirted with women passing by and admonished her angrily if she objected. When she was not present, Obama held back little. At last, a family friend who felt sorry for Ruth and her baby informed her in blunt detail about the scope of her husband's womanizing. Ruth decided she had had enough.

It was time to go home. Ruth knew she had to be discreet, for she too had heard the stories about women who had tried to leave unfaithful husbands and about how those husbands had tracked them down and beaten them. She would not let that happen to her with her little boy around. Secretly, she arranged for a friend to invite Obama to drive with him to

Kisumu for a weekend visit. Obama was always eager to return to Luoland and was not likely to turn down such a trip, which indeed he did not. The journey would give her a good couple of days to make her getaway.

Once Obama was gone, Ruth moved fast. Within days, Ruth and Okoth caught a one-way flight to Boston. Ruth was heartbroken. Although she still loved Obama deeply, she had decided that she could not endure a marriage with him, and her plan was to get a job in the United States and never return to Kenya. But Ruth's careful plan had failed to take one thing into account. Weeks later Obama bought an airplane ticket to Boston too. He was going to go and get her back.

8

LIONS, TIGERS, AND LIES!

By the time he reached his middle years, Maurice Joseph Baker had achieved many things of which he was proud.

His auto parts sales business was flourishing, even if it took him on the road more that he would have liked. His beloved daughter, Ruth, had graduated from Simmons College and gotten a job in a downtown law firm. And in 1958 he had become the proud owner of a brand new ranch home with a brick facade in suburban Newton, just nine miles from downtown Boston and the namesake of the infamous Fig Newton cookie. For the amiable Joe, who had grown up on the second floor above his parents' corner store in the blue-collar town of Malden, it was a considerable achievement.[1]

And so it was that when Ruth, his beloved "Ruthie" with her wry sense of humor and luxurious golden hair, took off and married an African man, he was devastated. That she chose a black man was just part of it. Joe had been raised in an orthodox Jewish home, and he had always presumed that his daughter would marry within the faith. After she left in 1964, Joe no longer dropped in at Pressman's Delicatessen in Chelsea where he had long been a regular, unable to face his longtime buddies.[2] Family members were told that Ruthie had upped and joined the Peace Corps and was working to improve the lives of the downtrodden Africans. But for a long time her cousins never heard much about what happened to her over there in Kenya. Mostly, Ruthie just seemed to be gone.

But then she came back. Ruth arrived at 16 Hartman Road in the summer of 1967 with a single suitcase and her one-year-old son, Okoth, in her arms. Thrilled to see her, the Bakers ushered her indoors and wept at the sight of their beaming grandson. But after they dried their eyes, they told Ruth unflinchingly that she and her coffee-colored baby would not be able to stay in the house. Her mother, Ida, placed several phone calls, and within a few hours she had located acquaintances in nearby Cambridge who would allow Ruth and Okoth to stay with them. Although deeply disappointed that she could not stay at home, the ever-forbearing Ruth forgave her parents their embarrassment. "It didn't bother me that much because I understood my mother," Ruth explained. "She was very conscious about how other people think. She wanted me away from her neighborhood because she could not explain that her white daughter had a black baby. And you know, that was okay. They still loved me, I knew that. And I loved them. Real love doesn't change."

Daunted by her African experience, Ruth was now determined to stay in the United States and to remake her life. She began to look for jobs and a place she could live long term. But before she could make much progress, a contrite Obama showed up at her door. Her parents had given him her address, partly hoping she would reunite with her husband—after all, he was the father of her child—and partly hoping that she would not. Ruth tried half-heartedly to turn him away. But Obama charmed her with an onslaught of entreaties. He *loved* her to the core of his being. He *adored* their son and had yearned for them every day they had been gone. If she would only return with him, he vowed that everything would be different. He would never pursue another woman again. He would not even look at another woman, he insisted.

What's more, he had already lined up a new job. Starting in October Obama was to be the senior development officer for the newly created Kenya Tourist Development Corporation (KTDC), a high-profile government corporation charged with overseeing the blossoming industry and directing public investment in a spate of new hotels and parks. As the second highest–ranking employee in the organization, Obama was to receive a handsome annual salary of 2,275 pounds.[3] It was a plum job that put Obama squarely in the league of the government's other ranking economists and at the forefront of an industry to which *Mzee*, the Swahili term of respect for an elder, Kenyatta himself was closely attuned.[4] It was not a permanent secretary's post like Philip Ndegwa had landed or even the top job at the KTDC, but it was a good job nonetheless. And it gave him a much-needed chance to rehabilitate himself.

Adding to Obama's bounty, the job came with a lovely home in the exclusive Woodley Estate west of the city's center, a neighborhood that the Nairobi City Council developed expressly for Europeans in the late 1940s.[5] Since independence, however, a handful of prominent Africans, including members of Parliament and government ministers, had trickled into the handsome homes flanked by high green hedges. Obama's house was a welcoming stone bungalow with a red tile roof, complete with a separate servants' quarters that could accommodate the trail of relatives that invariably followed him.

Ruth soon abandoned her plan of staying in the United States and agreed to return with him to Nairobi. But it wasn't because of Obama's promises of fidelity or even the goodies he dangled before her. "There was a connection between us, a passion, the type of love that holds a man and a woman together," said Ruth. "He loved me in a certain way, as much as he was able. It wasn't just because I was white because surely that wears off. For myself, he was a man I had a very strong passion for. I did not have that passion again in my life."

Once they were back in Nairobi, Obama's promises lasted only as long as it took Ruth to unpack her bags. No sooner had the couple settled into their new home than Obama resumed his carousing ways, leaving Ruth to juggle her secretarial job at Nestlé and caring for his extended family with only the help of a housekeeper. There were now three of his children living in the house along with a succession of visiting relatives. Roy, his eldest son, who would later be known as Malik, attended the prestigious Lenana School, once exclusively for whites. Rita, later known as Auma, attended a day school before eventually enrolling in the Kenya High School. Although Kezia regularly visited her children, bearing sweets and small gifts in the early years after they moved in with their father and his new wife, Kezia's tearful demeanor annoyed Obama, so he had her visits abruptly stopped. Auma would not see her birth mother for nearly seven years.[6]

There were also the young relatives who lived in the servant quarters out back. Not long after he returned from the United States, Obama had taken his first cousin Ezra under his wing. Ezra was a clever and amusing boy whose father, one of Hussein Onyango's brothers, was unable to pay for his son's schooling. So Ezra moved into the squat servants' quarters in 1967 and remained there for four years while Obama paid for his education. He was not alone. When Wilson Obama, another cousin, showed up in similar need, Obama agreed to pay for his education and offered him a place to stay for close to two years. Amir Otieno Orinda, Obama's half-brother with whom he shared the same mother, was in and out of the house as well. Zeituni Onyango, Obama's half-sister, stayed at the house for several weeks in the late 1960s and would later help to take care of Malik and Auma.[7] As those and other Obamas came and went from the busy household, Ruth sometimes found herself passing people in the hallway who, she says, "I hadn't the slightest idea who they were."

Obama, meanwhile, had once again become a habitué of the city's nightspots and would migrate from one elegant hotel barroom to the next. Buoyed by his new post and the keen interest others took in his command of econometrics, Double-Double now had *mingi*—Swahili for "many"—drinking companions. Flush with their new salaries and Harambee Avenue offices, a certain element of the new African elite cultivated a lifestyle richly steeped in alcohol. One of their favorite places was the bar at the newly opened InterContinental, called The Big Five in reference to the five most difficult and dangerous animals to hunt in Africa's far-flung game parks. The intimate retreat offered an eclectic mix. Patrons lounging on the plush leather stools could as likely rub shoulders with a dewy-eyed tourist from New Jersey, a minister who had just strolled out of the nearby Treasury building, or a World Bank project manager making notations on his napkin, all under the glassy-eyed gaze of the lion and gazelle mounted on the walls.

It also drew from the senior ranks of the civil service and the top echelon of the business community. Some of the regulars among the African elite were Mwai Kibaki, Kenya's current president and then Minister of Commerce and Industry, and Francis Masakhalia, Obama's old Maseno School friend and by then an economist/statistician with the Ministry of Economic Planning and Development headed by Tom Mboya. Members of the nearby Parliament and a host of Treasury officers were often a part of the mix. When Obama tired of his double shots there, he often headed to the Panafric Hotel for a chaser or two of Chivas or Martel cognac. To wrap up the evening he occasionally stopped at the Starlight Club for a spin around the dance floor before heading home to Woodley in the early hours of the morning.

By the time he got there Obama was often stumbling and barely coherent. If Ruth or one of the children made the mistake of locking up before they went to bed, Obama would hammer loudly on the door and angrily demand that someone let him in. Gladys Ogolah, the next-door neighbor who knew Obama from their days at Central Bank together, heard every word of it. "He would shout at Ruth, 'Open the door, woman. Open the door,'" Ogolah recalled. "He would say, 'Why are you sleeping when I am not back at home. Open the door *now*.' And then he would beat on the door, *boom, boom, boom*."

Ogolah was hardly the only Woodley resident keenly aware of their baritone-voiced neighbor. Even when Obama was sober, his thundering voice wafted over the hedges and shattered the neighborhood calm. Sometimes, he was just calling to his children without making any effort to keep his voice down. But on the nights when he and Ruth got into an argument, his domineering voice could be heard the length of the Loddon Grove road and sometimes beyond. Not long after they moved into the house, the Obamas had become a regular topic of neighborhood talk, little of it good. "Barack would come back from work or wherever he was in the middle of the night and they would fight very loudly," recalled Ndolo Ayah, who lived nearby. "Everybody knew about it. I think we all worried a bit about Ruth's safety. Barack was not a violent person, but he could be very violent in his language."

Gladys Ogolah and her husband, Boaz, got to know the Obamas well and not just because of the couple's ongoing fighting. Boaz Ogolah was also an economist who worked in the Ministry of Economic Planning and Development, and Obama respected his breadth of knowledge and experience. Sometimes Obama would drop in for a drink, and the two men would critique the other economists in government service whose academic credentials they considered inferior to their own. Obama would also talk openly of some of the beautiful women to whom he was attracted. "Barack was a Luo and a polygamist, and so this was no big deal to him," said Ogolah. "He was very open about it."

Just a few years younger than her neighbor, Gladys Ogolah grew to like her new American friend. Ruth clearly enjoyed Kenya and appreciated many of its customs. Unlike some *mzungu* who tended to stick with their own, Ruth counted African women among her closest friends. She was also devoted to all of Obama's children and even some of his closer cousins. She was the one who arranged their weekend outings swimming at the Panafric and Safari Park hotels or picnics in the countryside. And she was the one who drove them to their schools and doctors' appointments and, at times, shielded them from their father. "Ruth was a very great woman," said Ezra Obama, sixty-one and a retired manager of market development for Coca-Cola living outside Nairobi. "She treated all of us children the same and I respected her very much."

But no matter how much Ruth tried to make things run smoothly, Obama seemed always to have a complaint. And when his shouting developed into more aggressive behavior in the passing months, it was to Ogolah that Ruth often turned, running through the darkness to the safe haven of her neighbor's kitchen. "Sometimes, when he came home late he would order her to cook for him in the middle of the night and if she would not he would hit her about the shoulders and neck," recalled Gladys Ogolah. "Ruth would run screaming down the road to our house crying. She was tired of being hit and tired of being called names. She had a very, very rough time and I was always worried about her."

As a boy, Mark Ndesandjo was fearful of his towering father and tried hard to stay out of his way so he would not inadvertently trigger his rage. "What I felt from him was coldness. There was fear. That is what I recall," Ndesandjo said in an interview. "I was physically afraid of him. He was a large looming man and you did not know what to expect. Is he going to hit you or your mother or other people in your family? He did not smile except when he was drinking or when he was with friends."

Anxious as to what their father's condition would be on his return home each night, the children passed the afternoon following school with mounting apprehension. "Everyone in the house was totally on edge because you never knew when my father would be back," Ndesandjo said in an interview. "When he got there he would probably be drunk. And then the light would go on and you would hear thuds and shouts and my mother's voice rising and crying and screaming. You would hear sounds

like falling objects and it would go on and on and on and on. I instinc-
tively bonded with my mother because she was afraid and she was also
very protective of me. And that made my father even angrier. He resented
me because we were both now competing for my mother's attention. I was
my mother's firstborn and she had shifted some of her attention away
from him to me. Sometimes when she was holding me, he would shout at
her, 'Stop tending to that brat.'"

Nor was Obama's abuse of Ruth confined to their home. As he became
increasingly careless about shielding his attraction to other women,
Obama repeatedly humiliated his wife in public. "He would criticize me
and flirt with other women right in front of me. Always, there were other
women," Ruth sighed. "He took great pleasure in demeaning me because it
made him feel better."

Ruth endured for two reasons. The first was Mark Okoth, and the second would be named David Opiyo. Within a few months of their return to
Nairobi, Ruth learned that she was pregnant again and thus linked ever
more inextricably to her husband. Obama had made it clear to her that if
she ever left him, he would prohibit her from seeing their children, and in
Kenya's patriarchal culture she had little doubt that he could do so easily.
Determined to raise her children as best she could while struggling to preserve the marriage that had produced them, Ruth took stock of her situation. Her job at Nestlé continued to provide both a professional outlet and
much-needed emotional support. Best of all, it gave her a source of self-
esteem that she was not finding at home. She also had an extensive network of friends, some of whom strongly urged her to take the children and
flee under cover of night. But Obama had never struck any of the children.
As long as it was only she upon whom he inflicted his rage, she felt she
could manage.

But it wasn't easy. One night Obama came home drunk as usual, but
this time he had a pretty young woman clinging to his arm. It was not the
first time he had done so. In the past Ruth had simply turned tearfully
away as Obama and his woman friend slipped into one of the bedrooms
together. But on this particular night Obama insisted that Ruth leave their
house so that he could use their marriage bed without her interfering. He
was, after all, a Luo and had a right to any woman he might desire, he
declared, his voice growing steadily louder. But this time Ruth put her foot

down. She refused to move anywhere, and as she screamed out her hurt, the neighbors, as ever, got an earful.[8]

One of those neighbors was Achieng Oneko, one of the Kapenguria Six who were convicted in 1952 of supporting the Mau Mau rebels along with Kenyatta and sentenced to seven years in prison. Oneko, who had abandoned his old cellmate to join Odinga and the Kenya People's Union, was a legendary freedom fighter and a pioneering newspaper editor. He was also a former Maseno student, although he attended many years before Obama. Upset by the Obamas' domestic furor, Oneko picked up the telephone and called his friend Ndolo Ayah. "He said, 'You young people, you better talk to that friend of yours, Barack. He's making a mess of himself,'" Ayah recounted. "So I got another friend of mine and we headed on over to Obama's place to see what we could do."

The situation was chaotic. Ruth was screaming so forcefully that it took her awhile to realize that there were visitors in the house. Obama was drunkenly explaining to her that, according to Luo tradition, "he could bring any woman into the house at any time." said Ayah. "I said, well, he comes from a different Luo group than ourselves because we are Luo and you don't do this kind of thing. We tried to get Barack to come to Oneko's place so we could talk it out but he just told us to go to hell, you know. And so we left. I suppose at some level we felt it was none of our business."

As his marriage with Ruth grew increasingly strained, Obama turned to his first wife, Kezia, for solace—at least that is what she maintains. While working as a waitress in a Mombasa restaurant in the late 1960s, Kezia says that Obama occasionally visited her when he passed through town on business. On one of those trips Kezia became pregnant with a son she claims Obama fathered. In 1968 Sampson Nyandega, called Abo, was born. Two years later Bernard Otieno, whom she says is also Obama's son, was born.[9]

Many family members, however, do not believe that the boys are Obama's. They point out that he did not take them into his home, as he did with his other children, nor did he talk much about them. More compelling, the Nairobi High Court Judge who ruled on Obama's disputed estate in 1989 did not believe the evidence of Obama's paternity that Kezia presented and concluded that the boys were not his children. Judge J. F. Shields noted in a ruling that Kezia did not obtain the boys' birth certificates until after Obama died and did so then only in an effort to have them named as beneficiaries to his estate. Shields also wrote that Kezia had presented evidence of having access to Obama only during time periods after Bernard and Abo were born.[10] Whether or not Obama fathered the boys, Kezia is adamant that Obama remained her lover throughout his entire life regardless of whom he was married to or when. "Ruth, these other women, even Anna, I just said I do not care," Kezia shrugged, speaking in an interview. "Marry any of them. I am the first wife. Whoever wants to marry you, marry them. I do not care. He always came back to me."

AS RUTH UNDERSTOOD HIM, Obama's reckless behaviors stemmed from a couple of sources. The first were the rich and varied temptations of Nairobi life in the years after independence. Although Obama had managed to curb his more extreme inclinations while under scrutiny in the United States, once he returned to Kenya in the heady days of the mid-1960s, it was another story. On a scholarship in America, she noted, "he was being judged on a daily basis. He had to behave properly. There were parameters. But once he was back in Kenya and all his friends are saying, 'Let's go for the drink, let's go dancing, let's go find some women, let's do this and that,' he couldn't hold back. All those pressures were too much for him. He just didn't have the strength of character to resist. And the more he succumbed, the more he succumbed."

But Ruth believes the greater source of Obama's undoing lay deeply embedded in his gnawing lack of faith in himself, exacerbated by the perils of Kenyan politics. Kenyatta's chokehold on matters of state meant that little could happen without his sanction or that of members of his inner circle. Obama had already been blackballed for his aggressive critique of Sessional Paper No. 10, and his critical commentary at Central Bank hadn't helped matters. Much as he yearned to be a Big Man, Obama was far from it. That his fortunes were dependent on favors from others and the shifting sands of Kenya's powerful elites made matters only worse. Indeed, since his collision with Harvard administrators, he had found the doors to power closed to him at almost every turn. Uncertainty, coupled with the Luo habit of self-inflation, drove him to chronic exaggeration intended to compensate for his perceived shortcomings.

"One day he was charming, charming and loving and wonderful. He was just the way a woman wants a man to be. And then the next day he's beating you and abusing you," Ruth said. "You see, he was confused, very confused about himself. He had a great, enormous insecurity. He pretended to be this great fellow, but we all know that confident people do not have to blow their own horn like that. Nor do they have to drink all the time to give themselves false confidence."

Gladys Ogolah tried reasoning with him when he was sober. Why, she asked, do you beat on Ruth? "He'd say, 'Naaaaaah, I don't beat her. She just likes making noise.' I said that is not right. When my husband talked to him, he said he is just drinking too much and that is why he is loud."

Although Obama had abundant company in his heavy drinking, he was driven by more than the cultural excesses of the moment. Also contributing to his dark mood was the evolving cast of Kenyatta's inner circle, ever more authoritarian and intolerant of challenge. By the end of 1967 the mushrooming political schism between Kenyatta and the radicals led by Oginga Odinga had distinctly worsened. Kenyatta had tolerated the formation of the socialist Kenya People's Union, but far from yielding on his positions, he became increasingly trenchant as the months passed. He reviled the opposition's leftist platform, and at a public rally in Nairobi on Kenyatta Day he denounced KPU members, declaring that from then on they would be regarded as "snakes in the grass. . . . Let them try and re-examine their minds and return to KANU. If they do not do so, KPU should beware! The fighting for our Uhuru is on. Whoever has ears to hear, let him heed this. We say we are ready to fight for our Uhuru."[11]

Between 1966 and 1969 Kenyatta moved to stymie the opposition and isolate his Luo challengers. One means of effectively limiting the KPU's ability to expand was by refusing to authorize the registration of new party branches.[12] Those who attempted to organize opposition on a local level were overtly intimidated by KANU officials or else were likely to find the government withholding a sorely needed business permit or school document as a form of payback. As the government issued a series of laws and amendments that made it increasingly difficult for the KPU to compete with the dominant KANU party, it seemed likely that Kenyatta would soon crush the opposition altogether.[13]

With Odinga now effectively marginalized, Kenyatta's Kikuyu coterie began to look increasingly askance at Tom Mboya, who now stood as the likely heir apparent. Mboya was not only immensely popular among a broad swath of trade union members and members of parliament but was also believed to have the critical support of the Western countries, particularly the United States. As the aging Kenyatta's health began to deteriorate, many Kikuyus were increasingly alarmed at the possibility of the presidency falling to a non-Kikuyu. Rumors about Mboya's political intentions were rampant. That he was interested in the presidency was no secret. Some whispered that he was forging a secret alliance with Odinga to assume a spot within the KPU.[14] Others suspected a more devious agenda. Either way, the hostility of Kenyatta's inner circle toward Mboya escalated rapidly. As Mboya's biographer David Goldsworthy wrote, "Far from secure incumbency, his position was one of exposure, of vulnerability to the plottings of those who *were* securely incumbent. . . . By the later 1960s, [Mboya] was having to count his friends perhaps more intently than ever before."[15]

Of his enemies, there seemed to be no end. In December 1967 a sentry keeping guard at his home on Convent Drive fired a series of shots at Mboya's empty white Mercedes. The man, who was apprehended and jailed, was said to be mentally ill. Nevertheless, according to Goldsworthy, Mboya was increasingly fearful for his safety. After Robert Kennedy was assassinated in June of 1968, Mboya finally agreed to allow his American friends, William Scheinman and Frank Montero, both with the African American Students Foundation, and Robert Gabor, an official with the New York–based cultural funding organization, Peace with Freedom, to hire him a personal bodyguard.[16]

Unlike many who threw their lot with either one of the two Luo giants, Odinga or Mboya, Obama retained ties with both political camps, as he was drawn to aspects of each of their platforms. As he had expressed so forcefully in his critique of Sessional Paper No. 10, Obama believed that certain socialist principles that Odinga articulated should be a feature of the country's economic underpinnings. But he also saw a place for the capitalist principles that the West-leaning Mboya espoused. He was particularly incensed at the factions within KANU that were seeking to undermine Mboya, their own party's secretary-general. Although removed from Mboya's exalted circle, Obama continued to look to Mboya for guidance. Their relationship had grown more distant over the years as Mboya's star rose ever higher, but they nonetheless maintained a friendship throughout. Mboya's increasing political isolation gave Obama one more reason for dismay.

Like others disillusioned with the government's performance, Obama regarded Kenyatta as a bitter disappointment. In the months after he returned with Ruth, it seemed that much of what he had long dreamed for his country had failed to materialize. Far from standing as a boldly independent African nation, dependence on foreign capital still hobbled Kenya. At the same time, its domestic assets were being amassed in the hands of a privileged few. Obama was an economist who believed that free enterprise played a critical role in a democracy, but he also had a deep respect for African communalism. He felt strongly that the majority should share in the country's bounty. Instead, he saw unfettered capitalism and, increasingly, a rampant tribalism eroding the promises of *uhuru*.

Although Obama clearly had difficulty with authority of any kind, he was hardly alone in believing that his own Luo roots were coming to be a distinct liability. As he grew increasingly frustrated with the Kikuyus' tight grip on the country's politics, he began to drink ever more heavily. His frustration with the country's course coupled with his own personal failure to attain the heights that he believed should have been within easy reach were fast congealing into an acid stew of resentment. As was his habit, he did not hesitate to speak out. "He did not like the aggressive capitalism that Kenyatta was putting into place, the acquisition without taking into account all the poverty that there was," said Peter Aringo, Obama's longtime friend and an MP from Alego. "This sharing the crumbs from the table did not impress him and he said so. I pleaded with him to be moderate in what he said, but he would not. He took it very personally. He felt Africa needed someone who was courageous and he needed to speak out."

AS KENYA EMERGED FROM THE TURBULENT drive for independence, its new leaders turned to an unlikely group of people for an economic boost. They were *wazungu*—the plural form of *mzungu*—for the most part. They carried cameras. They knew little about Kenya and less about the African continent. But they generally had a generous amount of money in their pockets. In Swahili they were called *watalii*. Elsewhere they were known as tourists.

Tourism was hardly new in Kenya. Even before independence was declared in 1963, visitors predominantly from the United Kingdom, Europe, and the United States had journeyed to Kenya's interior on safari to photograph or bag the legendary game there. Others came to sample the undulating beaches of Mombasa and Malindi. In the two years after Kenya's rippling black, green, and red flag went up, the number of visitors coming on holiday leapt by 45 percent from 22,363 to 32,351. The number of visitors from the United Kingdom alone more than doubled from 1964 to 1965, whereas the total number of all visitors, including those doing business or in the military, peaked at 81,448.[17] Calculating that tourism would not only create employment more rapidly than any other sector of the economy but also generate substantial foreign exchange earnings, government leaders embarked on a major expansion of the accommodations and infrastructure that would stimulate the industry.[18] Their expectations were not modest. In the Kenya Tourist Development Corporation's five-year plan written in 1968, they projected that by 1973 the number of tourists coming to Kenya would reach 385,000 a year and would generate a net contribution to the economy of £16.2 million.[19]

To achieve that goal, the fledgling KTDC needed a highly skilled economist, someone who could attract foreign investors as well as parse the African tourist's appetite. Obama's name, invariably, arose from the small circle of Nairobi economists. But he was not the only one considered for the post of KTDC's senior development officer. Another candidate was Washington Jalang'o Okumu, a bright young economist who also happened to have a Harvard degree, a BA he received in 1962. Both men were unabashedly self-confident and impressed the KTDC board with their poise and performance. Both men were also impeccably turned out in the latest European attire. But in the end the board offered the post to Obama. Okumu went on to become a personal assistant to Kenyatta and an internationally acclaimed negotiator credited with mediating a critical 1994 compromise between South African presidents Nelson Mandela, F. W. de Klerk, and the Inkatha Freedom Party's Mangosuthu Buthelezi that paved the way for multiracial elections. "Obama was a very impressive man, very smooth and articulate," said Jeremiah Owuor, the general manager of the KTDC and Obama's immediate superior. "You could see immediately that he could deliver. The board was quite taken with him."

Indeed, Obama's economic skills must have dazzled the board, for they hired him despite the substantial liability of his spotty employment record. Although he beat out Okumu, Obama was assigned to a trial period of six months and placed on a full year's probation. The board instructed Owuor to "have a word with Mr. Obama" and to explain that the trial period was necessary due to some "adverse reports received from his former employers," according to the minutes of the KTDC's September 8, 1967, meeting. What's more, Owuor was advised to "keep a very tight control over [Obama] during this trial period. While problems such as over-drinking outside office hours may be considered personal they can no longer be considered personal if they affect and impair the performance of a member of the Corporation."[20] Less than two months later Obama was the subject of just the kind of headlines that KTDC board members had most feared.

"TOURISM OFFICER ON DRINKS CHARGE," the *Daily Nation* declared on November 4, 1967. Obama had been at a cocktail party before he collided with a milk handcart as he sped along the Ngong Road at 4 a.m. He had then pulled to the side of the road and telephoned police to report the accident. A medical report presented at his court hearing indicated that he had consumed "the equivalent of six beers or twelve whiskies," according to the news story. Pointing out that Obama had pleaded guilty to the charge and had a Harvard University degree, Obama's defense attorney asked for leniency. F. E. Abdullah, the magistrate hearing the case, was moved by what he called the "mitigating circumstances" in the case and fined Obama £50 and prohibited him from driving for one year. Adding that he could have decided to have him put in prison, Abdullah concluded, "The services of the accused to the nation will be more valuable outside prison."[21]

The KTDC board might have argued otherwise. Obama made good use of his formidable economic skills as an economist and forecaster during his three years at the KTDC, but his tenure there was a rocky one that culminated in disaster. He often showed up late for work smelling of alcohol and was chastised on a host of occasions for usurping his superiors. But his more egregious offense was his perennial impersonation of general manager Owuor while engaged in business in order to gain the perks of the other man's rank. Offended at having to work beneath a man he considered less educated than himself, Obama corrected the situation by simply giving himself a promotion. At the same time, his personal charm won him accolades from both tourists and investors alike, whom he regaled with dramatic stories of his childhood in the bush. Never mind that apparently few of them were true.

At the core of Obama's difficulties at the KTDC was his disdain for Owuor. Another Maseno graduate, Owuor was raised in a staunchly Christian family and was a keen believer in both his faith and personal discipline. Every Monday he called a meeting to review the week's work ahead, dubbing the meeting the "Monday morning prayer meeting," to Obama's great annoyance. Owuor had earned his BA and a MA in social sciences from universities in India, as had a number of other Kenyans of the period. But Obama, the Harvard man, was openly disdainful of his boss's education. And Owuor knew it. "You see, people who came back from getting an education in the United States, they had high expectations for themselves. They were going to rise very high," said Owuor. "And if you find yourself like Obama being under somebody trained in India, well, what is India? What is an education in India? Nothing. You're either from the UK, or America."

Compelled to work cheek by jowl, the two men chaffed from the start. "Jerry Owuor was a clean Christian, very strict. But Barack was a free man, so how were those two to get along?" asked Arthur Reuben Owino, Obama's old friend. "One was rather talkative and boastful, the other was a quiet and godly man. What would you expect to happen between them?"

One of a relatively small staff, Obama's responsibilities were multiple. His primary task was to assess the tourism industry's potential in Kenya, make projections of the number of tourists who could be expected to come to the country, and perform feasibility studies of hotel and park projects in which the KTDC had a financial interest. In order to evaluate the market, Obama was also required to interview tourists as they disembarked at the Nairobi airport and visit with them at their hotels. With the assistance of KTDC's other development officer, Nyaringo Obure, Obama periodically spent an evening with a group of tourists in order to develop profiles of their itinerary and their expectations. Piqued by their enthusiasm, Obama would often delight the visitors with yarns about his childhood experiences. Sometimes the stories involved savage, man-eating beasts; other times they revolved around inexplicable mystical spirits.

"We would all be sitting around the fire at night at the lodge and he would be doing most of the talking," recalled Obure. "He would make wild exaggerations. One story he told over and over was about how when he was a boy he was looking after the family cattle. Suddenly, a group of lions appeared and started to attack the cows. Barack pulls out his spear and kills the first lion by stabbing him in the chest. Then he goes for the rest, stab, stab, stab. Of course, I knew it was a lie. I don't think there were even lions in the area where he lived. But the tourists just loved it. Another time he said a buffalo attacked one of his relatives. Barack happened to be in a tree overhead and he dropped down on the buffalo's back and wrestled it to the ground. And so his stories went on and on."

To the managers of the hotels in which they stayed, Obama told a slightly different kind of story, but one just as untrue. During one of many tours of the Aberdare mountain region north of Nairobi while scouting possible hotel sites, Obama and Obure happened to get a flat tire on their car. At the time they were staying at the luxurious Outspan Hotel, a legendary country retreat in the heart of the coffee highlands. As neither of them could afford a new tire, Obama approached the general manager of the hotel. "He introduced himself as Dr. Obama, and explained that he was the general manager of the KTDC and could the man possibly give him a hand. I told him later it wasn't right to give himself such a title, but he just waved me away. And their manager couldn't have been more helpful. He gave us eight hundred shillings to buy the new tire and off we went."

During one of their long drives together, Obama happened to tell Obure a story so incredible that Obure just laughed in outright disbelief. Never one prone to talk much about his personal life, Obama spontaneously announced that he had a young son in America. In fact, the boy lived in Hawaii and had the same name as his own. "Well, of course I didn't believe a word of it," exclaimed Obure. "It was just Barack talking."

Obama soon began introducing himself as KTDC's general manager not just when he was in a fix but as a routine matter. Eager to please the ranking government officer, the hotel or restaurant staffers leapt to accommodate him. There were drinks on the house and the finest rooms available. There were small "loans" proffered under the table and lavish meals on top of it. The hotel's manager himself would often personally escort Obama out of the building to his waiting vehicle. Obure repeatedly admonished him to stop, to which Obama would reluctantly respond, "Okay, okay, I won't do it anymore."

But Obama kept right on. In time word of his impersonation filtered back to the real general manager toiling behind his desk in KTDC's office in Nairobi. Periodically, hotel managers would call him and inform him of Obama's high jinks. And when Owuor dropped in to the Panafric or Brunner's Hotel after work, the bar manager there would advise him that the general manager of the KTDC, a certain *doctor*, had already tried to get a few free rounds at the bar. Owuor took it all with a grain of salt until one day Obama went too far. When Obama was on a business trip in Tanzania, one evening he became so intoxicated that local police arrested and confined him to the army barracks jail. Owuor, back home, received a phone call. "It was the Tanzanian chief of police. He said that they had just locked up the general manager of the KTDC who had been arrested for drunkenness," recalled Owuor. "And then he said that he had been told that I was the KTDC accountant. He said the general manager had told him to get in touch with his accountant and he would bail him out."

Owuor understood that Obama's self-aggrandizing behavior was rooted in his conviction that he was the most qualified person to run the office, but Owuor was tired of it. So he sat Obama down and put it to him. "I said, 'You are an economist. That is your training,'" Owuor recalled. "'So, it doesn't matter how stupid the general manager is for there will still be an economist. You cannot have the general manager and the economist in one person. They are two jobs. If you tell people I know nothing about economics and so on, you are very right. But for my job, I do not need it. You are the economist. So, stick to your own side of the house.'"

By the time Obama's six-month trial period had run out, board members were concerned. They continued to receive reports of alcohol on

Obama's breath in the morning. They were also annoyed that he had received payment for taking part in televised group discussions without authorization.[22] The board, however, was not displeased with the work that Obama was doing. Tourism had continued to grow at a steady rate, holding its position as one of the most rapidly developing industries in the country. By the year's end a total of 262,000 foreigners would visit the country either on holiday or business. As part of an effort to increase tourist beds in the county's popular wildlife areas, the Kenya Safari Lodges and Hotels Ltd. had begun building two lodges in the Tsavo National Park, each with one hundred beds. At the same time, a beach hotel with two hundred beds had been launched in the seaside city of Mombasa. With Obama's financial counsel, the KTDC had emerged as the largest investor in the holding company managing all three of the projects.[23] Work had also begun on what would prove to be one of Kenya's most popular tourist attractions. Called the Ark, it was a lodge nestled in the treetops in the heart of the Aberdares from which a diverse assortment of game could be easily observed.

In downtown Nairobi, expansion plans were also under way. The owners of the Panafric, a popular international hotel, had agreed to nearly double its eighty-four-bed capacity and build a swimming pool with the help of a substantial equity loan from the KTDC. Hilton International had also committed to take over management of a six-hundred-bed hotel in the city's heart, and this was well under construction; they would assume operations of the well-known New Stanley Hotel several blocks away.[24] In order to staff all those hotels, the talk at KTDC had turned to developing a hotel training school, which was planned to open early in 1970. The industry, which employed a total of about twenty thousand people by 1969 and on which so many had pinned their hopes, seemed to be flourishing.[25]

At its June 1968 executive committee meeting, the board decided to confirm Obama's position, but it also advised the chairman to speak with Obama, "as there was still need to guide him and discipline him."[26] Obama was sufficiently satisfied with his own performance that in August, just two months after he had been taken off of probation, he boldly asked for a raise. In a letter to Owuor, Obama suggested that his salary be increased to the same level as that being paid to the chief planning officer for the Ministry of Economic Planning and Development. In other words, he was asking to be paid the same salary as Philip Ndegwa—or the salary that Ndegwa had been getting before he was promoted to Permanent Secretary of the ministry some months earlier. The board rejected his request, noting pointedly that the two jobs could not be compared.[27] Ndegwa continued to surge—steadily, infuriatingly—ahead of Obama.

Frustrated that his performance was not being given the recognition that he thought it merited, Obama continued to drink heavily. Now, his legendary order of a Double-Double was just an initial throat clearing at the bar before he got down to the serious job of drinking. At lunch he would down several beers in a row, ignoring Obure's suggestion that he slow down. Owuor was irked that on several occasions Obama had failed to attend the Monday "morning prayer meeting," presuming he was hung over from a drunken weekend. Obama also began to miss meetings he was assigned to attend, but when asked about his absence, he adamantly insisted that he had been present at the table. One Friday morning Obama did not show up to work at all, nor did he resurface over the weekend. By Tuesday a distraught Ruth showed up at the KTDC office frantically inquiring if anyone knew where her husband was. "We had no idea," recalled Obure. "But later that day the Kisumu police called to say that he had gotten drunk and driven all the way to Kisumu. He'd gotten completely lost and didn't know where he was. Ruth was very upset. It wasn't the last time he disappeared."

Nor was it the last time Ruth had to go looking for him. Not long after Obama had disappeared in Kisumu, Oyiro Ayoro was having a midday drink with him and several other government workers at the downtown Nyanza Bar. They were well onto their second drink when a visibly upset Ruth appeared. Beseeching Obama to come with her as the tears slid down her face, she exclaimed, "Why do you have to spend the whole day in the bar. We must go home," as Ayoro remembers it. "Barack was furious," Ayoro said. "He shouted, 'Go away before I hit you! A woman does not tell me where I should be or what I should be doing. Disappear, woman.' He made as if he was going to hit her and Ruth took off in a dash." Whenever he was flush, Obama was famously generous with his money. He would buy successive drinks for his friends at the bar and sometimes stand the entire room a drink or two. But spending at such a rate, he quickly exhausted his funds. When he was traveling on behalf of KTDC, some of those he ran into regularly learned to be wary of his spending habits when it came to alcohol. Leo Odera Omolo, a longtime friend of Obama's, was working as a press officer for the Brooke Bond Tea Company in Kericho on the road from Nairobi to Kisumu during the years Obama worked at KTDC. Obama often paused there for a couple of nights respite. The two men would start with a bottle of whisky at Omolo's home, but Obama soon insisted that they head to the tea plantation's club-like Tea Hotel, beloved by expatriate executives. Obama was eager to pick up some of the attractive women at the bar and restaurant there, or as Omolo recalls it, "white girls, black girls, any girls. He wanted to be drinking where there were beautiful women."

"But then he would leave me a disappointed man because he would drink many drinks and buy many more drinks for others and he would leave me with the bill," Omolo explained. "He would drink in one night the equivalent of one month's salary. Barack was a most entertaining fellow to drink with, but sometimes I avoided him. I would tell him that I would not be around when he was passing through and I would not come home until midnight. I could not afford his visits."

Obama's drinking companions were well versed in his disappointments and his rage at the Kikuyu bourgeoisie who seemed increasingly to monopolize the country's political and economic life. Many of them shared his feelings. But at the end of 1968 two American visitors appeared on Obama's doorstep for whom his tirades about the deep division in Kenyan politics were a wholly new conversation. The last time they had seen Obama he had been holding court outside of Hemenway Hall in Honolulu and heralding the days of Kenya's independence to come.

Neil Abercrombie and Pake Zane had been backpacking through Europe for over a year by the time they made their way to see their old friend in Nairobi. Exhausted from their travels, they collapsed at Obama's Woodley home and caught up on the past six years. Obama was pleased to see them both and took them on a tour of his favorite nightspots in the city. But Abercrombie noticed that Obama was drinking heavily and often disappeared so that he might be alone. He never mentioned Barack Jr. or asked if they had seen him. Nor did Zane or Abercrombie bring up the subject of his Hawaiian son. "Family life was secondary to work, just as it had been in Hawaii," recalled Abercrombie. "He was angry and disappointed that the government was not using him even remotely to the extent of his abilities. It was clear to me that he was drinking a very large amount. He was not so much drunk as he was drinking consistently. It was as though the drinking was now part of his existence."

Their two-week visit coincided with a day of national celebration marking the country's achievements and recognizing national unity. It was to be a special event in Nairobi, attended by Kenyatta and a host of government ministers celebrating the country's achievements. Representatives of all the country's different tribes were to be in attendance. Although Abercrombie and Zane were eager to attend, Obama refused to go. He told them he did not want to cross paths with the president and scoffed at the notion of celebrating unity in a country riven with tribal divisions. "The one thing Barack wanted was to do something for his country, but he felt he could not," said Zane. "He felt he was still part of Mboya's team in working for the country's economic development, but he was hemmed in on all sides. All the passion he had for Kenya when he was in Hawaii seemed to be smashing up against a wall of government and bureaucratic inertia. I really felt badly for him."

The situation would soon get much worse.

THE MORNING OF JULY 5, 1969, DAWNED cool and sunny in downtown Nairobi, a welcome respite from the rainy season that had recently subsided.

The streets were crowded with Saturday shoppers eager to get their purchases completed before the midday closing hour arrived. Obama was among them, strolling with the wife of his friend, Michael Kinyengi, as she surveyed the latest ladies' fashions in the store windows. As they rounded a street corner onto what was then called Government Road, Obama was pleased to see Tom Mboya pull up in front of Chhani's Pharmacy and get out of his car. Mboya had just returned from a meeting of the Economic Commission for Africa in Addis Ababa the day before. A photograph of him striding through the airport with Philip Ndegwa, his Permanent Secretary at the Ministry for Economic Planning and Development, was visible in the *East African Standard* on virtually every newsstand.[28]

Mboya paused and he and Obama talked for several minutes. Obama introduced Mboya to his companion and then jokingly observed that Mboya had parked his car illegally. "You have parked wrongly," laughed Obama. "You will get a ticket."[29]

The two men then parted company. Obama and Mrs. Kinyengi headed into a dress shop as Mboya entered the pharmacy to purchase some skin cream. About ten minutes later Mboya said farewell to the shopkeeper, his longtime friend, and stepped out on the street. Several feet from the door stood a slight man in a suit, holding a briefcase in his left hand with his right hand in his pocket. Two shots sounded. Mboya sank to the ground, blood staining his red shirt as pedestrians crowded anxiously around him. When he was pronounced dead on arrival at Nairobi Hospital shortly afterward, Kenya's future was changed forever.

In the hours after his death was announced, rumors surged across the country that the killer was a Kikuyu. It had to be, didn't it? First the Kikuyu had commandeered the heart of the government. Then they had effectively ousted Odinga from KANU. Now they had slain Tom Mboya in broad daylight. How could it not be a Kikuyu? The riots and demonstrations began by late afternoon. As shock and grief swept across Luoland, unruly mobs, churning with rage, began to roam through Kisumu. At a requiem mass at the Holy Family Cathedral three days later, a near hysterical mob of twenty thousand people, most of them Luo, surged outside. When President Kenyatta's car arrived, police were unable to hold back the angry protestors who attacked his car with sticks and stones, shouting, "*Dume!*" meaning bull, the symbol of the Kenya People's Union, in affirmation of their allegiance to Odinga. Mboya's murder seemed to have unleashed all the pent-up disappointment of the past five years and the subterranean tensions that had festered in the grip of Kenyatta's autocratic rule.

The rumors were right, in a way. Five days after Mboya was shot, a young man named Nahashon Isaac Njenga Njoroge was identified as a suspect and later charged with the murder. The announcement electrified the country. Njenga, it turned out, was a Kikuyu. And yet the evidence against him was far from decisive and no real motive could be discerned.

The trial that followed revealed little of substance except that the Smith and Wesson .38 revolver that killed Mboya was in fact Njenga's. The other piece of information to emerge was that during a preliminary hearing Njenga had asked a police superintendent, "Why do you pick on me? Why not the big man?" Njenga, a small businessman and low-level KANU activist, refused to identify the "big man." He was soon convicted and sentenced to death. Although the government announced that Njenga was hanged, the procedure was open to only a tiny group, and many believe he was never killed at all.[30] Many Kenyans suspect that Kenyatta or those among his inner circle arranged the assassination and that Njenga was simply the fall guy.

There were sixty-six witnesses at a preliminary hearing and more at Njenga's trial. The final prosecution witness was Barack H. Obama. According to newspaper accounts of his testimony, Obama said nothing incendiary. He testified only that he and Mboya chatted briefly and he related his own comments about Mboya's parking job. Mboya, he added, "did not say anything to me to indicate that he was frightened."[31] These were hardly the kind of words that would mark a man. But in the politically inflammatory moment, just taking the stand in Njenga's trial was a highly precarious thing to do. Since his provocative remarks about Sessional Paper No. 10 and his liquor-laced public rants, Obama was already known as a critic. Testifying in Njenga's trial was to wave a scarlet flag of defiance directly in Kenyatta's face.

Obama was in a highly vulnerable position. His longtime mentor was now gone. His post at the KTDC was anything but secure. Already underrepresented, Luos were sure to be even further marginalized as the Kikuyu reveled in their now-unobstructed dominance of the political system. As Caroline Elkins, the Harvard historian, put it, Obama's testimony was "the nail in the coffin. He had no one to protect him either way. So, it was a very bold move."[32]

Obama could easily have chosen not to testify. He could have remained silent and hoped that he would drift under the radar and his career would survive. But staying quiet had never been one of his strong suits. "I told him this was like suicide. If they killed Mboya, they can kill you," said Peter Aringo, shaking his head. "He said, 'No. I have to speak my mind.' He could not stand that Tom had been killed. He knew that he might be killed himself if he testified. He knew that Kenyatta wanted that case to die. But he went ahead and did it."

Some considered Obama a hero for doing so. "Tom's death was a shattering thing. The shock was as strong for us as it was in the United States with [John F.] Kennedy's killing," said Achola Pala Okeyo, a Kenyan anthropologist and international women's advocate. "It was unthinkable that Kenyatta, someone who had come out of the liberation movement, would preside over such a killing. People could not say anything or they would have been killed. Barack was one of the very few who were bold enough to speak out."

Obama may have known more than the little he revealed in the witness box. Years later Obama confided in two of his friends that he had seen Mboya's killer and believed that he was the only witness who could identify him. Of the nine eyewitnesses to the shooting who testified at the hearing, not one was able to identify Njenga in a police lineup.[33] Obama told Pake Zane, his friend from his Hawaii days, during a 1974 visit to Nairobi that he chose not to identify Njenga publicly because prior to the trial he had received a death threat on his family. He also claimed that a car that struck him while he was walking in the city in 1973 was a failed attempt on his life in retaliation for his testimony. In light of Pinto's death and now Mboya's, Obama had good reason to fear for his safety. Indeed, Mboya's murder remains so deeply shrouded in mystery and suspicion, to this day the Mboya family in Nairobi will not comment on whether Obama confided in them about what he had seen for fear of repercussions.[34] Many Kenyans who are unrelated to the incident decline to speak about it publicly. Zane, an American well removed from Nairobi's punishing political culture, would have appeared a safe and perhaps irresistible confidant. "Barack said he was the only one who witnessed the assassin and the only one who could identify him," Zane recalled. "But if he told he said he and his family would be killed. He did not say exactly who had threatened him. He just said 'the people who killed Mboya.' And I believed him. Barack had a lot of integrity and he was always very upfront with everything."

Evaluating Obama's statement in retrospect is difficult. Goldsworthy makes no mention of Obama in his meticulously researched biography of Mboya. Nor does he figure in any other accounts of the much written about Mboya assassination. It is also true that Obama clearly took liberties with the truth when it suited his purposes. At the time he made his revelation to Zane, embellishing the truth would have been tempting. A courageous patriot threatened by murderous political bosses made a much better story than an egotistical alcoholic having difficulties keeping his job. But nor can Obama's story be dismissed as impossible.

The blood of political assassinations runs deep through contemporary Kenyan history. Few found it surprising that none of the eyewitnesses in Njenga's case managed to identify him. Who, after all, wanted to take such a public stand and find themselves looking down the barrel of a gun? Among the political elite who lost their lives, Mboya was neither the first nor the last. Four years earlier Pinto had been shot. In January 1969 C. M. G. Argwings-Kodhek, a prominent activist lawyer, died in what was officially declared to be a car accident. But when his body was later exhumed, a bullet was found in his body and many believed he had been assassinated.[35] Then came J. M. Kariuki, a onetime personal secretary to Kenyatta who then turned and accused him of corruption and neglect of the poor. In 1975 he was found murdered in the Ngong Hills with several of his fingers missing. By the mid-1970s, as the historian and anthropologist David W. Cohen wrote, "a tradition of assassination was firmly in place as part and parcel of governance in Kenya."[36]

Cohen, coauthor of *The Risks of Knowledge: Investigations into the Death of the Hon. Minister John Robert Ouko in Kenya, 1990*, believes it is possible that Obama may well have been threatened as a consequence of his testimony. "What Obama did in testifying was highly risky," Cohen said in an interview. "Foes of the powers that be in Kenya are prone to be eliminated. Anyone who is a witness to this kind of thing are themselves potential victims of assassination."

Against this setting, Obama's claim of having received a death threat seems more plausible. Obama revealed to a second friend that he not only was able to identify Njenga, whom he had often seen around town, but that he was the one who gave the assassin's name and description to police, enabling them to make an arrest. Such information would have been critical. Furthermore, Obama said that investigators advised him not to testify to what he had done. The friend, a veteran of Kenyan political circles to this day, declined to be identified out of concern for his safety. But he said that when Obama spoke of the matter, he seemed uncharacteristically cowed. "Barack was a very vocal man who always spoke quite openly, but in this case he was very careful and he seemed quite scared," said the friend. "I think he carried that for the rest of his life."[37]

In the months after Mboya's killing, ethnic unrest spiraled out of control across the country and a political crisis loomed. With elections not too far off, Kenyatta embarked on an electoral tour in October of 1969 in large part to emphasize that he was firmly in control. But when he stopped in Kisumu—Odinga's political home base—to preside over the opening of a new hospital, Kenyatta was again heckled by young members of the Kenya People's Union who shouted "*dume*" and waved signs reading, "Where is Tom?" Enraged, Kenyatta launched a vicious verbal attack on Odinga, who was standing just a few feet away from him. If it were not for their friendship, Kenyatta declared, he would have had him locked in detention long ago. He commanded Odinga, "Tell these people of yours to desist. If not, they are going to feel my full wrath. And me, I do not play around at all. . . . I want to tell you, Odinga, while you are looking at me with your two eyes wide open, I have given my orders right now. Those creeping insects of yours are to be crushed like flour. They are to be crushed like flour if they play with us. You over there, do not make noise there. I will come over there and crush you myself."[38]

Now it was the crowd's turn to be furious. As protestors surged toward Kenyatta's departing vehicle as they hurled stones, police opened fire on the crowd. Seven people were killed and more than seventy injured in what came to be called the "Kisumu massacre." Kenyatta hurriedly left the scene, never to return to Nyanza for the rest of his life. Two days later Odinga and the other KPU leaders were arrested, and the KPU was finally banned. Odinga was confined to detention for two years. And with that Kenyatta had at long last vanquished the opposition and cleared the stage for his unchallenged one-man, one-party, and largely one-tribe domination of the nation. The yawning chasm that had been opened between the Kikuyu and Luo would divide the ethnic groups for generations.

For the Luos, the years to come would not be easy. Although some lost their jobs outright, they were more commonly stalled in their careers and their influence severely curtailed. Many who felt they were being turned down for a job because of the spelling of their name were often correct. In 1969 Kikuyus, who represented 20 percent of the population, held 30 percent of the government's senior bureaucratic jobs. Luos, who accounted for 14 percent of the population, held 10.8 percent of the posts. But three years later 41 percent of the senior positions were held by Kikuyus, whereas the Luos' share of those coveted jobs had shrunk to 8.6 percent.[39] With Mboya dead and Odinga incarcerated, Kenyatta was free to expand his political dynasty of extended family members and Kikuyu loyalists as broadly as he wished. The Luo had no choice but to hang on as best they could and remain discreet.

Obama did just the opposite. Far from muffling his rage over Mboya's death, he took every opportunity to denounce Kenyatta and his "betrayal of the Kenyan people," as he often described it. He insisted that Kenyatta had never received an education in London as he claimed and had personally amassed an immense personal fortune. He was a tribalist who had betrayed the promises of independence. And now Kenyatta had murdered his good friend Tom. In bars and restaurants he would approach Kikuyu patrons and insist that they take responsibility for the assassination. And the more he drank, the louder he got. "He was very abusive to the Kikuyus. He would walk right up to them and say, 'You Kikuyus, you killed Tom Mboya. You *killed* my brother.' He was very, very reckless to do that," said Joel Bonuke, a government economist in the 1960s and 1970s. "People would beg him to stop but he paid no attention. Was he brave, or was he foolish? You know, it depends on how you look at it."

Partly because of Obama's reputation as a highly skilled economist and partly because so few others were speaking out, his comments were widely noted. Soon Kenyatta himself took notice. "Obama always talked about being victimized," said Philip Ochieng, the *Nation* columnist. "But the truth was that he was too clever for many of the Kikuyu and they did not like him. Kenyatta was very angry with Obama for saying bad things about him and his clique. The Big Man was above criticism. Everyone knew that."

It is the conventional wisdom among many Luos, including the sprawling Obama family, that after Mboya's death Obama was punished for his own testimony and his subsequent tirade against the government. But though Kenyatta may have had his eye on him, Obama sowed the seeds of his decline. Two days before Mboya was shot the KTDC had a full board meeting to consider confidential reports on Obama's conduct. Although the minutes of the meeting do not specify what were the specific concerns,

Owuor was asked to write Obama to ask him to show cause why the board should not take action against him.

Six months later the board noted a specific and very egregious complaint against Obama. One of the KTDC's long-term pet projects was the creation of a *boma*, a traditional Kenyan village designed to showcase the country's culture and way of life and intended largely for tourists. Obama was a strong advocate of the project and had discouraged other developers from establishing competitive villages elsewhere in the country. Not long after the board had approved an expenditure on the proposed boma in January 1970, Obama unilaterally altered the terms offered to the contractor and architect. In doing so, he reduced the price tag on the project and shortened the time frame for its completion by ten weeks.[40] Without any authorization, he then awarded the contract under the revised terms.

Why he did so is unclear. But what alarmed the board members was not so much the specifics of the deal, for Obama had apparently negotiated terms more beneficial to the government. What upset them was that Obama lied about receiving authorization to take such a step. Obama maintained to the board that because general manager Owuor was out of the country at the time, he had conferred with the then chairman of the board, J. K. Ole Tipis, before he signed a contract with the architect. But the board considered his explanation "completely unsatisfactory." It noted that "there was no written evidence of any consultation between Mr. Obama and the then Chairman, and considered this to be a gross action of irresponsibility on the part of Mr. Obama."[41] The board had the architect contacted and immediately halted the project.

The issue flung open the floodgates. At a meeting of the board's executive appointments committee on May 11, 1970, board members began to talk about Obama and determined that he had lied about a number of things. One board member after another revealed offenses Obama had committed. Chairman Jan Mohamed told of a time when Obama informed him that Owuor had gone to Kisumu and had left Obama in charge, when in fact Owuor was sitting right at his desk. Board member G. M. Matheka recalled that before he was a board member he had once met Obama in Mombasa and that Obama had identified himself as the deputy general manager of the KTDC, a post that did not exist. K. S. N. Matiba, another board member, pointed out that in addition to Obama's lying about the boma matter, there was evidence of "other things he had done which would have warranted dismissal." Another member revealed that an earlier composition of the KTDC board had passed a resolution that Obama be dismissed and had been stopped only by the intervention of the Ministry of Tourism and Wildlife, which oversaw the KTDC. There was also Owuor's stack of reports about his drinking on the job, impersonations of Owuor, and absences from meetings. Alarmed about Obama's "image in public," the committee decided to recommend to the board that Obama be asked to resign. A senior development officer smelling of alcohol, never mind one prone to personal exaggeration, was not what they had in mind. If Obama would not agree to leave, "the board should dismiss him instantly."[42]

In the months leading up to Obama's firing, Owuor, seeing the writing on the wall, tried to get Obama to change his ways. It troubled him that a man of Obama's intelligence and ability did not carry himself with greater dignity. Owuor's own brother had known Obama in the United States, and Owuor felt some personal responsibility for his deputy. On a couple of occasions he invited both Ruth and Obama to his house and appealed to Ruth to see if there was something she could do to stop Obama's drinking and misrepresentations. But Ruth said she had already tried. "You know, it was not only Obama. There were others who came back from the U.S. and they did not hold themselves well," said Owuor. "They were very sophisticated and they thought that since they had earned their degrees, that since they could show that piece of paper, they were all set. But that was not the end of the story, of course. That was just the beginning. Look at Philip Ndegwa. He went to Harvard and he came back and he held himself as Harvard material. He was a man with dignity and a great deal of discretion. Obama did not hold himself as Harvard material. And that made all the difference."

When Obama learned of the board's action, he fought back. In a meeting with Chairman Mohamed, Obama demanded to know what the consequences would be if he refused to resign. He insisted that he receive several more weeks to consider his course of action. Mohamed refused to debate the matter any further, and in June 1970, less than a year after Mboya's assassination and the subsequent crackdown, Obama was terminated.[43] At thirty-four years old, he now had three failed jobs behind him, and his prospect of getting another job anytime soon, of getting any job at all, was less than promising.

Word of Obama's firing traveled swiftly through the ranks of government economists and planners, as Obama knew it would. Deeply despondent, he turned to the form of solace he knew best. Driving home from a bar alone late one night, he ran his car headlong into another vehicle parked at the side of the road. A few of his friends wondered if the accident might have been a suicide attempt. With one of his legs broken in multiple locations, Obama was hospitalized for nearly a month. As happened the last time he was laid up with two broken legs six years earlier, an envelope bearing bad news found its way to his bedside. This time the letter came from the Ministry of Internal Security and Defense. The government, or perhaps it was Kenyatta himself, had revoked his passport, making it impossible for him to do the kind of work at which he was so able.[44]

Winyo piny kiborne, as Hussein Onyango used to say: For the bird, the world is never too far. But the bird who had flown so high and so far now could fly nowhere at all.

9

"EVEN GOD DOES NOT WANT ME"

Shem Arungu-Olende had just returned from the United States in mid-1970 when he received a telephone call from his old friend Barack Obama. Olende, an electrical engineer with a passion for economic analysis, had recently concluded a year's stint as a visiting scholar at the Massachusetts Institute of Technology in Cambridge, Massachusetts, and had come home to consider his options. The two men had gotten to know each other several years earlier when they had discovered they shared a fascination with mathematical programming. Now Obama was calling to offer him a job. "He said he was setting up a consulting firm and he wanted me to work with him," recalled Olende, who would later become the secretary general of the African Academy of Sciences. "He said we'd make a great team. And you know, I was interested."

But as the two men talked, Olende was shocked to learn of Obama's circumstances. When they had met five years earlier Obama had recently returned from Cambridge. With his Harvard degree and elegant bearing, not to mention his attractive white wife, Obama seemed set to become a powerhouse among the newly emerging cadre of elite Africans who were slowly assuming control of the country's power structure. But here was Obama now without a job and his checkered employment record a matter of some talk in Nairobi circles. As Olende caught up with other old friends, he heard hair-raising stories about Obama's explosive domestic life and inexplicable behavior on the job. Nonetheless, Olende liked Obama and seriously considered teaming up with him. As it turned out he wound up taking a job with the United Nations, where he would remain for the next three decades. But he worried that Obama's reckless ways would eventually lead him into deeper trouble.

The consulting firm never happened. After Obama was fired from the KTDC, he managed to piece together stray bits of work, but none of them lasted long. He worked for the Kenya Water Department for some months and managed to parlay that job into a stint advising the World Health Organization on rural water supplies. But within a few months of losing his job Obama was adrift with neither a paycheck nor the prospect of one. Unmoored from the organizing rigors of a job and increasingly at odds with both his wife and children, Obama entered a period of fitful decline that lasted for nearly six years. Although he remained close with some of his older friends and continued to show up at his favorite watering holes— as long as someone else was buying—he periodically disappeared for long spells at a time. And when he emerged from this overcast period, he was a changed man, one whose world was considerably diminished.

With her husband now jobless and at large, Ruth struggled to keep the family afloat. She was now the sole support of the household. Not only did she pay the rent, the household expenses, and the wages of the housekeeper, she also signed the checks for five private school tuitions. In addition to Obama's own four children's schooling, there was Ezra's school bill and sundry other expenses for itinerant Obama family members. Nor did Obama assist much with the household logistics such as driving the children to school or to their sports activities. As in most any other Kenyan family of the same class, such tasks were left to Ruth or the household help.

Although Ruth tried to maintain a household routine as she juggled her job at Nestlé and ferrying the children, Obama came and went at odd hours. Most afternoons he retreated to the bar at Sans Chique or Brunner's and stayed there well into evening, railing against the failures of the government and the injustices that had befallen him. By the time he returned to the house, he was often stumbling and barely coherent. The children, cowering in their beds, listened as he crashed into furniture and cursed at his own clumsiness.

Auma heard the shouting too. As she told her brother Barack many years later, "The Old Man never spoke to Roy or myself except to scold us. He would come home very late, drunk, and I could hear him shouting at

Ruth telling her to cook him food," Barack recounted in *Dreams from My Father*. "Sometimes, when he wasn't home, she would tell Roy and myself that our father was crazy and that she pitied us for having such a father. I didn't blame her for this—I probably agreed."[1]

Obama had long vented his anger on Ruth with verbal onslaughts and a hail of blows to her head. But as he grew increasingly despondent in the months after he lost his job, his assaults on her grew more violent. Ruth took out a restraining order and worried constantly about what to do next. She was anxious that one day Obama would turn his frustration on the children and that, she had decided, would be the end. Nonetheless, she did not leave him because still, somehow, she loved him. And she believed that he loved her as well: "I loved him despite everything. I just had a great passion for the man. And I love my children. I'm a person who stays hoping that things will get better."[2]

But things didn't get better. They got worse. One night Obama returned from the bars in his usual ill humor, except this time he had a knife. "He came to the door one day, banging, banging and Auma let him in of course, being a child," Ruth recalled. "And when he came in he had that knife. He laid it against my neck as he shouted at me. I was terrified of course. He terrified me a number of times. But I did not think he would really kill me. He was a bluffer, just a bluffer. Even the children saw all of this happening. It was Roy who went and got a neighbor. She was a Luo friend of mine and she talked to Barack. She said, 'Don't do this, Barack. This is wrong.'"

Even then, Ruth did not leave. Instead, she started to contemplate a divorce. As she saw it, if she were able to get a divorce and gain custody of Mark and David, she would at last have some leverage over Obama. Part of Obama's singular authority over her was his ability to take them from her. Perhaps if she were able to negotiate from a position of greater strength, she could get Obama to change his behavior and stop his chronic drinking. That, at least, is what she hoped.

In November 1971 Obama made the surprise announcement that he was going on a lengthy overseas trip. Somehow he had gotten his passport back and was now eager to try to drum up some international consulting work again. Unable to find a job, Obama continued to pursue his hope of setting up a consulting firm and hoped to reconnect during his travels with some of his contacts from his days at the KTDC. No sooner had he walked out of the house with his suitcase did Ruth call her attorney. One of her friends and a cousin who visited the house frequently had witnessed Obama's abusive behavior on multiple occasions, and now they were ready to testify to what they had seen. "I knew the marriage wasn't going anywhere and I needed some leverage," said Ruth. "Divorce would give me the freedom so he didn't have any legal hold on me. That seemed very important."

While Ruth presented her case in a Nairobi courtroom, Obama was halfway around the world in Honolulu celebrating Christmas with the Dunhams, about whom he had told his current wife very little. He was also getting to know the little boy on the tricycle whose photograph he had religiously kept on his bureau for the past decade. That boy, Barack Obama II, was now ten years old and had decidedly mixed feelings about the looming dark figure with the slight limp who showed up on the doorstep a few weeks before the holiday. Since his father had left nine years ago, much had changed in his own young life. When the younger Obama was four years old, his mother had fallen in love with another foreign student, this one an amiable Indonesian who liked to wrestle with her young son. By 1968 Ann Dunham had married Lolo Soetoro, and the family settled in Jakarta. The marriage did not last long, however, and by the summer of 1971 Obama had returned to Honolulu to live with his grandparents and attend private school. Ann returned to celebrate the Christmas holiday that year, and eventually she and her young daughter had also returned to Honolulu to live, although she would not divorce her second husband for several more years.

Eying his father quietly from the corner of the living room on the day that he arrived, Obama observed that he was astonishingly thin, his bones pressing his trousers into sharp points at the knee. Wearing a blue blazer and a crisp white shirt with a scarlet ascot at his neck, he was overdressed compared to the casual island style. His cane was equally elegant with a rounded ivory head. But his eyes were a bleary yellow, "the eyes of someone who's had malaria more than once. There was a fragility about his frame, I thought, a caution when he lit a cigarette or reached for his beer."[3]

Obama stayed for one month. During that time he and the Dunhams visited island sites and the family's own architectural landmarks. They drove by the apartments in which the couple had lived, the Kapiʻolani Medical Center where their son had been born, and the trim one-story University Avenue house with the inviting veranda where Ann had ultimately retreated to live with her parents and her one-year-old son after her husband had left her. As the weeks passed, the watchful boy noted the power of his father's presence and the singular effect he had on other people. Obama generated an electricity, a vibration that made Gramps, as Stanley was called by his grandson, more vigorous. Even Madelyn, known as "Toot" for "Tutu," which is Hawaiian for "grandparent," was drawn into debate about politics and finance in the elder Obama's presence. When he waved his elegant hands in emphasis or recounted an amusing story in his commanding, all-enveloping voice, people listened. But between father and son there was not much conversation. "I often felt mute before him," his son wrote, "and he never pushed me to speak."[4]

Obama Sr.'s visit to Hawaii generated mixed emotions on both sides of the equation. For the elder Obama the sights and sounds of the island where he had lived in the flush of great promise were bittersweet. He did not look up many of his old friends and made no effort to connect with either Zane or Abercrombie. He sat, inexplicably, for a series of photographic portraits at the University of Hawaii, and these are filed in the school's archive bearing no explanatory label. In the photos Obama is dressed in a gray suit with a dark handkerchief tucked in his breast pocket, and he stares solemnly into the distance. There is little resemblance to the ebullient young undergraduate in shirtsleeves photographed amidst a throng of his friends in a photo shot a decade earlier.

Presumably aware that his marriage to Ruth was nearing a bitter end, Obama apparently initiated the Hawaii visit in part with the expectation that his former wife might return to Kenya with him. Ann, then twenty-nine, had her own marital troubles with Soetoro and likely intuited that her marriage was not to last long either. She was already talking about enrolling at the University of Hawaii in order to pursue a master's degree in anthropology. Although she considered Obama's suggestion, she concluded that she and her children were better off staying in Hawaii where their lives would be more stable. "He had come back and wanted her to go to Africa with him, finally," recalled Ann's old school friend, Susan Botkin Blake. "Of course this was what she had wanted all those years he had been away. But now, she told people, she could not face leaving again."

With the finality of Ann's refusal generating palpable tension, Obama's visit soon began to sour. Toot and Gramps were growing weary of Obama's presence and waited impatiently for him to retreat at the evening's end to the rented apartment in which he slept. The stress finally erupted one evening when young Barack turned on the television to watch the cartoon special *How The Grinch Stole Christmas!*, a favored Christmas ritual. Obama Sr. promptly ordered his son to turn off the television and head to his room to study. When Ann argued that the boy should be allowed to watch, the matter mushroomed into a fierce family squabble that consumed four highly irritated adults. As Barack Jr. watched the green Grinch alone behind his closed bedroom door, he "began to count the days until my father would leave and things would return to normal."[5]

His countdown ended two weeks later when Obama gave his son a farewell hug at the airport and disappeared into the blue skies overhead. Obama would never see his father again. For a time the two exchanged letters. But by the time Barack reached his twenties and was swept up in his own quest for rootedness and identity, the letter writing had stopped and the stack of aerogrammes from his father were stored neatly away in a closet. After the painful Christmas encounter, another two decades would pass before Barack turned to the pages of his memoir to sort out some of his complex feelings about his father.

On his return to Nairobi, Obama was dismayed to encounter still more rejection. In his absence Ruth had not only consulted with a lawyer about getting a divorce; she had managed to have their marriage terminated. Beside himself, Obama once again tried to talk her out of it, just as he had when she fled to the United States with their first son in 1967. But this time Ruth was not to be swayed. "He said don't go through with this, don't go through with this, please," said Ruth. "And I said, 'No, no, no. I *am* going through with it, Barack, because I've had enough of this nonsense.' I said I would still live with him even though we were divorced because you see then I had some leverage. I had the custody of the children now."

Ruth's hard-won leverage changed little. On the contrary, Obama continued with his dissolute lifestyle, seemingly impervious to his wife's outrage. Finally, one night he stumbled back into the house and raised his hand over his youngest son, David Opiyo, and struck him. With that, Ruth's seemingly inexhaustible forbearance came to an abrupt end. Days later, after Obama had headed out for the afternoon, a friend of Ruth's pulled his pickup truck in front of the Woodley house and Ruth swiftly filled it with her belongings. By nightfall she and her two sons and the family housekeeper were moved into a small rented house in Westlands. The following morning a furious Obama was banging loudly on their door. "He shouted at me, 'You prostitute, I am going to take the children. I am going to kill you.' You know, on and on. It was drunken rages, and more drunken rages. I think he followed me because he was ashamed. And I think part of the shame was that the community knew what was going on. They had witnessed it," Ruth said. "He kept coming back every week, the same thing, shouting and calling me names. It was very, very disturbing. It lasted for about a month and then we contacted the CID [Criminal Investigation Department of the Kenya Police] and they called him in. They said, 'Look Barack, stop bothering that woman.' And from that time on he never bothered me again. So, that was that."

Ruth wasn't the only one who had heard Obama raging at her door. Neighbors were horrified at his belligerent behavior, and in Nairobi's tight-knit social circles, the word got around. "The man was very much an outcast at that point," said Harris Mule, a high-ranking government economist then serving as deputy permanent secretary for planning in the Ministry of Finance and Economic Planning, whose wife was a friend of Ruth's. "Part of it was his personal history. I mean, Obama lived pretty much like an African. There were real horror stories of how he treated his wife. My own wife would tell me about this quite often so I would not think of such a thing myself. But the bigger problem, quite frankly, was the man was always broke. He would be a nuisance because he'd go to a bar without money and he would expect people to buy him drinks and he used to drink very expensive liquor which was whiskey. So his friends would get upset about that. They would try to avoid him."

With Ruth and the two younger boys gone by 1973, Obama was left virtually alone in the red-roofed Woodley house. The housekeeper had left with Ruth. Ezra had departed the previous year to take a job managing spare machine parts at Coca-Cola's Nairobi plant. Obama had landed him the job, a position that developed into a flourishing career that lasted for two decades. Malik, a student at the prestigious Lenana School, was also not around very much. Auma had recently been accepted at the Kenya High School and boarded during the week, returning home only on occasional weekends. More often than not, Obama found himself alone in the house with no one to cook for him or take the glass out of his hand when he fell asleep on the couch.

Auma, then thirteen, felt the breakup of the family deeply. Ruth had lived with the children since Auma was four years old, and she was the only mother Auma and Malik had ever really known. Now, not only were her "Mummy" and her younger brothers gone, but there was also no woman in the house to tend to her basic needs or to shield her from her father's self-destructive behavior. Often, when she returned to the empty house on vacations or on a weekend, she found the cupboards bare of food. Although Obama was able to borrow funds to pay for his necessities, he often gave the money to charities to maintain the illusion of prosperity. In the months after Ruth left, as Auma wrote in her 2010 memoir, *Das Leben kommt immer dazwischen* ("Life Comes In Between"), "a sad time began."[6] "It appeared that both my father and brother tried to escape from the stillness of our house as much as possible," Auma wrote. "Many times I was already asleep when they came home and often my father woke me up to talk with me."[7]

Inviting his daughter to come sit with him in the living room, Obama turned to the young girl for solace in the long lonely evenings. As Auma stared coolly at him from her end of the couch, Obama insisted that he deeply loved his children and was working as hard as he could to provide for them. As the night wore on, he played his beloved Schubert's Fifth Symphony on the record player while detailing the host of difficulties he had encountered in his life to his sleepy daughter. But Auma was unmoved by his sorrows. His late-night effort to forge a connection with a child he had long neglected was too little, too late. Engulfed in the dramatic cascade of flute and horns, she could not hear him. "I was far away from him. I did not understand his deep sadness and felt no compassion for his loneliness," she wrote. "At that time I was firmly convinced that the situation to which he had brought us was his own fault."[8]

To some extent Obama himself agreed. Although he publicly blamed Kenyatta and his Kikuyu coterie for his travails, Obama was painfully aware that in the end he was the one who was unable to provide for his children or his extended family. On his trips to Kanyadhiang he never mentioned that he had lost his job. On the contrary, he always arrived laden with food and gifts, purchased with funds he had borrowed from friends or the Kogelo Union Association. Dressed in his trademark European suits, now thinning at the elbow, he unfailingly presented himself as a flourishing government economist. But in private he mourned the sorry state of his fractured families to his closest friends and turned increasingly to drink. "It was a very, very tough time for him," said his old friend Peter Aringo, a former member of Parliament representing Alego. "I think he understood that the problem somehow lay within his own personality but he did not know how to correct it. It really broke his pride. So he blamed Kenyatta. It was Kenyatta who had made it impossible for him to take care of his families. Barack was fighting this huge monster and he could never win. By this time he had begun to drink a lot in the daytime. He really had nothing to occupy him."

What gnawed at Obama the most was his inability to pay for the education of his vast network of family members or even his own children. Ever since he had been a child performing math sums at Onyango's table, he had been taught that education was the passport to achievement and success. He had long preached the benefits of a college degree and proudly paid the school fees for countless young nephews and cousins. That he, Dr. Barack Obama, could no longer do even *that* galled him deeply. It was not for lack of trying. During the years that he was unemployed, Obama routinely dropped into the downtown office of the Institute of International Education, a U.S.-based nonprofit that provides international educational opportunities and training in hopes of securing funding for one or two of his relatives. Almost once a week Josephine Mitchell, director of the office from 1972 to 1975, who sometimes worked late into the evening, would look up to find Obama at the door. "He was looking for money," recalled Mitchell, now seventy-three years old and living in Vancouver

Island. "He always had a long list of family members in mind. He'd say, 'I have this brilliant nephew you must let me tell you about,' or 'Here are the schools I have in mind for him,' or, 'Did you know that these are the schools I went to?'"

Mitchell found his determination moving. But she found the strong smell of alcohol on his breath distinctly less appealing. "He was usually quite tight," added Mitchell. "If you got him in the morning, he'd be OK. But he had a few at lunch and a few more on the way home. By evening he was pretty wasted. You know, by then he was someone people had really cast aside. He just wasn't much use in the scheme of things anymore. It was really very sad."

Although some of Obama's colleagues and friends kept their distance, Omogi Calleb did not. Calleb was not just a man of similar tastes but was also born not far from Kanyadhiang in the same year as Obama. For a short while the two had attended school together. A gregarious and amiable man, Calleb owned a popular new restaurant in Westlands with a dance floor famous for its Congolese bands. Worried that his old friend was slipping into a perilous state, Calleb took him under his wing. He made sure Obama had ample funds for his Double-Doubles and provided him a bed in his own home for months at a time. On some weekends the two of them hit the road looking for excitement. They went to the beaches in Mombasa, stayed in fine hotels in Tanzania, and ate at luxurious restaurants in Nairobi. And sometimes they arranged to meet some young women at their ultimate destination. "We liked going out with pretty young ladies," said Calleb. "We had a philosophy which was that they must be presentable. So sometimes we did that. But to be fair to Barack, this was not always his practice. At this point in his life, what he really liked was his *pombe*, his alcohol, and always the general company of other people drinking."

Like others, Calleb worried about Obama's alcoholic intake, and he was especially worried when Obama was behind the wheel of his car. During the early 1970s Obama had a series of minor traffic accidents, most of them at night, and the police frequently lectured him for his perilous driving habits. But driving under the influence of alcohol was hardly uncommon, and Obama paid the police little mind. As Obama's mother had done some years ago, Calleb warned Obama that he would meet his end in a car crash if he was not careful. "I said, 'Your death will be caused by drunkenness,'" recalled Calleb. "He said, 'To hell with it. If that's the cause of my death, so be it.'"

Inevitably, Obama wound up in yet another serious car accident. This time he not only broke both of his legs but also shattered his left knee cap. The knee required a cast for three months and a hospital stay of twice that duration.[9] During his recuperation Obama sunk into deeper gloom. Unable to walk during much of his hospitalization, Obama could no longer manage even the small amounts of contract work that had kept him financially afloat. When he was finally released from the hospital on crutches toward the end of 1973, he walked with a limp that would stay with him for much of his life. Obama, Harvard graduate and son of Hussein Onyango, was now a man with a physical handicap, no means of support, and a dwindling number of friends. "He was ostracized mostly because of his penury, having no money," said Mule. "In Kenya, if you have no money that's a big problem."

Obama believed he had a much larger problem—bigger than his damaged legs, bigger even than his financial worries. And that was a vengeful Kikuyu determined to pay him back for his role in Njenga's trial. Although it is unclear whether Kenyatta's regime in fact targeted Obama in any way or threatened his family with death as he told a handful of friends, his fear seemed genuine. When his old Hawaii friend Pake Zane and his then girlfriend, Julie Lauster, arrived in Nairobi for a visit in 1974, they were both struck by Obama's fixation with Kenyatta's government. Not only had the president betrayed the country with his capitalist ways and nepotistic practices, Obama declared, but he had sought to assassinate Obama himself. He explained that his leg had been injured when a car had tried to run him down on a city street, which he called "a direct attempt on my life," recalled Zane. Obama appeared to be in near constant pain, and his anger was unrelenting. Accompanying him on his circuit of downtown bars at night, Zane found listening to his diatribes difficult. "He'd go out and get wasted and piss off all of his friends," recalled Zane. "We'd be at an outside bar and he'd pour out his anger at someone for their stance on this or their opinion on that or something they had done. He'd be sarcastic and right in their face. He'd point at someone and say, 'That man is a fool,' or 'He has no understanding of what he is talking about.' You couldn't get a word in edgewise. It was really hard to be around all that rage."

Zane and Lauster had intended to stay at a campground just outside the city during their week in Nairobi but had instead moved to Obama's house at his insistence. After a few days staying with Obama, however, they decided to move back to the campground. "He was funny and charming and a real bore," declared Lauster. "We went back to the park because it was much calmer there."

Sometimes when Obama went off on a rant about the miserable state of Kenyan affairs, fistfights would develop. Aringo recalls a night at the Nyanza Bar when Obama was crowing so loudly about his Harvard degree that others in the bar turned to look at him as the room grew quiet. "And then a voice from the back of the bar called, 'Go to hell,' and that was that," said Aringo. "Obama went after the man and there was a huge fistfight. We finally separated them. Obama was very apologetic the next day. I said, 'You cannot fight in public like that. You are far too senior.'"

Then came the ultimate humiliation. In the administrative office of the Kenya High School, Auma Obama's tuition was often unpaid for weeks beyond the due date. Not just once, but repeatedly. Each time, Auma was summoned to the bookkeeper's office, where she was given a bill for the derelict amount and told to return home until the account was settled. And each time, when she arrived home, Obama contacted several of his friends who agreed to cover the debt. But Obama knew full well that they had little intention of doing so. Refusing to acknowledge his inability to pay for his daughter's education, Obama briskly wrote out a check as though doing so would somehow replenish his empty account. Auma solemnly trudged the two-mile distance back to school, painfully aware that the check in her hand was worthless.[10] "So I was more than once again sent home a few days later and again had to ask my father for the payment," wrote Auma. "With each visit I had to grow a thicker skin to be able to cope with this terrible situation. My skin became thicker and thicker until I totally distanced myself from my father and the pain I saw in his face."[11]

After several such instances, a headmistress at the school learned of Auma's plight and stepped forward to offer her a scholarship. Auma was able to continue her schooling and returned home as little as possible.[12]

By the end of 1975 there was no real home to return to. Unable to pay the rent, Obama was forced to leave the Woodley house in which he had lived for six years. Virtually homeless, he slept on the couches of his friends Aringo and Calleb or at the home of his nephew Ezra. When he was able to borrow money or claim a favor from a friend, he stayed alone in a hotel room.

Despite his abject financial state, Obama continued to frequent his favorite bars, usually able to find an acquaintance who would stand him a round or two. One day, as he maneuvered slowly through the lobby of the Intercontinental Hotel, still favoring his injured leg, he ran into his young friend Oyuko Mbeche. It was in Cambridge that Obama had met Mbeche, the high school student who had been so inspired by Obama's eloquent articulation of mathematical principles that he had changed his career from medicine to engineering. Mbeche, who had spent many a night in Obama's Cambridge apartment listening raptly to the older man's stories, had since earned a couple of university degrees himself and was now a lecturer at the University of Nairobi. Taken aback by Obama's slender frame and his halting stride, Mbeche said he was sorry to hear about Obama's accident. "Obama said, 'Well, you see, now even God does not want me,'" recalled Mbeche. "Here he'd had this accident in which he should have died but . . . as he saw it, not even God wanted him."

THE YEAR 1975 BROUGHT A SERIES OF pivotal developments that broke the free fall of Obama's life. It opened with a political tragedy that tore at the Kenyan heart. But it ended with Obama's surprising personal resurrection, a renaissance that was initiated, fittingly enough, over double shots of whiskey at an elegant bar.

The politics came first. In the years after Tom Mboya's death and the banning of Odinga's KPU, Kenyatta enjoyed a period of relative political peace during which the voices of his perennial critics remained quiet. But it did not last. Josiah Mwangi Kariuki, a colorful member of Parliament known as J. M., had once been a personal secretary to Kenyatta and a devotee of the aging oligarch. But like some other dissident Kikuyus, Kariuki had grown increasingly unhappy with what he considered to be the administration's disregard for the poor and its gradual accumulation of riches. Championing himself as a man of the people, Kariuki famously declared that "We do not want a Kenya of ten millionaires and ten million beggars."

Kariuki was no mere gadfly warning against the perils of class formation, another naysayer to be squashed. He was a popular former insider with a following in parts of Kikuyuland. And so it was that he had to be eliminated. On March 3, 1975, two Masai elders found his body in a thicket in the Ngong Hills. He had been shot several times and several of his fingers had been cut off.[13] The assassination prompted widespread outrage as students boycotted lectures on the University of Nairobi campus and members of Parliament denounced the government and formed a committee to probe the murder. The banner headline of the *Daily Nation* on March 14 trumpeted, "WE WANT THE TRUTH."

Once again, as he had in the case of the Kisumu rioting after Mboya's death, Kenyatta came down hard on his enemies. A report critical of the government investigation into the matter was shelved, and several critics in Parliament were either detained or forced out of office. Kenyatta may have been an old man showing signs of senility, but he was still capable of slapping down his opponents with an iron hand in an iron glove when he wanted to. At the annual Kenyatta Day celebration several months later, Kenyatta concluded his remarks with the chilling words, "The hawk is in the sky. It is ready to descend on chickens who stray from the pathway."[14]

Like many Kenyans, Kariuki's murder deeply disheartened Obama, as it came only six years after Mboya's assassination. For months afterward it was the topic of heated, if somewhat guarded, conversation in the bars and restaurants around town. Indeed, Obama and Aringo had been discussing the political consequences of the administration's crackdown over drinks one October afternoon at a table at the Intercontinental Hotel when they noticed Mwai Kibaki, then the Minister of Finance and Economic Planning, stride across the room toward his usual spot at the bar.

Kibaki, an able economist, had already worn a number of hats in his career and had gotten to know Obama when he worked as Tom Mboya's deputy in the planning ministry in the mid-1960s. Although a Kikuyu who commanded a prominent government post, Kibaki had a soft spot for Luos, partly stemming from his days with Mboya. He had even been aligned temporarily with Odinga over some internal KANU struggles in the pre-independence days. Kibaki not only shared Obama's appetite for whiskey, but he had also been deeply impressed by the other man's mathematic skills and economic modeling. And so when Obama approached him at the bar that day, Kibaki held out his hand. Obama got right to the point, as Aringo recalls it. "He said, 'I have no job so I cannot buy myself a drink. Why is it that you have a job and yet I am twice the economist that you are?' Kibaki really liked Obama. He understood him and the way he talked. So he bought him his double shots of whiskey and then he told Barack to come to his office in another week. There would be a job for him there."

Obama was deeply pleased. At long last he faced the prospect of serious work and could begin to piece together a semblance of his old life. In early November 1975 Obama walked into the Finance Ministry on Harambee Avenue, the same building in which Edgar Edwards had him turned down for the job of chief planning officer on his return from the United States eleven years earlier. Obama was instructed to report to Harris Mule, the deputy permanent secretary in charge of planning, and Mule was not displeased to see him. Although he took issue with aspects of Obama's domestic life and was well aware of his problems at KTDC, he also admired Obama's abilities and felt he could make a valuable contribution.

Mule and others had carefully considered what kind of job to give Obama, keenly aware of his sometimes abrasive personality. They had concluded that he would be best suited for a technical job, one without any of the fiscal or management responsibilities that had led him into trouble at KTDC. Obama was made planning officer for commerce development in the Industry and Infrastructure Section. The job, strictly crunching numbers, was at a level usually reserved for recent college graduates.[15] He was to be paid 1,446 pounds a year, significantly lower than his salary at KTDC. That the graying Kenyatta apparently did not object to Obama's hiring indicated that either he was simply unaware of it or could not be troubled by such a low-level posting. "The man was qualified and I knew he could do the job," said Mule. "At KTDC he had been assigned to help run an institution but his personality quite frankly was not up to it. What we were giving him was a behind the scenes job where you sit down and get information and crank it up and come up with the product in the end. And that is what he did."

Obama recognized a lot of the faces on the second floor, many of them economists with whom he had started out and who now held positions far more exalted than his own. Although the number of economists and planners in the Ministry had significantly increased over the past decade, they still shared a camaraderie and zeal for their mission that Mboya had fostered. Edwards, the professor from Texas who had turned him down so many years ago, was still there working as a senior adviser. Philip Ndegwa, whom he had tutored at Harvard, had recently left his post as Permanent Secretary of the Ministry of Finance and Planning to take a job at the United Nations. And Francis Masakhalia, who had been a few years behind him at the Maseno School, was now chief economist in the planning department and Obama's new boss. Masakhalia, who was deeply fond of Obama, welcomed him warmly. "I had all the sympathy for my old friend and I was glad to see him back," said Masakhalia. "Here was a very well educated individual who was not being utilized in our society. And that pained us."

Not everyone was so pleased to see Obama reporting to work. Some who knew him were uncomfortable, even a bit embarrassed, to see Obama at such a low rank. Others were concerned that the grandstanding and drinking about which they had heard so much would become a problem. But when another permanent secretary questioned Obama's employment, Masakhalia leapt to his defense. In a letter to the secretary, Masakhalia wrote, "regarding Mr. Obama's tendencies, let me assure you that the latter have been common knowledge to everyone who has known Mr. Obama for some time. . . . We, however, have been made to believe that Mr. Obama has reformed considerably. Furthermore, he has been advised of the conduct and discipline that he has to maintain while in the Civil Service."[16]

Two weeks later deeply saddening family news dampened the buoyancy that Obama had felt on returning to work. The Old Man, Hussein Onyango, frail and nearly blind at eighty, had died. As the oldest son, Obama was responsible for pulling together the funeral. Because he had just started work and had not yet been paid, Obama had to request an advance on his salary to do so. Five months later he requested a second advance in order to pay for myriad other expenses. It was just the beginning. Throughout his years in the Ministry of Finance, Obama was forever short of funds, frequently raising the specter of family tragedies or personal problems for which he needed immediate cash. His requests were almost always granted. "I just do not have any money at all," Obama wrote to Masakhalia in a November 1975 letter asking for an advance. "Could you please arrange for the money to be paid to you, then hand it over to Olweny Ogutu, who is my nephew?"

In May 1976 he politely requested an advance of 1,000 Kenyan shillings. In a letter to the Treasury's senior personnel officer, Obama wrote that he was plagued by financial problems. Not only was his oldest son, Malik, sick in Kisumu and about to start private school, "I also have to pay quite a lot of money in school fees and uniforms for all my children going to school. Added to this I just lost my father recently and as such I find myself very much squized [sic] financially."

So "squized" was he that he was unable to pay his rent on an apartment he had taken on Race Course Road in 1977. In February 1978 Joseph K. Muriungi, Obama's landlord, wrote to the department's personnel officer and asked for help in recovering 4,200 Kenyan shillings that "Dr. B. H. Obama owed him." Muriungi had not had much luck in his own efforts to extract the money. "I have called [Obama] on several occasions and in all he speaks to me very rudely," Muriungi wrote. "He has even gone so far as asking me whether I don't know that he is a doctor."[17]

Despite his financial problems, Obama was, once again, working as an economist and speaking the language that he understood so intuitively. But the tasks he was initially assigned had little relation to the multiple regression analysis and sophisticated modeling technique that he had learned while at Harvard. Obama was dealing instead with the most basic fundamentals of Kenya's transportation needs: The Kilifi ferry on the northern coast needed to be expanded and made more efficient. Axle load limitations called for special enforcement as overweight commercial trucks were causing heavy damage to the Nairobi/Mombasa and Kericho/Busia corridors.[18] Even as the work grew more complex in the passing months, Obama was often drafting memos or responding to queries on behalf of either Masakhalia or Mule. But Obama's lengthy memos are strikingly articulate and comprehensive, with no detail left untended.

The Barack Obama who uncomplainingly wrote those memos on behalf of his higher ups was a changed man. Although he had resurrected the title *Dr. Obama* with aplomb and continued to visit the plush hotels like the elegant Nairobi Serena and the legendary Norfolk with his flusher friends, the old flourish was missing. A white pickup truck had replaced the gleaming Mercedes. Some friends joked he had made the change to · limit the number of people who could drive with him. Instead of pricey Benson and Hedges cigarettes, he now smoked 555s or the local Sportsman. The pipe belonged largely to the past. Although Obama continued to beat out a rhumba with any young girl who might join him, the days when he pulled on his elegant white suit and strutted on to the dance floor at the Starlight Club before an admiring crowd were over. There was about him a quieter and more subdued air, especially when he was in the office or with people he did not know well. Obama could always manage to find a battle in which to take a side, not unlike the debates in which he so excelled during his Maseno School days, but the larger war was over. "Even when he finally had the job, the damage had been done. It was too little, too late," said Aringo. "He had accumulated a great deal of debt and he could not stand that he could not maintain the village family in the manner that he should be able to do as a senior person. His children were not doing particularly well either and that weighed on him."

But there also was much about Obama that remained the same. Just as Masakhalia and Mule aimed to reduce Obama's interactions with other employees, to limit his engagement on teams, for example, so Obama did his best to steer clear of those in the office whom he considered his inferior. He whispered not so quietly that they were "intellectual dwarfs." When he arrived in the Ministry's Treasury Department, Obama met another economist named James Otieno who worked as a planning officer in the Natural Resources Section. A Luo like Obama, Otieno and he shared a network of associations back home. Otieno was an intense, highly skilled economist himself and could easily hold his own with the newcomer in infrastructure. Otieno had little of Obama's boisterous sense of humor, but the two men shared both a passion for intellectual debate and a large appetite for cigarettes and alcohol. Some laughingly likened the pair to "The Two Ronnies," a popular British comedy show at the time about two men named Ronnie. "Jim was a bit temperamental, a bit touchy, not as social as Barack," said Alex Obondo, an insurance executive and a close drinking friend of Obama's. "But they got along well because they were very brilliant and their brains worked on the same level."

Impatient with the detritus of the daily office interchange, Otieno also preferred to keep his distance from others. And so it was that Otieno and Obama adopted their own personal working schedule. They arrived at the office as early as 5 a.m., well before the Treasury corridors began to fill, and toiled quietly in their separate offices. By noon they were done. They then headed to the Kaloleni Public Bar, where they would pass the rest of the day until others on a more conventional schedule began to show up toward the late afternoon.

The Kaloleni bar, with its red tile roof and colorful liquor logos painted on the walls, was a favored Luo watering hole at one end of the historic residential estate. On the more downscale east side of the city, far from the five-star hotels and towering office buildings in the city's center, the Kaloleni drew a mix of mid-level civil servants, laborers, and small businessmen. The economists and planners favored the outdoor seating area under a sprawling jacaranda tree, where they could keep an eye on the spare ribs and the marinated skewers of beef called *mishkaki* simmering on the outdoor spit. The talk wandered from work to politics or the outcome of the football game at the nearby City Stadium. Obama and Otieno routinely passed the afternoons there with their drinks in hand—local Tusker beer for Otieno and Johnnie Walker for Obama. Otieno was generally the first to head out in the early evening. Obama lingered on and, usually too inebriated to drive, got a ride home from someone else. "They were like conjoined twins," explained Meshack J. Onyango, an economist then working at the Central Bank and one of the regulars among the Kaloleni drinking crowd. "They came in early because they didn't want anybody to bother them. And whatever assignment you gave them they would finish it on time and leave it there for you. That's why they were prized. These were just two brilliant people."

And as long as the "Two Ronnies" got their work done, they were pretty much allowed to come and go as they pleased. "The truth is Obama was not in the office much during the day," said Johnson M. Hungu, the senior planning officer in Human Resources who later became the Permanent Secretary of the Ministry. "People tolerated him because they knew they could not change him. He knew what he was talking about so he could get away with it. He'd work until noon and then he'd go drink his lunch. The day was over."

Well, almost over. If a matter arose in the afternoon that needed the attention of either of them, the Ministry often dispatched a car over to the Kaloleni. "If there was something urgent in the office that required them the car would go and bring one of them back," said Gondi Hesbon Olum, an economist who worked at the Central Bureau of Statistics in the same ministry. "Or the driver would say, 'So and so is stuck. What do you think, or what would you advise we do?'"

Although just forty years old himself, Obama was older than many in the Treasury corridors, and his Harvard training still carried considerable clout. More than a few found Dr. Obama, as he insisted the younger economists call him, a highly entertaining mentor who was more than willing to discuss the latest econometric formulas and mathematic technique. Meshack Onyango, nearly fifteen years younger than Obama, had just completed a course on financial programming not long after Obama had been hired when he ran into him at the Big Five. The two immediately plunged into a conversation about domestic credit and its relation to foreign assets, and Onyango was deeply impressed. "He was a really a genius at financial programming," says Onyango. "I think he was the first Kenyan who did econometrics. He was just very, very good at analysis and simulations, all of that."

After nine months on the job Obama's status was made permanent in August of 1976.[19] With that, he was given steadily greater responsibility and soon began to travel on behalf of the government. Two projects in particular defined Obama's years in the Treasury. The first was a long-running plan with Ethiopia to develop the Lake Turkana-Omo River Basin along their joint border. Turkana, the largest desert lake in the world, is fed by the Omo River in Ethiopia and is the site of extensive prehistoric research. The project, which the European Economic Community was to fund, called for the development of the region's basic infrastructure and improved management of the wildlife, fisheries, and tourism in the area. Obama was assigned to develop projections on the project's financing and oversee a feasibility study that an international consultancy was preparing. By 1980 Dr. B. H. Obama, as he was referred to in government documents and press accounts of the projects, was often the lead negotiator for the Kenyan delegation in a series of meetings held in Addis Ababa.

Obama was also instrumental in several road development projects with neighboring countries considered critical to developing markets outside the country as well as for the enhancement of tourism. The largest was a proposed road link between Kenya and Sudan, a 580-kilometer stretch that would connect Lodwar to Juba in southern Sudan. By 1979 Norway had committed to finance the engineering study, but Kenya had to secure the financing for the bulk of the project. Obama traveled extensively to Europe and the Sudan starting in the late 1970s to consult with both technical committees considering the project and potential financiers.[20]

Obama's higher profile was made possible in part by the death of Jomo Kenyatta on August 22, 1978. The death of the *Mzee*, the Swahili term of respect for an elder, the father of the Kenyan nation, was mourned throughout the country, as many of his flaws and excesses were forgiven in the grief over his passing. His legacy was mixed: He left behind a country that had benefited from relatively steady economic growth, but it remained heavily dependent on Western countries for funds and guidance. Although human rights in Kenya had largely been safeguarded, Kenyatta's intensely autocratic, heavy-handed style of governing had allowed freedom of speech for only a sanctioned few. The election of Kenya's second president, Daniel arap Moi, a longtime political presence and the vice president for eleven years, marked the beginning of a very different era, at least in the beginning.

Moi, of the Kalenjin ethnic group, acted quickly to earn the good will of the Kikuyu elite by bringing several Kikuyu leaders into his government, one of them Mwai Kibaki, who became his vice president. At the same time, the genial former teacher declared an end to political factionalism and corruption as he released Kenyatta's political detainees and assembled a broad multiethnic coalition. The more relaxed political atmosphere eased the career limitations on Luos, many of whom remained stagnant in government and the private sector since Mboya's death. Moi's domestic programs, including a national literacy campaign and free milk for school children, also won broad-based support.[21] The economic problems that would plague his presidency, stemming in part from worldwide recession, would take more than a year to develop.

By 1980 Obama was promoted to Planning Officer I, a position with more seniority and a slightly higher salary. But Obama had never surrendered the belief that he was chronically underemployed, and once again he began to give himself occasional promotions. It began with small elevations of his title. Particularly when meeting people who did not know him, he often presented himself as a senior economist or other high-ranking officer. Masakhalia, who by then had been promoted to permanent secretary of the Ministry of Economic Planning and Development, got wind of Obama's exaggerations. But Masakhalia was not overly concerned. By this time Obama's quirky behavior—his use of the title Dr., his claim of higher positions, and even his routine drinking on the job, any of which would easily have gotten him fired back in the United States—had been accepted as part of his character. Government officials from the highest level downward seemed willing to tolerate it in return for his high level of expertise. "The fact is that in general conversations with audiences he would attempt to throw his weight around and assume titles he did not have," said Masakhalia. "His demeanor was always that of an important man and he wanted people to think of him that way. But what did it really matter. Nairobi at the time was a small place and everybody knew who he was. I did not think it something I needed to take action about."

Masakhalia, who went on to work as an adviser with the UN Development Programme and served as a member of the Kenyan Parliament for several years, acknowledges that he found it difficult to take a firm hand with Obama. "You see the thing is we were friends," he shrugged. "Our friendship began a long time ago."

Emboldened, Obama became more daring. On a trip to Ghana in 1980 Obama was a member of an advance team assigned to prepare Ghanaian officials on the Kenyan team yet to arrive. But in the meetings Obama claimed to be the Minister of Economic Planning and Development himself, a position actually occupied by Dr. Z. T. Onyonka.[22] When Onyonka arrived the following day and introduced himself, the Ghanaian negotiators looked at him in astonishment, presuming he was an imposter. When Onyonka finally figured out what had happened, he dispatched Johnson M. Hungu to have a sharp word with Obama. "Like everyone else, Onyonka knew how Barack behaved and so he wasn't too upset," said Hungu.

"I took Barack out for a beer and I told him what he had done was improper and he had to stop doing it. He just laughed it off."

Although Obama made good use of his salary increase and had rented a narrow two-story, government-owned townhouse at Mawenzi Gardens, a significant comedown from his lush Woodley estate, his financial problems continued to plague him. His worn pink personnel file, held in what is now the Ministry of Planning, National Development and Vision, bulges with requests for salary advances, international cables begging for funds to pay for his hotel bills, and demands for payment of unpaid bills from utilities and merchants. Funeral expenses topped the list. A sister-in-law and her unborn baby had died. A first cousin was shot in Kampala. Another cousin died in Mombasa. A son was kicked out of school "because I had not paid the fees for 2d term and I have not paid for this third term. I would have paid all these fees but because I have had two deaths, one in July and one in August, 1977, all my money went for these funerals." Adding that his son's school would not permit the boy to sit for his exams until the fees were paid, Obama urgently requested an advance, writing, "This would be disastrous particularly when I have spent so much for his education for so long."[23]

Obama's file also contains multiple requests beginning within months of his hiring for funds to cover the costs of traveling on home leave to Alego with his "wife and five children." At that time, however, he had no wife living with him. Two of his children, Mark and David, were living with Ruth, and Auma and Malik were often living at boarding school. Another child lived in Hawaii, and Bernard and Abo lived with their mother, Kezia. Nonetheless, the Ministry routinely approved funds for rail fare for the mythically happy family to travel together.

Nor had Obama's heavy drinking slowed in the slightest. "Double-Double" drank consistently on the job and most people knew it. In fact, some of his colleagues observed that he performed better with alcohol in his system than without it. During one trip to Addis Ababa to discuss the Lake Turkana project in 1980, members of the Ethiopian delegation watched in consternation as Obama downed one whiskey after the other during the course of the evening, alarmed that he would be unable to function at their meeting the next day. But by the following morning

Obama was in high-performance mode and stunned the Ethiopians as he rattled off statistics and details of the project that they could barely recall.[24]

Not long after Kenyatta's death, Mule was promoted to the position of permanent secretary of the Ministry of Economic Planning and Development.[25] Even in his high-ranking job, Mule managed to keep an eye out on Obama, of whom he was fond. And when he felt that Obama was stuck on a particular task or could not make his calculations work out as they should, Mule handed him fifty shillings and suggested he go get a shot of whiskey at his own favorite bar down on Moi Avenue—or maybe two shots.

"I encouraged him to go get a drink," said Mule. "I knew that he had difficulty working without any whiskey in him so if I saw he was having a mental blockage of some kind, I'd just send him off to Tina's. And then he would come back and do a wonderful job."

Sometimes, however, Obama's alcohol intake was less than conducive to work. Most Mondays, Obama's colleagues noticed that he smelled of alcohol, the residue of his heavy weekend intake. More than once Obama managed to burn through his travel advance while on assignment, and sometimes he did so before he had even left town. Sebastian Okoda, an assistant secretary in the Ministry of Finance who briefly shared an apartment with Obama, tells of a night in 1976 when Obama had a travel advance of 7,000 Kenyan shillings burning a hole in his pocket. Instead of heading to the airport and preparing for his journey, Obama decided to take half a dozen of his friends out drinking at the popular Revolving Tower Restaurant on the twenty-seventh floor of the iconic Kenyatta International Conference Center that dominates downtown Nairobi. By early the next morning the group was still cavorting at the bar and Obama was broke. "Barack had to borrow money from everyone for the trip and then he raced off to the airport," Okoda said.

Obama's alcoholic exploits were easily tolerated among the largely male crowd with which he drank. Nairobi was a hard-drinking culture, so heavy consumption was de rigueur. As some of his friends saw it, Obama was just a bit extreme. That his mother and a handful of close friends had pleaded with him to stop drinking was a telling measure of how extreme his drinking had become by the late 1970s, but anyone unfamiliar with his drinking patterns and the way in which the Ministry indulged him found his demeanor shocking. For instance, Clive Gray was a consultant with the Harvard Institute for International Development working with the Kenyan Ministry of Agriculture in 1981 when he happened to see Obama walking down a corridor in the ministry. Gray had been a graduate student at Harvard at the same time as Obama and instantly recognized him. He was thinner, yes, but Gray couldn't mistake that broad face and the heavy-rimmed glasses. As he watched, Gray noticed that Obama was staggering slightly, raising his hand to the wall to steady himself. Clearly, Obama was drunk. And it was still an hour before lunch. "I asked a friend what had happened to him. You know, I remembered him from Harvard," recalled Gray. "And I was told that he was drunk most of the time. It was a shame, just a real waste."

IN JUNE 1980 BARACK OBAMA TURNED forty-four years old. He was by then a middle-aged man with a complex domestic history, even by Luo standards. He had three wives in his wake and five or seven children, depending on who was doing the counting. His relationship with virtually all of them was strained at best. And then things got even more complicated.

Obama met a woman.

Her name was Jael Atieno. In the Dholuo language, Atieno means "born at night." She was tall and soft-spoken with long braids that reached down her back. When his half-sister, Marsat, with whom she attended school, introduced Jael to him, she was twenty years old—the same age as Obama's only daughter, Auma, and twenty-four years younger than him. The following year she moved in with him and the two agreed that they would marry. Because Jael was pregnant, the traditional dowry payment of cows could not be made. According to traditional Luo custom, payment of dowry when a woman is pregnant results in bad luck such that the baby might die. But one of Obama's brothers paid her mother 1,000 shillings in *ayie*, the first step of a Luo wedding process that is a gesture of appreciation to the bride's mother and an indication that both sides are committed to continue with the marriage. The wedding ceremony was scheduled to take place in December of 1982, when the baby would be about six months old.[26]

For Obama, the union with Jael provided a stability to his life that had long been lacking. Like many African men, Obama continued his nightly visits to the bars in town with his male friends, leaving his young wife at home. But he now had home-cooked meals and someone to look after him. Their lifestyle in the boxy Mawenzi Gardens complex, with its cement block walls and tiny outdoor patio, was a far cry from that to which he had once been accustomed, but it was a vast improvement over the dingy hotel rooms and bachelor pads of recent years. Obama also felt that at long last he had gained some recognition for his hard work on the Lake Turkana and Sudan road projects. Early in 1982 he was selected to partake in the country's fifth national development plan covering the years 1984 to 1988, considered a vital government project. Obama was to chair a planning group on roads and housing that would review the country's progress since independence and establish goals for the future. Seven years after he had been confined to a behind-the-scenes accounting post, he was now overseeing dozens of government workers at regular committee meetings each week. It wasn't a division head or even an official promotion, but the position gave Obama a bit of the authority he felt he deserved.

Establishing development goals in Kenya of 1982, however, was a daunting task. President Moi's honeymoon period had lasted barely a year when the deepening world recession began to have a severe impact on the Kenyan economy, and the country faced an acute shortage of foreign exchange. As a scarcity of goods became commonplace, a series of strikes shook the country and many grew alarmed about the adequacy of the country's food supply—and for good reason. In an effort to maintain control of the increasingly turbulent situation, Moi began to crack down on dissent and increased the army's size in a deliberate show of muscle. On August 1, 1982, the country's air force personnel staged an attempted coup d'état and seized control of the Voice of Kenya radio station, claiming they had taken over the government. The maneuver was short lived, as army troops managed to regain control within hours, although looting and chaos on the streets continued for days. For weeks afterward a curfew remained in place, as the deeply shaken nation struggled to regain an equilibrium.

As the year drew toward an end, Jael found herself anxious about her husband. Their baby, named George Hussein Onyango Obama after a cherished cousin, had been born in May. Although the birth of another son invigorated Obama, he remained anxious about his finances and how he would be able to pay for yet another round of school fees. He was also deeply upset about the country's state of economic crisis and Moi's drift to the right. The specter of a return to the bad old years, even a pale version of them, left him despondent. When Obama headed out in the evenings, Jael cautioned him to be circumspect, worried that he might antagonize one of the soldiers patrolling the streets and wind up in jail. Amir Otieno Orinda, Obama's half-brother by his mother, who was visiting the couple, agreed. "She told him not to go outside," recalled Orinda. "She knew he was a hot-headed man and that he would not be afraid of the patrol. He kept saying the country was *piny rach* or 'the country is no good.'"

There was still another matter that contributed to Obama's dark mood. His old nemesis, Philip Ndegwa, had just reached an unprecedented pinnacle and his shadow fell longer than ever. Ndegwa had held a succession of high-profile positions in recent years, including serving as adviser to newly elected president Moi and then as chairman of the Kenya Commercial Bank. But in November of 1982 it became clear that Ndegwa was going to be named governor of the Central Bank of Kenya, one of the most influential positions in the Kenyan government. Ndegwa, who of course had been famously tutored by Obama back in their Harvard days, was now the commander of the same bank that had dismissed Obama after ten months as a graduate trainee fifteen years earlier. Ndegwa's posting, which would become effective in December, was galling.

On a day in late November Obama came home with some chilling words. He told Jael that if he should die, she must make sure that George went to the best schools. And if he should die before the boy turned eighteen, she must make sure that all of his children received an equal share of whatever he had. He was adamant that he did not want "[unclear] to get five cents out of this."[27] Although Jael pressed him repeatedly to explain why he was saying such things, Obama refused to say anything further.

Three days later Obama was dead. On November 26 Obama's pickup truck had slammed into a eucalyptus stump as he was heading home at night from the Kaloleni bar. No one knew exactly how the accident had occurred, and some in his circle of drinking pals promptly questioned if it was an accident at all. On that day Obama had worked later than usual. He

was preparing for an upcoming committee meeting on the fiscal con-
straints that were expected to shape the fifth development plan and had
wound up in the office later than expected. As he was leaving the building
early in the evening, en route to the Kaloleni, he happened to run into
Edgar Edwards in the basement garage. Edwards, the senior economic
adviser, could tell from Obama's thick speech that he had put away a few
drinks already. As he often did when he encountered Obama in such a
condition, Edwards took a few minutes to urge Obama to drink less so
that he could make better use of his substantial talents. Obama listened
noncommittally, as he usually did to Edwards's admonishments. "He was
always very reserved around me," recalled Edwards. "He listened and nod-
ded his head, but he would never respond positively or negatively. He just
listened respectfully."

Obama continued on his way and dropped in at the Intercontinental for
a couple more drinks. By the time he reached the Kaloleni at around 8
p.m., he was in exceptionally high spirits. The score of regulars there were
also well into their cups and the place was humming. Otieno was hunched
over the table, deep in conversation. So too were Obondo and Olum.
Obama headed to the bar, where he ordered his trademark Double-
Double set of whiskies and bought a round of drinks for several other cus-
tomers. At 10:30 p.m. Obama asked a friend, David Owino Weya, who
often bought him drinks when he was out of money, to walk with him to
his car. On that night the man who usually drove Obama home when he
was in no condition to drive himself was otherwise engaged. A few people
offered to drive him, but Obama was adamant that he could drive himself.
"He was a bit tipsy but in quite a good humor," said Weya. "When we got
to his car he gave me two hundred shillings. He said, 'I am leaving but you
go and buy yourself some drinks. I will see you tomorrow at lunchtime.'"

Weya was the last person to whom Obama spoke. A half hour later
Obama drove into a broad stump at the edge of the Elgon Road a short
distance from his home. He died instantly. The police came upon the
wreckage several hours later and moved his body to the mortuary. As
word of his passing spread quickly during the day, a handful of stunned
relatives hurried to his side to say their final goodbyes.

Speculation about the accident mushroomed just as quickly. Not surprisingly, the elements of Obama's death were as mysterious to his family

and friends as were fundamental aspects of his life. Family members, many of whom attribute Obama's employment difficulties to payback for his brazen outspokenness, believe that nameless government enemies murdered him. It is a matter of gospel among them that Obama's body was unscathed in the accident and his car undamaged—the very windshield unbroken. Even his eyeglasses, they maintain, were intact.[28] If Obama had careened drunkenly into a tree, surely his body would have been brutally broken, his car a shattered wreck. He must have been killed in some other manner and his body placed in the car in such a way as to make it appear that he had an accident. Or so their reasoning goes.

Others were convinced that Obama's death was a suicide. How else to explain his curious remarks to his wife? Obama's rage about the arc of his own life and his aching disappointment in his country's path was hardly a secret. Nor was his self-destructive habit of drinking. Peter Aringo, traveling outside the country, remembered in one of his last conversations with his old friend that Obama had been despondent about his children, as they were scattered so widely and, in some cases, doing poorly. "It weighed on him greatly," said Aringo. "So I was not surprised to hear that he had died."

By far the most plausible scenario is that Obama died in a drunken car accident, just as the police said. Both Obama and his car were crushed in the accident. The *Nairobi Times* reported that Obama's car was so badly destroyed that his body "had to be wedged out of the car."[29] As for Obama, doctors concluded that he had died as the result of "bleeding due to ruptured heart due to a traffic accident."[30] Whether Obama deliberately turned his car into the stump will never be known for sure, but the fact is that at the time of his death Obama had at long last arrived at a place of some peace. He was doing work that he loved and had regained some semblance of dignity. That he was a father again meant that he had the opportunity to do it differently this time, to be the kind of nurturing parent he had never had himself.

The funeral, an elaborate event that lasted for several days, took place at the family homestead in Alego. After years of feeling he was insufficiently appreciated, the list of notables who attended would have delighted Obama. There were members of Parliament and dozens of his colleagues from the Treasury. Peter Aringo and the Minister of Foreign Affairs,

Robert Ouko, both spoke in tribute to his fierce intelligence and passion. Obama's mother, Habiba Akumu, frail and tearful, sat mournfully by his wooden coffin, the grief over her eldest son's death etched in the deep lines of her face. Dressed in a white floral dress and blue head kerchief, she sat protectively by his coffin as though she might protect him in death from the disappointments that had plagued him in life.

OBAMA IS BURIED next to his father on the Obama family compound about an hour's rough drive north of Lake Victoria. His grave is covered in broken yellow tiles and bears the Dholuo words *ibed gi kwe*, or "peace be with you." If Barack Obama were to have sung a Luo praise song of his own life, he would have dwelled not on the tumult of his final decade but rather on the extraordinary and unlikely journey of a child born in a thatched hut in Kanyadhiang. The bird had flown high and far. Although Obama fell short of the exacting heights to which he aspired, he achieved ambitions that many Kenyans of his generation could not have begun to fathom.

Emerging from a bruising childhood, Obama rose swiftly above the red African dust. With his fierce intellect as his passport, he was not simply a man firmly of the twentieth century but one who stood at the fulcrum of a changing world as his country emerged from the tyranny of colonialism. Obama came within inches of the Harvard doctoral degree that he so coveted, the academic jewel that would have served as the bedrock for the career he envisioned. But Harvard denied him that. So broken was Obama by Harvard's summary judgment of him that he returned to Nairobi unable to even look at the dissertation that he had initiated with such high hopes. When, in a moment of despair, he claimed that paper had been stolen by thieves, what had really been lost was a deeper faith in himself.

Obama never fully recovered from that disappointment, but it did not prevent him from taking the stage at a vital moment in his country's life. At a time when many more cautious men retreated from a new imperious government that lashed out at dissent, Obama spoke truth to power. Confronted with the challenges of newly independent Kenya, a place radically changed from that which he left as a hopeful young man, Obama struggled to reconcile his ideals for his country with a bitterly disappointing reality. He refused to knuckle despite the enormous personal consequences. In the end, it was not, as his friend Ndolo Ayah said, that Barack Obama did not finish the race; rather, he finished too early to see what he had wrought.

Nearly every day tourists from the farthest reaches of the world contemplate the cracked yellow tiles on his grave and take photographs of the resting place of President Barack Obama's father for their albums back home. As the next page of history has turned, Obama's impact has proved to be profoundly greater than he could have imagined. Although he never knew it, his legacy was to produce the most powerful man in the world. The other Barack would have liked that.

ACKNOWLEDGMENTS

That any project of substance requires a village of helpers is a cliché. It is also true. This project enlisted the support of a global metropolis. During the two and a half years it took to produce this book, I have relied on an army of assistants around the world. I bow first to my team of friends and advisors in Nairobi and Kisumu. A heartfelt thanks to the four who burrowed so deep and traveled so many kilometers and then went back again: Okoth Beatrice Akoth, Leo Odera Omolo, Terry Wairimu, and Felgona Atieno Ochieng. Each of them committed themselves to finding the truth despite the sometimes daunting obstacles.

Many in the Obama family gave me their time and assistance. I am particularly thankful to Ezra Obama and Obama Kobilo, who made the drive with me to Kendu Bay more than once, and to the ever-welcoming Hawa Auma. Thanks also for their generosity and reflection to Francis Masakhalia, Fred Okatcha, Bitange Ndemo, Achola Pala Okeyo, Johnson Hungu, Peter Aringo, Edgar Edwards, and Chukwuma Azikiwe.

Among the many who supported the cause in Hawaii, there is first and foremost Ken Kobayashi, a determined reporter and my colleague on the ground for nearly two years. I thank you. Also, much gratitude to Gov. Neil Abercrombie, Hal Abercrombie, Pake Zane, and Naranhkiri Tith.

To Team Jacobs, the heart of it all: Shi Shi and Streett Jacobs, Grace Hamada, Sandra May, Jayson Walker, Jane Beal, Tabby, Castro, and Dixie. Each of them endured—and sometimes even looked at—the elaborate flow-charts left behind when I headed out on the road.

To my extraordinary friends who always made time to read and reflect, even when they didn't have it, Larry Tye and Judy Rakowsky, a heartfelt hallelujah. I am deeply grateful also to Kim Blanton, Sarah Wesson, Dudley Clendinen, and Phil Bennett. For their expertise and patience, John Lonsdale, Dharam Ghai, David W. Cohen, Parker Shipton, Dominique Connan, and Celia Nyamweru.

I am also most grateful to the families of Elizabeth Mooney and Helen Roberts for sharing their wealth of letters and photographs and letting me tell the extraordinary story, at last. If it weren't for Miss Mooney, who delivered the first Barack Obama to the United States, there might not be an Obama in the White House at all.

To others who made a difference along the way Lois Beckett, David Arnold, Liz Cooney, Paul Nyangani, Azinna Nwafor, Dorothy and Bob Stephens, Gitau Warigi, Barbara and M. F. Scherer, Richard Parker, Roger Noll, Ann Trevor, and Brendan Bannon.

Last, but certainly not least, I am indebted to the *Boston Globe* for giving me the time to work on this book and for taking me back when it was done.

NOTES

CHAPTER 1

1. Peter Firstbrook, *The Obamas: The Untold Story of an African Family* (London: Preface Publishing, 2010), 52; David W. Cohen, "The River Lake Nilotes from the Fifteenth to the Nineteenth Century," in *Zamani: A Survey of East African History*, ed. Bethwell A. Ogot and J. A. Kieran (Nairobi, Kenya: East African Publishing House, 1968), 149.

2. Grace Kezia Aoko Obama, affidavit in Succession Cause No. 233 of 1985, in the matter of the estate of Barack Hussein Obama, High Court of Kenya, Nairobi, November 1988.

3. Habiba Akumu, affidavit in Succession Cause No. 233 of 1985, in the matter of the estate of Barack Hussein Obama, High Court of Kenya, Nairobi, November 1988.

4. Ruling by Judge J. F. Shields, June 1989. Succession Cause No. 233 of 1985.

5. From Ruth Ndesandjo, Ezra Obama, and W. E. Obama Kobilo interviews.

6. Barack Obama, *Dreams from My Father: A Story of Race and Inheritance* (New York: Random House, 1995), 212.

7. From Abong'o Malik Obama interview.

8. Obama, *Dreams from My Father*, 217.

9. Auma Obama, *Das Leben kommt immer dazwischen* (Cologne, Germany: Bastei Lubbe GmbH & Co. KG, 2010), 123.

10. Andrew Jacobs, "An Obama Relative Living in China Tells of His Own Journey of Self-Discovery," *New York Times*, November 4, 2009.

11. Obama, *Dreams from My Father*, 344.

12. From Mark Ndesandjo interview.

13. Mark Ndesandjo, *Nairobi to Shenzhen* (San Diego: Aventine Publishing, 2009), 6.

14. Ibid., 133.

15. George Obama with Damien Lewis, *Homeland: An Extraordinary Story of Hope and Survival* (New York: Simon and Schuster, 2010), 48.

16. Ibid., 269.

17. Obama, *Dreams from My Father*, 129.

18. Ibid., 221.

19. From Neil Abercrombie interview.

CHAPTER 2

1. Ronald Hardy, *The Iron Snake* (New York: G. P. Putnam's Sons, 1965), 308.

2. Assa Okoth, *A History of Africa*, vol. 1: *African Societies and the Establishment of Colonial Rule, 1800–1915* (Nairobi, Kenya: East African Educational Publishers, 2006), 198–99.

3. Oginga Odinga, *Not Yet Uhuru: The Autobiography of Oginga Odinga* (Nairobi, Kenya: East African Educational Publishers, 1967), 1.

4. Barack Obama, *Dreams from My Father: A Story of Race and Inheritance* (New York: Random House, 1995), 397.

5. Ibid., 398.

6. David W. Cohen, "The River Lake Nilotes from the Fifteenth to the Nineteenth Century," in *Zamani: A Survey of East African History*, ed. Bethwell A. Ogot and J. A. Kieran (Nairobi, Kenya: East Africa Publishing House, 1968), 142.

7. Ibid., 154.

8. Ibid.

9. Bethwell A. Ogot, *A History of the Luo Speaking Peoples of East Africa* (Nairobe, Kenya: Anyange Press, 2009), 512; Peter Firstbrook, *The Obamas: The Untold Story of an African Family* (London: Preface Publishing, 2010), 47.

10. Obama, *Dreams from My Father*, 395.

11. From Charles Oluoch and Elly Yonga Adhiambo interviews.

12. Caroline Elkins, *Imperial Reckoning: The Untold Story of Britain's Gulag in Kenya* (New York, Henry Holt and Co., 2005), 7.

13. Odinga, *Not Yet Uhuru*, 2.

14. Carol E. DePré, *The Luo of Kenya: An Annotated Bibliography* (Washington DC: Institute for Cross-Cultural Research, 1968), 26.

15. Uganda Railway, Publicity Department poster, Dewar House, Haymarket S.W., undated.

16. Elkins, *Imperial Reckoning*, 14.

17. Odinga, *Not Yet Uhuru*, 23.

18. Richard D. Wolff, *The Economics of Colonialism: Britain and Kenya, 1870–1930* (New Haven, CT: Yale University Press, 1974), 119–20.

19. Obama, *Dreams from My Father*, 425

20. That figure does not take into account the rate of inflation affecting the British shilling as compared to the U.S. dollar.

21. Obama, *Dreams from My Father*, 426.

22. From Penina Ndalo interview.

23. Bethwell A. Ogot, "British Administration in the Central Nyanza District of Kenya, 1900–60," *Journal of African History* 4, no. 2 (1963), 256.

24. Ibid., 258.

25. From Saad Khairallah interview.

26. Obama, *Dreams from My Father*, 403.

27. Barack Obama's date of birth is unclear. His earliest school records bear no birth date. His University of Hawaii transcript records his birthdate as June 18, 1934. His marriage certificate and résumés indicate he was born in 1936. U.S. immigration records show his year of birth as both 1934 and 1936. Family members say they believe he was born in 1936, so I have used that date.

28. Paul Mboya, *Luo Kitgi Gi Timbegi*, trans. Jane Achieng (Nairobi, Kenya: Atai Joint Limited, 1938), 88.

29. Ibid., 45.

30. Parker Shipton, *The Nature of Entrustment: Intimacy, Exchange, and the Sacred in Africa* (New Haven, CT: Yale University Press, 2007), 51.

31. Mboya, *Luo Kitgi Gi Timbegi*, 54.

32. Onyango's drinking habits are described by Charles Olouch, Hawa Auma, and Obama Madoho in their interviews with the author.

33. Mboya, *Luo Kitgi Gi* Timbegi, 137.

34. From Sarah Obama interview.

35. Timothy H. Parsons, *The African Rank-and-File: Social Implications of Colonial Military Service in the King's African Rifles, 1902–1964* (Portsmouth, NH: Heinemann, 1999), 2.

36. Obama, *Dreams from My Father*, 409.

37. Ogot, "British Administration in the Central Nyanza District of Kenya, 1900–60," 269.

38. Tiyambe Zeleza, "Kenya and the Second World War, 1939–1950," in *A Modern History of Kenya, 1895–1980*, ed. W. R. Ochieng (London: Evans Brothers, 1989), 166.

39. Bethwell A. Ogot, "Kenya under the British, 1895 to 1963," in *Zamani: A Survey of East African History*, ed. Ogot and J. A. Kieran (Nairobi, Kenya: East African Publishing House, 1968), 282.

40. Ogot, "British Administration in the Central Nyanza District of Kenya, 1900–60," 270.

41. Matthew Carotenuto and Katherine Luongo, "Dala or Diaspora? Obama and the Luo Community of Kenya," *African Affairs* 108, no. 431 (2009): 197–219.

42. Odinga, *Not Yet Uhuru*, 102.

43. This view of Mboya comes from interviews by author and Beatrice Akoth with villagers, including Charles Ogun Yamo, Charles Oluoch, Elly Yonga Adhiambo, and Penina Ndalo.

CHAPTER 3

1. From Obama Madoho interview.

2. From Dominick Odida interview.

3. Ibid.

4. Barack Obama, *Dreams from My Father: A Story of Race and Inheritance* (New York: Random House, 1995), 415.

5. John Oywa, "Tracing Obama Snr's Steps as a Student at Maseno School," *The Standard*, November 4, 2008.

6. Oginga Odinga, *Not Yet Uhuru: The Autobiography of Oginga Odinga* (Nairobi: East African Educational Publishers, 1967).

7. Bethwell A. Ogot, *My Footprints on the Sands of Time: An Autobiography* (Kisumu, Kenya: Anyange Press, 2003), 38.

8. The year that Obama entered the Maseno School is unclear. School officials say he entered in 1951, but classmates and Obama family members place him there as early as 1949.

9. Bethwell A. Ogot, *My Footprints on the Sands of Time*, 38.

10. Odinga, *Not Yet Uhuru*, 62.

11. Oywa, "Tracing Obama Snr's Steps as a Student at Maseno School."

12. For a description of the "lorry" hairstyle, see Oscar Obonyo, "Kaloleni Home of Ex-Uganda Leader," *The Sunday Nation*, August 15, 2004.

13. Obama, *Dreams from My Father*, 419.

14. Caroline Elkins, *Imperial Reckoning: The Untold Story of Britain's Gulag in Kenya* (New York, Henry Holt and Co. 2005), 26.

15. William Robert Ochieng, *A History of Kenya* (London: Macmillan, 1985), 130.

16. Obama, *Dreams from My* Father, 417.

17. Ibid.

18. Ben Macintyre and Paul Orengoh, "Beatings and Abuse Made Barack Obama's Grandfather Loathe the British," *The Sunday Times*, December 3, 2008.

19. Obama, *Dreams from My Father*, 418.

20. David Anderson, *Histories of the Hanged: The Dirty War in Kenya and the End of Empire* (New York: W. W. Norton and Co., 2005), 41.

21. The Kikuyu did not keep birth records, so the year of Kenyatta's birth is unknown. His biographer writes that he was likely born in the late 1890s. Jeremy Murray-Brown, *Kenyatta* (New York: E. P. Dutton, 1973), 37.

22. Anderson, *Histories of the Hanged*, 5; Elkins, *Imperial Reckoning*, xiii.

23. Elkins, *Imperial Reckoning*, xvi.

24. Anderson, *Histories of the Hanged*, 2.

25. Obama, *Dreams from My Father*, 419.

26. David Goldsworthy, *Tom Mboya: The Man Kenya Wanted to Forget* (New York: Africana Publishing Company, 1982), 17.

27. Tom Mboya, *Freedom and After* (London: Andre Deutsch, 1963), 29.

28. Goldsworthy, *Tom Mboya*, 14.

29. Ibid., 93.

30. From Alfred Obama Oguta interview.

31. From Grace Kezia Obama interview.

32. Paul Mboya, *Luo Kitgi Gi Timbegi*, trans. Jane Achieng (Nairobi, Kenya: Atai Joint Limited, 1938), 65.

33. Ibid., 66.

34. Ibid., 80.

35. Bethwell A. Ogot, "The Decisive Years, 1956–63," in *Decolonization and Independence in Kenya, 1940–93*, ed. Bethwell A. Ogot and William Robert Ochieng (London: J. Currey, 1995), 51.

36. Ibid., 56

37. Dan Schecter, Michael Ansara, and David Kolodney, *The CIA Is an Equal Opportunity Employer* (Cambridge, MA: Africa Research Group, 1970).

38. Goldsworthy, *Tom Mboya*, 159.

CHAPTER 4

1. Elizabeth Mooney, letter to Frank Laubach, December 21, 1958, Syracuse University, Frank C. Laubach Collection.

2. Elizabeth Mooney, letter to Frank Laubach, February 16, 1959, Syracuse University, Frank C. Laubach Collection.

3. Caroline Blakely and Robert S. Laubach, *Literacy Journalism at Syracuse University: A Thirty-Year History, 1952–1981* (Syracuse, NY: Lit-J Alumni, 1996), 80.

4. Jeni Klugman, Bilin Neyapti, and Frances Stewart, *Conflict and Growth in Africa, Vol. 2: Kenya, Tanzania and Uganda* (Paris: The Organization for Economic Co-operation and Development, 1999), 36.

5. Frank Charles Laubach, *Forty Years with the Silent Billion: Adventuring in Literacy* (Old Tappan, NJ: The Fleming H. Revell Co., 1970), 13.

6. Frank Kay, "Teaching Adult Africans How to Read and Write Makes Two-Year Scheme," *East African Standard*, 1957.

7. "No, Miss Mooney," *The Sunday Post*, September 22, 1957, Records of U.S. Foreign Assistance Agencies, Office of Educational Services, Africa and Europe Program Division, RG 469, The U.S. National Archives and Record Administration, College Park, MD.

8. Elizabeth Mooney, letter from to her friends, May 31, 1957, provided by the E. M. Kirk family.

9. Jim C. Harper, *Western Educated Elites in Kenya, 1900–1963: The African American Factor* (New York: Routledge, 2006), 63, 65.

10. *The Key*, a publication of *Kenya Adult Literary News*, iss. 5 (February 1959): 5.

11. Helen Roberts, letter to Muriel McCrory, May 1959, provided by her son, Don Roberts.

12. Harper, *Western Educated Elites in Kenya, 1900–1963*, 3, 10.

13. Mboya, *Freedom and After* (London: Andre Deutsch, 1963), 142.

14. Harper, *Western Educated Elites in Kenya, 1900–1963*, 5, 94.

15. Mboya, *Freedom and After*, 143.

16. Mansfield Irving Smith, "The East African Airlifts of 1959, 1960, and 1960" (PhD dissertation, Syracuse University, 1966), 18.

17. The International Monetary Fund, International Financial Statistics database derived from the United Nation's Department of Economic and Social Affairs (updated March 2011).

18. Smith, "The East African Airlifts of 1959, 1960, and 1960," 14.

19. David Goldsworthy, *Tom Mboya: The Man Kenya Wanted to Forget* (New York: Africana Publishing Company, 1982), 76.

20. Tom Shachtman, *Airlift to America: How Barack Obama, Sr., John F. Kennedy, Tom Mboya, and 800 East African Students Changed Their World and Ours* (New York: St. Martin's, 2009), 49.

21. Smith, "The East African Airlifts of 1959, 1960, and 1960," 27.

22. Harper, *Western Educated Elites in Kenya, 1900–1963*, 124.

23. Smith, "The East African Airlifts of 1959, 1960, and 1960," 38.

24. Mboya, *Freedom and After*, 139.

25. Elizabeth Mooney, letter to her brother Mark Mooney, January, 28, 1959, provided by the E. M. Kirk family.

26. Ibid.

27. Elizabeth Mooney, letter to Marjorie Mooney, February 16, 1959, provided by the E. M. Kirk family.

28. Obama, *Dreams from My Father*, 421.

29. Frank J. Taylor, "Colorful Campus of the Islands," *The Saturday Evening Post*, May 24, 1958, 39.

30. Obama, *Dreams from My Father*, 427.

31. Helen Roberts, *The Unfolding Trail*, unpublished biography, 179, provided by Roberts's son, Don Roberts.

32. Elizabeth Mooney, letter to Marjorie Mooney, March 31, 1959, provided by the E. M. Kirk family.

33. From Dora Mumbo interview.

34. Smith, "The East African Airlifts of 1959, 1960, and 1960," 37.

35. *Ramogi*, July 7, 1959, 3.

36. Elizabeth Mooney, letter to Frank C. Laubach, March 23, 1959, Syracuse University, Frank C. Laubach Collection. Used with the permission from the E. M. Kirk family.

37. Ibid.

38. Barack Obama, letter to Frank C. Laubach, July 28, 1959, Syracuse University, Frank C. Laubach Collection.

39. Goldsworthy, *Tom Mboya*, 120–23.

40. Elizabeth Mooney, letter to Frank C. Laubach, August 5, 1959, Syracuse University, Frank C. Laubach Collection.

CHAPTER 5

1. "Jet Age Makes Debut in Hawaii," *The Honolulu Advertiser*, July 1, 1959.

2. Robert C. Schmitt, *Demographic Statistics of Hawaii 1778 to 1965* (Honolulu: University of Hawaii Press, 1968).

3. "First African Enrolled in Hawaii Studied Two Years by Mail," *Ka Leo O Hawaii*, October 8, 1959.

4. *Honolulu Advertiser*, October 10, 1959.

5. "Isle Inter-Racial Attitude Impresses Kenya Student," *Honolulu Star Bulletin*, November 28, 1959.

6. "First African Enrolled in Hawaii Studied Two Years by Mail."

7. Robert M. Kamins and Robert E. Potter, *Mālamalama: A History of the University of Hawai'i* (Honolulu: University of Hawaii Press, 1998), 4.

8. University of Hawaii, Chancellor's office. Figures provided to the author by Debra Ann C. Ishii, executive assistant to the chancellor in August 2009.

9. Frank J. Taylor, "Colorful Campus of the Islands," *Saturday Evening Post*, May 24, 1958, 96.

10. Barack H. Obama, "Terror in the Congo," *Honolulu Star-Bulletin*, June 8, 1960.

11. *Ka Leo O Hawaii*, November 5, 1959, 1.

12. Lyle H. Dahling (Immigration and Naturalization Service administrator), "Memo for File," April 1961, Barack Obama's "A" file.

13. "Applications to Extend Time of Temporary Stay," July 1960 and August 1961, Barack Obama's "A" file.

14. Barack Obama's transcript from the University of Hawaii, Syracuse University, Frank C. Laubach Collection.

15. From Susan Botkin Blake interview.

16. Barack Obama, *Dreams from My Father: A Story of Race and Inheritance* (New York: Random House, 1995), 127.

17. Ibid., 124.

18. Schmitt, *Demographic Statistics of Hawaii 1778 to 1965*, 210.

19. Peggy Pascoe, *What Comes Naturally: Miscegenation Law and the Making of Race in America* (Oxford: Oxford University Press, 2009), 242.

20. Dahling, "Memo for File." Dahling wrote, "Subject claims to have been divorced from his wife in Kenya in this method."

21. David Mendell, *Obama: From Promise to Power* (New York: Harper Collins, 2007), 29.

22. Obama, *Dreams from My Father*, 126.

23. Ibid., 422.

24. From Susan Botkin Blake interview.

25. From Neil Abercrombie and Pake Zane interviews.

26. Dahling, "Memo for File."

27. Obama, *Dreams from My Father*, 12.

28. Dahling, "Memo for File."

29. Certification of Life Birth, released by the Obama presidential campaign.

30. Barack Obama's "A" file.

31. Elizabeth Mooney Kirk, letter to Tom Mboya, May 8, 1962, The Hoover Institution archives at Stanford University, Tom Mboya papers.

32. Obama, *Dreams from My Father*, 126.

33. Barack Obama, letter to Tom Mboya, May 29, 1962, The Hoover Institution Archive at Stanford University, Tom Mboya papers.

34. Helen Roberts, letter to Alice Sanderson, May 15, 1962, quoted with permission from Roberts's son, Don Roberts.

35. Helen Roberts, letter to Alice Sanderson, July 4, 1962, quoted with permission from Roberts's son, Don Roberts.

36. Helen Roberts, letter to Alice Sanderson, August 21, 1962, quoted with permission from Roberts's son, Don Roberts.

CHAPTER 6

1. Barack Obama, letter to Sylvia Baldwin, December 20, 1962, in the possession of Baldwin.

2. Morton Keller and Phyllis Keller, *Making Harvard Modern: The Rise of America's University* (New York: Oxford University Press, 2001), 301–305. The Kellers describe the continuing struggle over parietals in the 1960s.

3. Fred Hechinger, "Harvard Debates Mind-Drug Peril," *New York Times*, December 14, 1962.

4. "Struggle for Integration Must Continue, King Says," *Harvard Crimson*, Oct. 25, 1962.

5. Richard Norton Smith, *The Harvard Century: The Making of a University to a Nation* (New York: Simon and Schuster, 1986), 224.

6. James Reston, "Nothing Left at Harvard but Radcliffe," *New York Times*, December 30, 1960.

7. Donald E. Graham, "Kennedy Will Host Overseers Tonight as Board Begins Two-Day Meeting," *Harvard Crimson*, May 13, 1963.

8. Smith, *The Harvard Century*, 13.

9. Ibid., 216.

10. "Report of the President of Harvard College and Reports of Departments, 1962–63," October 26, 1964, Official Register of Harvard University, vol. LXI, no. 28: 569, 570.

11. The number of black students is calculated by consulting a number of sources. The Report of the President of Harvard College 1970–71 states that the number of minorities on campus a decade earlier was less than 1 percent. Werner Sollers, Caldwell Titcomb, and Thomas A. Underwood, eds., *Blacks at Harvard: A Documentary History of African-American Experience at Harvard and Radcliffe* (New York: New York University Press, 1973), estimates that in 1963 "blacks constituted about one percent of the student body" (xxiv).

12. Ellen Lake, "Police Arrest 2 Nigerians In Bickford's," *Harvard Crimson*, May 27, 1964.

13. Lawrence W. Feinberg, "Africans, Afro-Americans Form Club," *Harvard Crimson*, April 27, 1963.

14. "The AAAAS and Discrimination," editorial, *Harvard Crimson*, January 13, 1964.

15. Barack H. Obama's "A" file, maintained by the U.S. Immigration and Naturalization Service (INS), Form 1-20A. Certificate by Non-Immigrant Student Under Section 101(a)(15)(F)(1) of the Immigration and Nationality Act, signed by Barack H. Obama, August 1962.

16. W. E. B. DuBois, *The Autobiography of W. E. B. DuBois: A Soliloquy on Viewing My Life from the Last Decade of Its First Century* (New York: International Publishers, 1968), 136.

17. From Stephen A. Marglin interview. Marglin received a PhD from Harvard University in 1965.

18. From Richard E. Sylla interview. Sylla received a PhD in economics from Harvard University in 1969.

19. From Peter D. McClelland interview. McClelland received his PhD in economics from Harvard University in 1966.

20. Barack Obama, letter to Sylvia Baldwin, December 20, 1962, in possession of Baldwin.

21. From Harris Mule interview. Mule was Obama's boss in the 1970s.

22. From Oyuko Onyango Mbeche, Moses Wasonga, Otieno Wasonga, and George Saitoti interviews.

23. Omar Obama's birth date is unclear. According to alumnae records at the Buckingham Browne & Nichols school, Omar Okech Onyango Obama was born March 10, 1945. Information provided by Beth Jacobson, BB&N director of alumnae affairs. The Massachusetts Registry of Motor Vehicle records list his birth date as June 3, 1944.

24. "The Status of Airlift Students," memo to Tom Mboya, September 7, 1963, the Hoover Institution at Stanford University, Stanford, California, Tom Mboya papers.

25. Buckingham Browne & Nichols alumnae records. Information provided by Beth Jacobson, BB&N director of alumnae affairs.

26. Newton North High School records. Information provided by the principal's office.

27. Omar's name change appears in court records and on his registration with the Massachusetts Registry of Motor Vehicles.

28. Secretary of the Commonwealth of Massachusetts, Corporations Division, the Wells Market, Inc., 1760 Dorchester Ave., Dorchester, Massachusetts, registration March 16, 1992.

29. Maria Sacchetti, "Obama's Aunt Is Granted Asylum," *The Boston Globe*, May 18, 2010.

30. From Zeituni Onyango interview.

31. K. D. MacDonald, memo to J. A. Hamilton, January 31, 1964. Contained in Obama's immigration file maintained by the former U.S. Immigration and Naturalization Service. Per department policy, some names are deleted for privacy reasons.

32. M. F. McKeon (immigration inspector), memo, April 28, 1964. Contained in Obama's INS file.

33. M. F. McKeon, memo, May 19, 1964.

34. David D. Henry, letter to Barack H. Obama, May 27, 1964. The letter is contained in Obama's "A" file

35. "Memo for File," June 18, 1964, signed by Dep. Sec. Mulrean, Boston. Contained in Barack Obama's "A" file.

36. From Ruth Ndesandjo interview, April 7, 2010.

37. Barack H. Obama Curriculum Vitae. Contained in Obama's personnel file, held by the Kenyan Ministry of Planning, National Development and Vision.

38. E. Golden (immigration inspector), memo, August 28, 1964. Contained in Obama's "A" file.

CHAPTER 7

1. "There's No Need To Get Lost!" *The Nation*, May 8, 1964.

2. Republic of Kenya, Statistical Abstract 1967, Nairobi Government Printer, 1967, p. 14. Figures from Population Census of 1962, as published in Cherry J. Gertzel, Maure Leonard Goldschmidt, and Donald S. Rothchild, eds., *Government and Politics in Kenya; A Nation Building Text* (Nairobi, Kenya: East African Publishing House, 1969), 22.

3. Jim C. Harper, *Western-Educated Elites in Kenya, 1900–1963: The African American Factor* (New York: Routledge, 2006), 124. Harper says there were less than five hundred with degrees from overseas at the time of independence. One year later dozens more had returned from attending college overseas, putting the figure at close to six hundred.

4. From Mwaura Ngari interview.

5. From Leo Odera Omolo interview.

6. David Goldsworthy, *Tom Mboya: The Man Kenya Wanted to Forget* (New York: Africana Publishing Company, 1982), 139. Goldsworthy characterizes Ayodo's relationship to Mboya as close.

7. Jared Onono, interview with author, February 2010.

8. From Ezra Obama and Charles Oluoch interviews. Both men discuss the importance of a lady's legs in general and Ruth's legs in particular.

9. From Leo Odero Omolo interview.

10. From Jared Onono and Peter Aringo interviews.

11. Celia Nyamweru, "Letting the Side Down: Personal Reflections on Colonial and Independent Kenya," in *Global Multiculturalism: Comparative Perspectives on Ethnicity, Race, and Nation*, ed. Grant Hermans Cornwell and Eve Walsh Stoddard (London: Rowman and Littlefield, 2001), 185.

12. Andrew Hake, *African Metropolis: Nairobi's Self-Help City* (New York: St. Martin's Press, 1977), 74.

13. Certificate of Marriage, Nairobi Registrar's Office, 1964, no. 47. A copy of the certificate is in the case file of Succession Cause No. 233 of 1985 in the Nairobi High Court in Nairobi.

14. Goldsworthy, *Tom Mboya*, 216.

15. Bethwell A. Ogot and William Robert Ochieng, eds., *Decolonization & Independence in Kenya, 1940–93* (London: J. Curry, 1995), 85.

16. Norman Miller and Rodger Yeager, *Kenya: The Quest for Prosperity* (Boulder, CO: Westview Press, 1994), 31.

17. Goldsworthy, *Tom Mboya*, 248. Goldsworthy describes Mboya's state of mind about the job as well as how others regarded the appointment.

18. Gertzel et al., *Government and Politics in Kenya*, 349.

19. "African Socialism and Its Application to Planning in Kenya," Sessional Paper no. 10, Statement by the President, copy available in the Kenya National Archives.

20. Dharam Ghai, "African Socialism for Kenyans," *East Africa Journal*, June 1965, 17–19.

21. Barack H. Obama, "Problems Facing Our Socialism," *East Africa Journal*, July 1965, 29.

22. Ibid.

23. Ibid.

24. Ibid., 33.

25. Ibid.

26. David W. Cohen, "Perils and Pragmatics of Critique: Reading Barack Obama Sr.'s 1965 Review of Kenya's Development Plan" March 2010, an unpublished paper prepared for the University of Cape Town and the University of KwaZulu-Natal, p. 8. This quotation comes from comments Cohen presented to the journalist David Remnick on April 15, 2009, and included in the paper cited here. Quoted here with the permission of the author.

27. Ibid., 27.

28. From David Cohen interview.

29. *East Africa Journal*, April 15, 1966.

30. Miller and Yeager, *Kenya*, 40.

31. From Kevin Abiero and Leo Odera Omolo Erastus Amondi Okul interviews.

32. From Wilson Ndolo Ayah and Ruth Ndesandjo (April 2010) interviews.

33. From Kezia Obama interview.

34. Harvard University registrar, letter to Barack H. Obama, November 16, 1965. Contained in Obama's "A" file.

35. Herufi is the Swahili word for "statistics."

36. "Historical Facts of Banking in Kenya & The Central Bank of Kenya" (Central Bank of Kenya), 16.

37. From Duncan Ndegwa interview.

38. Ibid.

CHAPTER 8

1. From Dr. Marty Singer interview.

2. From Florence Pressman interview.

3. "Boards, Agendas and Minute Meetings," Kenya Tourist Development Corporation (KTDC), December 14, 1967, AHC/3/12, Kenya National Archives.

4. "Boards Agendas and Meetings," Draft Annual Report of the KTDC, December 1969, AHC/3/12, Kenya National Archives. This document provides an overview of the tourism development corporation and notes many of Kenyatta's remarks about the industry.

5. Andrew Hake, *African Metropolis: Nairobi's Self-Help City* (New York: St. Martin's Press, 1977), 257.

6. Auma Obama, *Das Leben kommt immer dazwischen* (Cologne, Germany: Bastei Lubbe GmbH & Co. KG, 2010), 28.

7. Ibid., 27.

8. From Ruth Ndesandjo interview (April 2010).

9. From Kezia Obama interview.

10. High Court of Kenya at Nairobi, P&A No. 233 of 1985, ruling issued 1989. This document is included in the files concerning both Succession Cause 233 of 1985 and Succession Cause 63 of 1990.

11. Jomo Kenyatta, *Suffering without Bitterness: The Founding of the Kenya Nation* (Nairobi, Kenya: East African Publishing House, 1968), 343.

12. Susanne D. Mueller, "Government and Opposition in Kenya 1966-9," *Journal of Modern African Studies* 22, no. 3 (September 1984): 408.

13. Ibid., 415.

14. Bethwell A. Ogot and William Robert Ochieng, eds., *Decolonization & Independence in Kenya, 1940–93* (London: J. Curry, 1995), 101.

15. David Goldsworthy, *Tom Mboya: The Man Kenya Wanted to Forget* (New York: Africana Publishing Company, 1982), 267.

16. Ibid., 274.

17. Republic of Kenya, Central Bureau of Statistics Economic Survey, June 1966, p. 52, table 36, Kenya National Archives.

18. W. P. Gamble, *Tourism and Development in Africa* (London: Murray, 1989), 32–34.

19. "Boards Agendas and Meetings," Draft Annual Report of the Kenya Tourist Development Corporation, December 1969, AHC/3/12, , p. 6, Kenya National Archives.

20. All references to the terms of Obama's employment at the KTDC come from "Boards, Agenda and Minutes," KTDC executive committee meeting, September 8, 1967, AHC/3/12, Minute no. 27/67/EC. Kenya National Archives.

21. "Tourism Officer on Drinks Charge," *The Daily Nation*, November 4, 1967.

22. Minutes of the fifth meeting of the KTDC executive committee, June 18, 1968, AHC/3/12, Minute no. 14/68, p. 3, Kenya National Archives.

23. "Boards Agendas and Meetings," Draft Annual Report of the Kenya Tourist Development Corporation, December 1969, AHC/3/12, pp. 4–5, Kenya National Archives.

24. Ibid., 3.

25. Joseph P. B. M. Ouma, *Evolution of Tourism in East Africa: 1990–2000* (Nairobi, Kenya: East African Literature Bureau, 1970), 103.

26. Minutes of the fifth meeting of the KTDC executive committee, June 18, 1968, AHC/3/12, Minute no. 14/68, p. 3, Kenya National Archives.

27. Minutes of the sixth meeting of the KTDC executive committee, August, 13, 1968, AHC/3/12, Minute no. 26/68, p. 5, Kenya National Archives.

28. Goldsworthy, *Tom Mboya*, 279.

29. "Mboya Murder Defence Evidence Today," *The Daily Nation*, September 9, 1969, 1, 24.

30. Hilary Ng'weno, "Thomas Joseph Odhiambo Mboya's Murder and the Return of One-Party State," *Afro Articles*, December 7, 2007, http://www.afroarticles.com/article-dashboard/Article/Thomas-Joseph-Odhiambo-Mboya-s-murder—-the-return-of-one-party-State/62356.

31. "Mboya Murder Defence Evidence Today."

32. From Caroline Elkins interview.

33. Goldsworthy, *Tom Mboya*, 284.

34. From Susan Mboya interview.

35. Peter Firstbrook, *The Obamas: The Untold Story of an African Family* (London: Preface Publishing, 2010), 218.

36. David William Cohen and E. S. Atieno Odhiambo, *The Risks of Knowledge: Investigations into the Death of the Hon. Minister John Robert Ouko in Kenya, 1990* (Athens: Ohio University Press, 2004), 5.

37. From "Anonymous" interview.

38. E. S. Atieno Odhiambo, "Ethnic Cleansing and Civil Society in Kenya, 1969–1992," *Journal of Contemporary African Studies* 22, pt. 1 (2004): 29–42.

39. John R. Nellis, *The Ethnic Composition of Leading Kenyan Government Positions* (Uppsala: The Scandinavian Institute of African Studies, Nordiska Afrikainstitutet, 1974), 14–15.

40. Minutes of the second meeting of the Kenya Tourist Development Corporation, May 4, 1970, AHC/3/12, Minute no. 13/70, Kenya National Archives.

41. Ibid.

42. Minutes of the first meeting of the executive appointments committee of the KTDC, May 11, 1970, AHC/3/12, Minute no. 1/70, Kenya National Archives.

43. Minutes of the second meeting of the KTDC executive committee, June 15, 1970, AJ/2/8, Minute no. E5/70(b), Kenya National Archives.

44. From Nyaringo Obure interview.

CHAPTER 9

1. Barack Obama, *Dreams from My Father: A Story of Race and Inheritance* (New York: Random House, 1995), 215.

2. From Ruth Ndesandjo interview (February 2010).

3. B. Obama, *Dreams from My Father*, 65.

4. Ibid., 66.

5. Ibid., 68.

6. Auma Obama, *Das Leben kommt immer dazwischen* (Cologne: Germany: Bastei Lubbe GmbH & Co. KG, 2010), 27.

7. Ibid., 63.

8. Ibid., 64.

9. Barack Obama [Sr.], letter to the Ministry's personnel officer March 11, 1978, Barack Obama's personnel file, held by the Ministry of Planning, National Development and Vision.

10. A. Obama, *Das Leben kommt immer dazwischen*, 72.

11. Ibid., 72.

12. B. Obama, *Dreams from My Father*, 217.

13. David Kariuki and Blamuel Njururi, "M.P.s Demand Full Probe into J.M.'s Murder," *The Daily Nation*, March 14, 1975, 4.

14. Norman Miller and Rodger Yeager, *Kenya: The Quest for Prosperity* (Boulder, CO: Westview Press, 1994), 52.

15. From Harris Mule interview.

16. Y. F. O. Masakhalia, letter to the Permanent Secretary of the Ministry of Commerce and Industry, November 14, 1975, Barack Obama personnel file.

17. Joseph K. Muriungi, letter to the Ministry of Finance and Economic Planning's personnel officer, February 15, 1978. Contained in Barack Obama's personnel file.

18. Ministry of Finance and Planning records, National Archives in Nairobi, folios 104 through 110.

19. Y. F. O. Masakhalia, memo, August 6, 1976, Barack Obama Personnel File.

20. Obama wrote dozens of memos about the project that are contained in the Ministry of Finance and Planning records, Nairobi National Archive, folios 18, 31. Details of the project are spelled out in two specific memos:"Brief on the Kenya-Sudan Road Link," prepared by Obama for Harris Mule, May 28, 1979, EPD/A/132/79/01; and "Brief on Kenya/Sudan Joint Projects," prepared by Obama, September 12, 1980, EPD/A/132/79/01.

21. David. K Leonard, *African Successes: Four Public Managers of Kenyan Rural Development* (Berkeley: University of California Press, 1991), 1, 69.

22. From Johnson M. Hungu interview.

23. Barack Obama, memo to the Ministry's Personnel supervisor, November 3, 1977, Barack Obama personnel file.

24. From Owino Okongo interview.

25. Leonard, *African Successes*, 202.

26. Jael Atieno testimony, April 1989, Succession Cause No. 233, High Court of Kenya.

27. Ibid.

28. That Obama might have met with foul play on the night of his death is a view shared by many family members. It was discussed in detail in interviews with Hawa Auma, W. E. Obama Kobilo, Ezra Obama, Charles Oluoch, and Amir Otieno Orinda.

29. William Onyango, "Economic Planning Man Dies in Crash," *The Nairobi Times*, November 30, 1982, 5.

30. Certificate of Death No. 109369, Nairobi, Kenya. This document is available in the files of Succession Cause No. 233 in the High Court of Kenya.

BIBLIOGRAPHY

Adams, Ayin M., ed. *African Americans in Hawai'i: A Search for Identity.* Ka'a'awa, HI: Pacific Raven Press, 2010.

Allen, Gwenfread E. *The YMCA in Hawaii 1869-1969.* Honolulu: Young Men's Christian Association, 1969.

Anderson, David. *Histories of the Hanged: The Dirty War in Kenya and the End of Empire.* New York and London: W. W. Norton and Company, 2005.

Ayodo, Awuor. *Luo (The Heritage Library of African Peoples).* New York: Rosen Publishing Group, 1996.

Berman, Bruce and John Lonsdale. *Unhappy Valley: Conflict in Kenya and Africa.* Athens, OH: Ohio University Press, 1992.

Bienen, Henry. *Kenya: The Politics of Participation and Control.* Princeton, NJ: Princeton University Press, 1974.

Chesaina, Ciarunji. *Oral Literature of the Embu and Mbeere.* Nairobi: East African Educational Publishers Ltd., 1997.

Cohen, David William and E. S. Atieno Odhiambo. *The Risks of Knowledge: Investigations into the Death of the Hon. Minister John Robert Ouko in Kenya, 1990.* Athens, OH: Ohio University Press, 2004.

Cohen, David William and E.S. Atieno Odhiambo. *Siaya: The Historical Anthropology of an African Landscape.* Nairobi: Heinemann Kenya, 1989.

Daws, Gavan. *Shoal of Time: A History of the Hawaiian Islands.* Honolulu: University of Hawaii Press, 1974.

DuPré, Carole E. *The Luo of Kenya: An Annotated Bibliography.* Washington, DC: Institute for Cross-Cultural Research, 1968.

Elkins, Caroline. *Imperial Reckoning: The Untold Story of Britain's Gulag in Kenya.* New York: Henry Holt and Company, 2005.

Firstbrook, Peter. *The Obamas: The Untold Story of an African Family.* London: Preface Publishing, 2010.

Gertzel, C. J., Maure Goldschmidt, and Don Rothchild, ed. *Government and Politics in Kenya; A Nation Building Text.* Nairobi: East African Publishing House, 1972.

Glauberman, Stu, and Jerry Burris. *The Dream Begins: How Hawai'i Shaped Barack Obama.* Honolulu: Watermark Publishing, 2009.

Goldsworthy, David. *Tom Mboya: The Man Kenya Wanted to Forget.* New York: Africana Publishing Company, 1982.

Hake, Andrew. *African Metropolis: Nairobi's Self-Help City.* New York: St. Martin's Press, 1977.

Hardy, Ronald. *The Iron Snake.* New York: G. P. Putnam's Sons, 1965.

Harper, Jim C. *Western-Educated Elites in Kenya, 1900-1963: The African American Factor.* New York: Routledge, 2006.

Hazlewood, Arthur. *The Economy of Kenya: The Kenyatta Era.* New York: Oxford University Press, 1979.

Huxley, Elspeth. *The Flame Trees of Thika: Memories of an African Childhood.* New York: Penguin Books, 2000.

Jacobs, Ron. *ObamaLand: Who is Barack Obama?* Honolulu: Trade Publishing, 2008.

Judith Mariann Butterman, "Luo Social Formations in Change; Karachuonyo and Kanyamkago, c. 1800–1945" (PhD diss., Syracuse University, 1979).

Kamins, Robert M. and Robert E. Potter. *Mālamalama: A History of the University of Hawai'i.* Honolulu: University of Hawaii Press, 1998.

Kaplan, Irving and others. *Area Handbook for Kenya,* 2nd ed. Washington, DC: U.S. Government Printing Office, 1976.

Kariuki, G. G. *The Illusion of Power: Reflections on Fifty Years in Kenya Politics.* Nairobi: Kenway Publications, 2001.

Kenyatta, Jomo. *Suffering Without Bitterness; The Founding of the Kenya Nation.* Nairobi: East African Publishing House, 1968.

Klugman, Jeni, Bilin Neyapti, and Frances Stewart. *Conflict and Growth in Africa, Vol. 2: Kenya, Tanzania and Uganda.* Paris: OECD Publishing, 1999.

Laubach, Frank C. *Forty Years with the Silent Billion*: Adventuring in Literacy Old Tappan, NJ: Fleming H. Revell Company, 1970.

Laubach, Frank C. and Robert S. Laubach. *Toward World Literacy: The Each One Teach One Way.* New York: Syracuse University Press, 1960.

Leonard, David K. *African Successes; Four Public Managers of Kenyan Rural Development.* Berkeley: University of California Press, 1991.

Leys, Colin. *Underdevelopment in Kenya: The Political Economy of Neo-Colonialism.* Berkeley and Los Angeles: University of California Press, 1975.

Malo, Shadrack. *Luo Customs and Practices,* trans. Jane Achieng. Nairobi, Kenya: Sciencetech Network, 1999.

Margaret Jean Hay, "Economic Change in Luoland; Kowe, 1890–1945" (PhD diss., University of Wisconsin, 1972).

Mboya, Tom. *Freedom and After*. London: Andre Deutsch Limited, 1963.

Mendell, David. *Obama: From Promise to Power*. New York: HarperCollins, 2008.

Miller, Norman and Rodger Yeager. *Kenya: The Quest for Prosperity*. Boulder and Oxford: Westview Press, 1994.

Munuhe, Kareithi. *J. M. Kariuki in Parliament*. Nairobi: Gazelle Books Company, 1975.

Murray-Brown, Jeremy. *Kenyatta*. New York: E. P. Dutton & Co., Inc., 1973

Ndegwa, Duncan Nderitu. *Walking in Kenyatta Struggles*. Nairobi: Kenya Leadership Institute, 2006.

Ndesandjo, Mark Obama. *Nairobi to Shenzhen*. San Diego: Aventine Publishing, 2009.

Nicholls, C. S. *Red Strangers: The White Tribe of Kenya*. London: Timewell Press Limited, 2005.

Nwosu, Uchenna. *The Rejected Stone*. USA: Xlibris Corporation, 2009.

Obama, Auma. *Das Leben kommt immer dazwischen*. Germany: Lübbe, 2010.

Obama, George and Damien Lewis. *Homeland: An Extraordinary Story of Hope and Survival*. New York: Simon & Schuster, 2010.

Ochieng, W. R. *A Modern History of Kenya, 1895–1980*. London: Evans Brothers Limited, 1990.

Odhiambo, E. S. Atieno and John Lonsdale, ed. *Mau Mau & Nationhood*. Athens, OH: Ohio University Press, 2003.

Odhiambo, E. S. Atieno, T. I. Ouso, and J. F. M. Williams. *A History of East Africa*. Harlow, England: Longman Group UK Ltd., 1977.

Odinga, Oginga. *Not Yet Uhuru: The Autobiography of Oginga Odinga* Nairobi: East African Educational Publishers, 1976.

Ogot, Bethwell A. *My Footprints on the Sands of Time: An Autobiography*. Victoria, British Columbia: Trafford Publishing, 2003.

Ogot, Bethwell A. *Reintroducing Man into the African World: Selected Essays 1961–1990*. Kisumu, Kenya: Anyange Press Ltd., 1999.

Ogot, B. A. and J. A. Kieran, ed. *Zamani: A Survey of East African History*. Nairobi: East African Publishing House, 1968.

Ogot, B. A. and W. R. Ochieng', eds. *Decolonization & Independence in Kenya, 1940–1993*. Athens, Ohio: Ohio University Press, 1995.

Ouma, Joseph P. B. M. *Evolution of Tourism in East Africa (1900–2000)*. Nairobi: East African Literature Bureau, 1970.

Parker, Richard. *John Kenneth Galbraith: His Life, His Politics, His Economics*. Chicago: University of Chicago Press, 2005.

Parsons, Timothy H. *The African Rank-and-File: Social Implications of Colonial Military Service in the King's African Rifles, 1902–1964.* Portsmouth, NH: Heinemann, 1999.

Reed, Ishmael, ed. *MultiAmerica: Essays on Cultural Wars and Cultural Peace.* New York: Penguin Books, 1998.

Rake, Alan. *Tom Mboya: Young Man of New Africa.* Garden City, New York: Doubleday & Company, 1962.

Remnick, David. *The Bridge: The Life and Rise of Barack Obama.* New York: Afred A. Knopf, A Division of Random House, 2010.

Shachtman, Tom. *Airlift to America: How Barack Obama, Sr., John F. Kennedy, Tom Mboya, and 800 East African Students Changed Their World and Ours.* New York: St. Martin's Press, 2009.

Shipton, Parker. *Mortgaging the Ancestors: Ideologies of Attachment in Africa.* New Haven, CT: Yale University Press, 2009.

Shipton, Parker. *The Nature of Entrustment: Intimacy, Exchange, and the Sacred in Africa.* New Haven, CT: Yale University Press, 2007.

Smith, Mansfield Irving, "The East African Airlifts of 1959, 1960 and 1961" (PhD diss., Syracuse University, 1966).

Smith, Richard Norton. *The Harvard Century: The Making of a University to a Nation.* Cambridge, MA: Harvard University Press, 1986.

Sollors, Werner, Caldwell Titcomb, and Thomas A. Underwood, ed. *Blacks at Harvard: A Documentary History of African-American Experience at Harvard and Radcliffe.* New York: New York University Press, 1993.

Stephens, Dorothy. *Kwa Heri Means Goodbye: Memories of Kenya 1957–1959.* New York: iUniverse, 2006.

White, Luise, Stephen F. Miescher, and David William Cohen, ed. *African Words, African Voices: Critical Practices in Oral History.* Bloomington, IN: Indiana University Press, 2001.

Wolff, Richard D. *The Economics of Colonialism: Britain and Kenya, 1870–1930.* New Haven and London: Yale University Press, 1974.

PERIODICALS

Mueller, Susanne D., "Government and Opposition in Kenya 1966–1969," *Journal of Modern African Studies,* Vol. 22. No.3 (September 1984).

Nellis, John R. "The Ethnic Composition of Leading Kenyan Government Positions." *Scandinavian Institute of African Studies,* 1974, 14–15.

Ng'weno, Hilary. "Thomas Joseph Odhiambo Mboya's Murder and the Return of One-Party State. *Afro Articles,* Dec. 7, 2007.

Odhiambo, Atieno E. S. (2004), "Ethnic Cleansing and Civil Society in Kenya, 1969–1992, *Journal of Contemporary African Studies,* 22, 29–42.

Taylor, Frank J. "Colorful Campus of the Islands." *Saturday Evening Post,* May 24, 1958.

INTERVIEWS

The following is a list of telephone interviews that took place with the author.

Abercrombie, Hal; multiple interviews
Abiero, Kevin; August 2010
Achola, Milcah; May 2009
Aguda, Osewe; March 2010
Alberti, Peggy; June and September 2009
Ayot, Henry; April 2010
Azikiwe, Chukwuma; multiple interviews

Baldwin, Sylvia; August 2009
Benjamin, Ed; April 2010
Blake, Susan Botkin; multiple interviews
Bonuke, Joel; February 2010
Brimble, Maureen and Michael; January 2010
Butler, Jack; February 2010

Chirls, Diane; August 2010
Cohen, David; multiple interviews
Connan, Dominique; May 2010

Dewey, Alice G.; November 2009
Dukakis, Kitty; February 2010
Dulo, Paul; April 2009

Ekpebu, Larry; April 2010
Eldridge, Pal; August 2009
Elkins, Caroline; October 2008 and March 2010
Enright, Ernest; September 2009
Epstein, Judy; November 2009

Frost, Ellen; April and September 2009
Geller, Laurel; February and September 2009
Gerald, Kimo; December 2009
Ghai, Dharam; March 2009 and November 2010
Gilpin, Peter; multiple emails

Gray, Clive; September 2008
Gregor, Dorothy; September 2009

Harper, Jim; November 2010
Harvey, David; July 2009
Hesselmark, Gunilla; January 2011

Jacobson, Beth; March 2009

Khairallah, Saad; October 2010
Kirk, John; December 2009

Laubach, Bob; April and June 2009
Levine, Judy; May 2010
Lonsdale, John M.; multiple interviews
Lucas, David; January 2010

Maganjo, Mwangi; September 2010
Mandell, Stuart; June and September 2009
Marglin, Stephen; May 2009
Mboya, Susan; multiple interviews
McCabe, Sumi; August, 2009 and April 2011
McCauley, David; July 2009
McClelland, Peter D.; June 2010
McCroskey, James C.; November 2009
Metaxas, Georgia; July 2010
Mitchell, Josephine; June 2010
Mooney, Esther; October 2010
Murashige, Juditha Clark; November 2009
Muriuki, Godfrey; April 2009

Ndesandjo, Mark; November 2009
Njiiri, Ruth; November 2009 and February 2010
Nachmanoff, Arnold; April 2009
Ngari, Mwaura; October 2009
Noll, Roger; multiple interviews
Nottingham, John; April and October 2009
Nwosu, Uchenna; multiple interviews
Nyamweru, Celia; June 2010

Obama, Said; October 2008 and February 2010
Odaga, Asenath Bole; February 2009
Ogolah, Gladys; February and August 2010
Okoda, Sebastian Peter; July and October 2010
Okul, Erastus Amondi; April 2010
Omolo, Leo Odera; multiple interviews
Omondi, Arthur; January 2009
Otunnu, Olara; July 2010
Pala, Taa O.; February 2011
Pressman, Florence; September 2010

Rait, Barbara; February 2010
Rajula, Nick; March 2009
Rege, James; November and December 2009
Roberts, Charleen multiple interviews
Ruenitz, Robert M.; April 2009
Ruthazer, Debby; April 2009

Saffarian, Jane; January 2010
Sandberg, Lars Gunnarsson; October 2009
Schydlowsky, Daniel; multiple interviews
Shipton, Parker; multiple interviews
Singer, Marty; February 2010
Smith, Bruce R.; October 2010
Sylla, Richard; July 2010

Tith, Naranhkiri; multiple interviews
Toutonghi, Mary; August 2009

Ugoh, Sylvester; February 2010

Wairagu, Lazarus; December 2009 and March 2010
Wanyee, Lydia; August 2010
Weiss, Cora; February 2009
Weya, David Owino; March 2010
White, Larry; August 2009
Wilson, Catherine; November 2009
Woodward, Kathryn Roen; December 2009

Zeckhauser, Richard; May 2009
Zeigler, Lee; July 2009

The following interviews were conducted in person with the author, unless otherwise indicated.

Kenya
Adhiambo, Elly Yonga, in Kanyadhiang, February 2009
Akello, Joseph, in Nyangoma, November 2009 and March 2010
Aringo, Peter, in Nairobi February and June 2009 and March 2010
Arungu-Olende, Shem, in Nairobi, March 2010
Asiyo, Phoebe, in Washington, DC, May 2009, and Nairobi, March 2010
Ayah, Wilson Ndolo, in Nairobi, March 2010
Ayodo, Damaris, in Nairobi, February 2010
Ayoro, Oyiro, with Beatrice Akoth in Gem Kodiaga, June 2009
Ayot, Henry, in Nairobi, June 2009

Calleb, Omogi, in Kendu Bay, October 2009

Hungu, Johnson, in Nairobi in May and November 2009 and March 2010

Isigie, Peter, in Nairobi, February 2009

Kagumba, Helga and Mboya, in Achego, May 2009
Kinyua, Wilson, in Nairobi, June 2009
Kobilo, W. E. Obama, multiple interviews in Kenya, 2009 and 2010
Kut, Julius, in Ng'iya, February 2009

Madoho, Obama, in Alego, February 2009
Masakhalia, Francis, in Lavington, February and May 2009, and in Nairobi, March 2010
Mbeche, Oyuko Onyango, in Nairobi March 2010
Mboya, Dan, in Gendia, Karachuonyo, October 2009
Mboya, Susan, in Nairobi, November 2009
Muga, Richard, with Beatrice Akoth in Kendu Bay, November 2009
Muguku, Faith Njeri, in Nairobi, May 2009
Mule, Harris, in Nairobi, March 2010
Mumbo, Doris, in Nyangoma, March 2009

Ndegwa, Duncan, in Mombasa, October 2009
Ndemo, Bitange, in Nairobi, March 2010
Ndesandjo, Ruth, in Nairobi, February 2010, and Boston, April 2010
Ndolo, Penina, by Beatrice Akoth in Kanyadhiang, March 2009
Ndungu, Owen, in Nairobi, February 2010
Ng'weno, Hilary, in Nairobi, February 2009

Obama, Ezra, multiple interviews in Kenya throughout 2009 and 2010
Obama, George Hussein Onyango, in Nairobi, June and November 2009
Obama, Grace Kezia, in Bracknell, England, December 2008
Obama, Hawa Auma, in Oyugis, June 2009
Obama, Rajab Ouko, multiple interviews in Nairobi
Obama, Said, in Kisumu, February 2009
Obama, Sarah, in Alego, February 2009
Obama,Wilson, in Kisumu, March 2009
Obama, Wycliffe, in Kisumu, February 2009
Obama, Zeituni Onyango, in Boston, November 2008 and April 2009
Obondo, Alex, in Nairobi, March 2010
Obure, Nyaringo, in Nairobi, November 2009
Ochieng, Philip, in Nairobi, October 2009
Ochieng, Stephen, in Nairobi, March 2009
Odida, Dominick, in Ng'yia, June 2009
Odour, Allan, in Nairobi, June 2009
Ogembo, William Onyango, in Nairobi, February 2009
Ogutu, Alfred Obama, in Kanyadhiang, October 2009
Ogutu, Dibo, in Nairobi with Felgona Atieno Ochieng,
    November 2009
Okatcha, Fred, multiple interviews in Nairobi in 2009 and 2010
Okeyo, Achola Pala, Nairobi, March 2010
Okumu, Joash Muga, in Kital village by Beatrice Akoth,
    March 2010
Okun, Joseph Muga, with Beatrice Akoth in Kendu Bay, June 2009
Olum, Gondi Hesbon, in Nairobi, October 2009
Oluoch, Charles, in Kanyadhiang, February and May 2009
Omondi, Peter, in Nairobi, February 2009
Omolo, Leo Odera, in Kisumu throughout 2009 and 2010
Onono, Jared, in Nairobi, February 2010
Onyango, Meshack J., in Nairobi, May 2009
Opar, David, with Beatrice Akoth in Kendu Bay,
    November 2009
Orinda, Amir Otieno, in Kosele, March 2010
Orinda, Razik Otieno, in Kosele, March 2010
Otula, Paul, in Maseno, February 2009
Owino, Arthur Reuben, in Kodiaga in Gem, November 2009
Owino, Okongo, in Kisumu, June 2009
Owuor, Jeremiah, in Nairobi, June 2009
Oyiro, Ayoro, with Beatrice Akoth, Karachuoyno,
    November 2009

Oyucho, Manasseh, in Nyangoma, October 2009

Rabuku, John, in Nyangoma, November 2009

Saitoti, George, in Nairobi, February 2010
Schramm, Paula, in Nairobi, March 2010

Wamae, Matu, in Nairobi, February 2010
Wasonga, Otieno O., in Nairobi, February 2010
Wasonga, M. Kings, in Nairobi, February 2010

Yamo Charles, by Beatrice Akoth in Gendia, April 2009

England
Obama, Grace Kezia, in Bracknell, England, December 2008

United States
Abercrombie, Neil, in Honolulu, Hawai'i, June 2009

Coleman, Joyce Kirk, in Dallas, Texas, February 2010

DeMello, Edward, in Honolulu, Hawai'i, June 2009

Edwards, Edgar O., in Poultney, Vermont, April 2009

Harvey, David W., in Syracuse, New York, May 2009
Hasegawa, Edward, in Honolulu, Hawai'i, June 2009
Holmes, Stephen, by David Arnold in Exeter, New Hampshire,
    December 2009

Ikeda, George, in Honolulu, Hawai'i, June 2009

Krim, Bob, by David Arnold in Boston, Massachusetts, December 2009

Laubach, Bob, in Syracuse, New York, May 2009
Lauster, Julie, in Honolulu, Hawai'i, June 2009

Nwafor, Azinna, multiple interviews in Cambridge, Massachusetts,
    with Judy Rakowsky, 2009 and 2010
Nyangani, Paul, multiple interviews in Cambridge,
    Massachusetts, 2009 and 2010

Obama, Zeituni Onyango, in Boston, Massachusetts,
    November 2008 and April 2009

Parker, Richard, in Cambridge, Massachusetts, August 2009
Prather, Donna, in Honolulu, Hawai'i, June 2009

Stephens Dorothy and Robert, in Marblehead, Massachusetts, July 2009

Varez, Dietrich, on the Hawai'i Volcanoes National Park, the Big Island,
    Hawai'i, June 2009

Wells, Mary Beth, in Cypress, California, June 2010

Zane, Pake, in Honolulu, Hawai'i, June 2009

INDEX

The letter n after a page number indicates a note.

Sally H. Jacobs lives in Belmont, Massachusetts, with her two children. She is a veteran reporter at the *Boston Globe*, where she has covered national, international, and breaking news for over two decades. She has won several journalism awards including the George Polk Award. She has specialized in political reporting and profiles including the famously reclusive Joan Kennedy, Michelle Obama, and Pat Patrick, Deval Patrick's father. This is her first book.

PublicAffairs is a publishing house founded in 1997. It is a tribute to the standards, values, and flair of three persons who have served as mentors to countless reporters, writers, editors, and book people of all kinds, including me.

I. F. Stone, proprietor of *I. F. Stone's Weekly*, combined a commitment to the First Amendment with entrepreneurial zeal and reporting skill and became one of the great independent journalists in American history. At the age of eighty, Izzy published *The Trial of Socrates*, which was a national bestseller. He wrote the book after he taught himself ancient Greek.

Benjamin C. Bradlee was for nearly thirty years the charismatic editorial leader of *The Washington Post*. It was Ben who gave the *Post* the range and courage to pursue such historic issues as Watergate. He supported his reporters with a tenacity that made them fearless and it is no accident that so many became authors of influential, best-selling books.

Robert L. Bernstein, the chief executive of Random House for more than a quarter century, guided one of the nation's premier publishing houses. Bob was personally responsible for many books of political dissent and argument that challenged tyranny around the globe. He is also the founder and longtime chair of Human Rights Watch, one of the most respected human rights organizations in the world.

•   •   •

For fifty years, the banner of Public Affairs Press was carried by its owner Morris B. Schnapper, who published Gandhi, Nasser, Toynbee, Truman, and about 1,500 other authors. In 1983, Schnapper was described by *The Washington Post* as "a redoubtable gadfly." His legacy will endure in the books to come.

Peter Osnos, *Founder and Editor-at-Large*